The Politics of Association in Hellenistic Rhodes

New Approaches to Ancient Greek Institutional History

Series editors: Mirko Canevaro, University of Edinburgh; Edward Harris, Durham University; David Lewis, University of Edinburgh

This series will showcase new trends in the study of Greek political, legal, social and economic institutions and institutional history. It will create a fruitful dialogue between Greek institutional historians and the political and social sciences – and in particular the New Institutionalisms.

Books in the series will go beyond a traditional approach to offer theoretical and methodological reflection on the importance of institutions and on how we should study them. They will appeal to Greek historians and to political and social scientists alike.

Books available in the series
The Ideology of Democratic Athens: Institutions, Orators and the Mythical Past
Matteo Barbato

The Politics of Association in Hellenistic Rhodes
Christian A. Thomsen

Visit the series web page at: edinburghuniversitypress.com/series-new-approaches-to-ancient-greek-institutional-history

The Politics of Association in Hellenistic Rhodes

Christian A. Thomsen

EDINBURGH
University Press

Edinburgh University Press is one of the leading university presses in the UK. We publish academic books and journals in our selected subject areas across the humanities and social sciences, combining cutting-edge scholarship with high editorial and production values to produce academic works of lasting importance. For more information visit our website: edinburghuniversitypress.com

© Christian A. Thomsen, 2020

Edinburgh University Press Ltd
The Tun – Holyrood Road, 12(2f) Jackson's Entry, Edinburgh EH8 8PJ

Typeset in 11/13 Bembo Std by
IDSUK (DataConnection) Ltd

ISBN 978 1 4744 5255 7 (hardback)
ISBN 978 1 4744 5257 1 (webready PDF)
ISBN 978 1 4744 5258 8 (epub)

Contents

List of Tables and Figures

Acknowledgements

I believe that all men through their lives contribute *eranoi* for themselves.
Not only the kind which one collects, but others also.

(Dem. 21.184)

This book began as a dissertation and research was made possible through the generous grant of a three-year stipend by the Independent Research Fund Denmark, awarded by the Danish Research School for History.

Over the years, I've collected not a few *eranoi* from my colleagues at the Saxo Institute, University of Copenhagen, in the form of helpful discussions and comments on several aspects of private associations in the ancient Greek world. Thanks are due especially to the members of the Copenhagen Associations Project, Annelies Cazemier, Stella Skaltsa, Mario Paganini, Jan-Mathieu Carbon and Kasper Evers, but most of all Vincent Gabrielsen, who supervised my work at the Saxo Institute and whose knowledge on the subject of Hellenistic Rhodes and associations is surpassed only by his patience. At various stages other colleagues have discussed the manuscript with me: Alain Bresson, John K. Davies and Peter F. Bang examined the dissertation, and David M. Lewis, Edward M. Harris and Mirko Canevaro greatly improved the manuscript (without necessarily subscribing to any or all of the views expressed therein).

I am indebted also to Anastasia Dreliossi-Herakleidou, Vasso Patsiada, Eriphyle Kaninia and their colleagues at the Ephorate of Dodecanese Antiquities who helped me access inscriptions and archaeological sites, and not least to Carol McDonald and Sarah Foyle at Edinburgh University Press.

The *eranoi* collected from my family over these many years are far too large and far too many to mention. I have committed each and every one to heart and memory knowing full well that they, for their own part, never kept accounts.

Copenhagen, December 2019

Abbreviations of Epigraphic Corpora

AD	*Archaiologikon Deltion*
AE	*Archaiologike Ephemeris*
AEMÖ	*Archäologisch-epigraphische Mitteilungen aus Österreich-Ungarn*
Agora 16	Woodhead, A. G. *The Athenian Agora 16: Inscriptions: The Decrees.* Princeton. 1997.
AIV	*Atti dell'Istituto Veneto di Scienze, Lettere ed Arti, Classe di Scienze morali e Lettere*
Annuario	*Annuario della Scuola Archeologica di Atene e delle Missioni Italiane in Oriente*
ARW	*Archiv für Religionswissenschaft*
Cl. Rhodos	*Clara Rhodos: Studi e materiali pubblicati a cura dell' Istituto storico-archeologico di Rodi*
I. Ephesos	Wankel, H. et al. *Die Inschriften von Ephesos (IK 11–17)* Bonn. 1979–84.
IIR I	Kontorini, V. *Inscriptions inédites relatives à l'histoire et aux cultes de Rhodes au IIe et au Ier s. av. J.-C.: Rhodiaka.* Louvain. 1983.
I. Magnesia	Ihnken, T. *Die Inschriften von Magnesia am Sipylos: Mit einem Kommentar zum Sympolitievertrag mit Smyrna.* Bonn. 1978.
I. Pergamon	Fränkel, M. *Die Inschriften von Pergamon: Altertümer von Pergamon, 8, 1–2.* Berlin. 1890–5.
JÖAI	*Jahreshefte des österreichischen archäologischen Instituts in Wien*
Lindiaka VI	Blinkenberg, C. *Les Prêtres de Poseidon Hippios. Étude sur une inscription lindienne. Lindiaka VI.* Copenhagen. 1937.
Lindos II	Blinkenberg, C. *Lindos: Fouilles de l'Acropole II, 1902–1914: Inscriptions.* Copenhagen. 1941.

MDAI(A)	*Mitteilungen des deutschen archäologischen Instituts: Athenische Abteilung*
NSER	Pugliese Carratelli, G. 'Nuovo supplemento epigrafico rodio'. *Annuario* n.s. 17–18 (1955–6). 157–81.
NSill	Maiuri, A. *Nuova silloge epigrafica di Rodi e Cos.* Florence. 1925.
Paphos V	Nicolaou, I. *The Stamped Amphora Handles from the House of Dionysos.* Nicosia. 2005.
PdP	*La parola del passato: Rivista di studi antichi*
RIPR	Bresson, A. *Recueil des inscriptions de la Pérée rhodienne.* Paris. 1991.
SER	Pugliese Carratelli, G. 'Supplemento epigrafico rodio'. *Annuario* n.s. 14–16 (1952–4). 247–316.
Tit. Cam.	Segre, M. and G. Pugliese Carratelli. 'Tituli Camirenses'. *Annuario* n.s. 11–13 (1949–51)141–318.
Tit. Cam. Supp.	Pugliese Carratelli, G. 'Tituli Camirenses Supplementum'. *Annuario* n.s. 14–16 (1952–4). 211–46.
TRI	Badoud, N. *Le temps de Rhodes: Une chronologie des inscriptions de la cité fondée sur l'étude de ses institutions.* Munich. 2015.

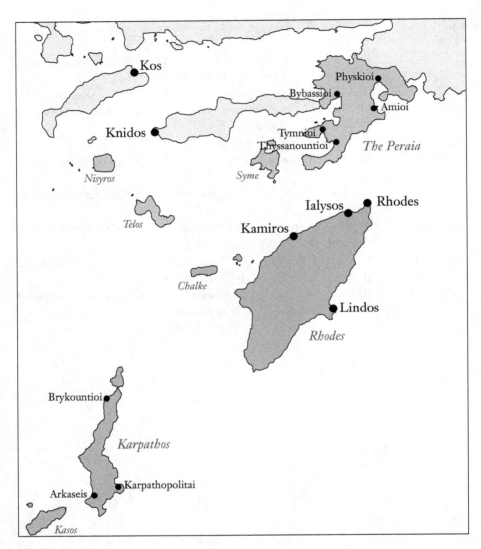

Map 1 The Rhodian state (without Megiste).

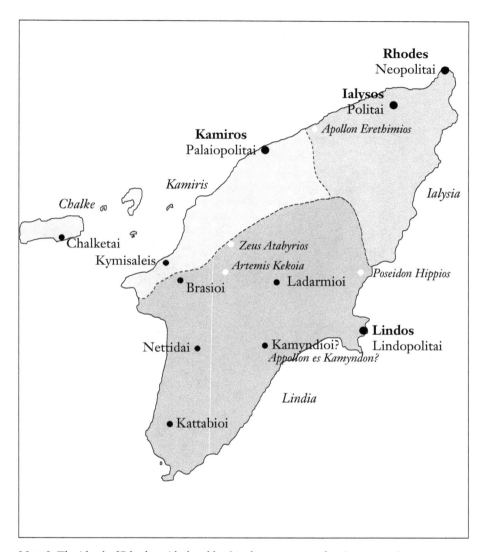

Map 2 The island of Rhodes with the old *poleis*, deme centres and major sanctuaries.

CHAPTER I

Introduction

D emocracy is arguably among the most fascinating aspects of ancient
Greek society. From its inception in the murky years of the late sixth
century BCE, a democratic form of government became closely associated with
Athens, the leading state of Classical Greece, and eventually spread to practically all corners of the Greek world, becoming, in turn, synonymous with
legitimate government of the Greek *polis*.[1] It is scarcely possible to overstate
the prominence of Classical Athens in the study of ancient democracy. For the
Classical period this is first and foremost a reflection of the state of our source
material. In addition to a thoroughly Athenocentric literature comprising histories and court, council and assembly speeches – even a political pamphlet
and a political treatise on the subject – hundreds of inscribed documents have
allowed historians to examine political institutions and practice in ever greater
detail. By comparison the evidence from Classical democracies outside Athens
is as scarce as it is fragmented.[2]

In terms of evidence, the playing field becomes somewhat more level
when moving into the Hellenistic period. This first of all reflects the drasti-
cally diminished availability of literary evidence. Nothing comparable to the
extant speeches or philosophical treatises have survived from the Hellenistic
period, and even the histories that have do not allow a sustained view of any
polis comparable to that provided by Herodotus, Thucydides and Xenophon
for Classical Athens. On the positive side, however, the widespread of the

---

[1] The name *demokratia*, however, is only attested from the late fifth century BCE in Athenian
literature and inscriptions (Harris 2016a: 44 with n. 3. Cf. Sealey 1987: 98–102).
[2] Robinson 2011. Cf. Robinson 1997.

so-called epigraphic habit across the Hellenistic *poleis* affords us a direct and in some cases sustained – but of course by no means complete – view of several more ancient democracies.[3] So many, in fact, that historians can confidently say that in the course of the early Hellenistic period democracy had come to be regarded as not only the default, but also the only acceptable, form of political organisation.[4] In terms of quantity, at least, there should be wide agreement that the heyday of ancient Greek democracy came in the centuries after the end of the Classical period.

DEMOCRACY, CLASSICAL AND HELLENISTIC

For these reasons, the Greek democracies of the Hellenistic period ought to provide fertile empirical ground for expanding our understanding of ancient democracy; in particular we should be able to investigate how democracies outside Classical Athens differed from or compared to their Athenian predecessor.

The study of democracy in the Hellenistic period, however, has hit upon a number of problems. One, and perhaps too obvious even to mention, was the once widespread belief that the ancient Greek *polis* had simply ceased to exist as a political community with the conquest of Philip and Alexander in the late fourth century. Though few contemporary historians would now dispute Louis Robert's famous remark that the Greek *polis* did not die at Chaironeia, or with Alexander, or at any point during the Hellenistic period, the death of Alexander is still thoroughly entrenched as a conventional end point of the history of the Greek *polis* and democracy, and attempts to transcend the dividing line – wherever exactly the line is drawn – remain few and far between.[5] This is not, of course, to suggest that democracy in the Hellenistic period has suffered total neglect; far from it, but the Classical/Hellenistic divide as it manifests itself in scholarship on ancient democracy contributes to a second problem for our understanding of democracy in the Hellenistic period, namely that of generalisation.

It has long been the practice among historians of the Hellenistic period to speak of 'the Hellenistic *polis*' and by extension of 'Hellenistic democracy'.[6] In the latter case in particular, the shift in perspective from the study of a single democracy (Athens in the fifth and fourth century BCE) to a

---

[3] See, for instance, the case studies by Grieb (2008) and Carlsson (2010).

[4] O'Neil 1995: 103–20; Gauthier 1993: 217–18.

[5] Robert 1969: 42. For an example of unease with the convention, see Sealey 1976: 491–2. Histories that bridge the gap between Classical and (early) Hellenistic Athens: Gauthier 1985, and to some extent Habicht 1995; Bayliss 2011.

[6] Jones 1940: 168; Hansen 2006: 132–4.

'synthetic' Hellenistic democracy constructed from evidence collected from
several *poleis* scattered across space and time, and ostensibly descriptive of
as many or even more (even all?) *poleis* in the period between 322 and 31
BCE, is connected with two changes in source material. First of all, the
ancient historical narratives available for the period (above all Polybios)
focus on the Hellenistic kingdoms and Rome as the agents of history, leaving less sustained attention to individual *poleis*. Secondly, and perhaps more
importantly, the greatly increased, but also largely fragmentary epigraphic
evidence may be said to have invited a 'synthetic' approach. But differences between *poleis* were profound, especially in regard to their political
proximity to hegemonic powers, be they Hellenistic kingdoms, leagues or,
eventually, the Romans.[7] This becomes a particularly pertinent problem
when dealing with Hellenistic Rhodes, a city which by most criteria usually
employed to distinguish between Classical and Hellenistic *poleis* comes off
as a thoroughly 'Classical' *polis*.[8] To take just the yardstick of independence:
from the mid-fifth to the late fourth century BCE Rhodes was a subject of
the imperial aspirations of, first, Athens and Sparta before it fell under the
sway of Carian dynasts, which lasted until Alexander's army swept through
southern Asia Minor and in passing installed a garrison on the Rhodian
acropolis.[9] Only after the death of Alexander and the ousting of his garrison did the Rhodians gain their independence, which they successfully
defended against the attempted conquest by Antigonos and his son Demetrios, and rose to be an important military power of the Eastern Mediterranean and a hegemon in their own right. For the Rhodians, it would seem
the traditional narrative of decline was in fact inverted, and one might
argue that Rhodes had been a 'Hellenistic' *polis* for much of the Classical
period, only coming into its own as an independent 'Classical' *polis* after
the death of Alexander and remaining so throughout the Hellenistic period,
even if the room for independent manoeuvring in foreign affairs diminished
considerably as Roman influence began to manifest itself in the Aegean
and beyond.[10] Surely, other *poleis* had equally complex relationships with
other states and undoubtedly other historical variables should be taken into
account.[11] For these reasons it is difficult not to agree with Patrice Hamon's

---

[7] Gauthier 1993: 212 (cf. Mann 2012: 19); Dmitriev 2005: 331–3.

[8] Hansen (2006: 132–4) sets out the significant differences between the Archaic and Classical *polis*
and its Hellenistic successor: (1) the loss of *autonomia*, (2) the loss of military organisation and
(3) the diminished significence of public associations. Though the subject is ostensibly 'the
Hellenistic *polis*', Hansen's examples are invariably drawn from (Hellenistic) Athens.

[9] Berthold 1984: 19–37.

[10] Berthold's notion (1984: 213–32) of the 'long twilight' overstates the case and downplays the
continued military importance of Rhodes in the following century (Wiemer 2002: 328–39).

[11] Carlsson 2010: 101–47.

judgement, that any talk of 'the Hellenistic *polis*', and by extension 'the Hellenistic democracy', is in fact still premature and must await the completion of more studies devoted to individual ancient democracies.[12]

The third problem concerns the definition of democracy. Traditionally scholars of 'Hellenistic democracy' have argued that although the *poleis* of the period were in possession of all the institutional trappings of the Classical Athenian democracy, political life had come to be dominated by a relatively small group of wealthy citizens (often, and particularly in the case of Hellenistic Rhodes, described as an 'aristocracy') who, as the financiers of chronically impoverished states, could easily bend the will of their fellow citizens. Consequently, 'Hellenistic democracy' to some extent became shorthand for 'fictional democracy' or oligarchy in disguise.[13] 'Fictional democracy', of course, assumes that there was in fact such a thing as real democracy with which to contrast it, and, whether explicitly stated or not, that real democracy is ever that of Athens in the fifth and fourth centuries BCE.[14] Crucially, Classical Athenian democracy has remained the yardstick of ancient democracy even as certain aspects of the traditional orthodoxy on Hellenistic democracy have been questioned. It may be noted in passing that one scholar of the Hellenistic period, critical of too sharp a divide between Classical and Hellenistic democracy, has attempted to take the fight to the opposition, as it were, by pointing to indications of 'oligarchisation' even in Classical Athens.[15] A more sustained critique of the traditional view has revolved around what is believed to be the continued vitality of democratic institutions in the Greek *poleis* of the Hellenistic period. According to this line of reasoning, democratic institutions like those associated with Classical Athens were widely adopted and maintained by democracies in the course of the late fourth and third centuries BCE (the now widely accepted 'High Hellenistic Period'), with oligarchisation only setting in from around the middle of the second century (the 'Low Hellenistic Period') as the influence of the Romans was more directly felt by the Greek *poleis* in and around the Aegean. This, paired with institutional developments, such as permanent boards of magistrates or executive power invested in councils, fundamentally changed the political institutions of the, now former, Hellenistic democracies. This reinvigorated, but traditional, institutional approach, however, is susceptible to a number of interconnected methodological problems. First of all, employing the example of Classical Athens as both model and criterion for true democracy

---

[12] Hamon 2009: 379.
[13] The classical formulation is that of Veyne (1990 [1976]) and Quass (1993), who introduced the concept of a 'Honoratiorenschicht' and 'Honoratiorenregime' to German scholarship. Cf. O'Neil 1995.
[14] O'Neil 1995: 107.
[15] Habicht 1995.

leaves little room for variation, in as much as variation potentially disqualifies any polity from being considered as democratic.[16] As a consequence, the discussion is to a large extent reduced to one about *when* precisely ancient democracy became 'Hellenistic'.

In a recent study of Hellenistic democracy Susanne Carlsson rightly points out that such an approach is fundamentally Athenocentric in as much as it disqualifies any other institutional arrangement from consideration. Instead Carlsson, with inspiration from Robinson's study of early Greek democracy, suggests guarding against it by applying a set of criteria for democracy drawn from the political theorist Robert Dahl.[17] The approach has merit in as much as it ought to allow the historian to look beyond a pre-defined set of institutions and open our eyes to other forms of democracy. The problem, then, is where to look, and Carlsson's answer to that question, namely to look at four Hellenistic *poleis* in full possession of democratic institutions broadly similar to those of Classical Athens, is as good an indication as any that such institutions must – perhaps inevitably – be the starting point. The exclusive focus on democratic institutions, however, runs the risk of reductionism, and recent contributions to the debate about Hellenistic democracy have tended to equate political institutions with political practice. If democratic institutions allowed for, or even encouraged, the equal participation of all citizens, it is argued, then there is no reason to suppose that all citizens did not particpate, and do so equally.[18] In such cases, however, where the evidence consists entirely of the epigraphic output of democratic institutions – and this is true for an overwhelming majority of *poleis* in the Hellenistic period – the argument becomes dangerously circular.[19]

What is more, it also partly misses the question. The challenge to 'true democracy', envisioned by earlier scholarship on Hellenistic democracy, came not from formal restrictions on the right of every citizen to participate in government, but from a relatively small group of citizens with greater desire to be involved, and greater availability of time, ability (real or perceived), and wealth as well as other social resources, than that of the average citizen.[20] In

---

[16] Carlsson (2010: 13–17), for instance, frames the question of Hellenistic democracy as one of 'fact or fiction'.

[17] Carlsson 2010: 45–54. Cf. Robinson 1997: 13–16.

[18] Carlsson (2010: 17) inverts Lewis's (1997: 57) question and asks: 'if the democratic formulas in the Classical period revealed democratic government, how can we know that this was not also the case in later periods?' Eventually Carlsson concludes that 'all choose leaders *from all*' (my emphasis) since 'all male citizens had access' to the assembly and since 'the holding of office is not dependent on property'. Grieb (2008: 356) concurs: 'Die politische Gleichberecthtigung der einzelnen Bürger lässt sich im weiteren an den politischen Institutionen der Poleis deutlich ablesen.'

[19] Robinson 2011: 221.

[20] On the balance between 'mass and elite' in Classical Athenian democracy, see Ober (1989: 293–339 and throughout). For measures apparently aimed at minimising the wealth and educational gap among the citizens in Taras and Thurii, see Robinson 2011: 118–19, 244–5.

this regard, ancient democratic institutions, at least on the Athenian model, embodied a paradox not unfamiliar to democracies of the present day, by insisting on the political equality of all citizens while simultaneously accepting profound social and economic inequalities. This view of ancient democratic institutions was first formulated in the context of Classical Athenian democracy by Mogens H. Hansen. In Classical Athens, politics was the privilege of the citizen, and not only the citizen, but the citizen free from social restraints.[21] Hansen reminds us of the process that shaped policy in Classical Athens, the ancient democratic *polis* par excellence: 'An initiative was taken by *ho boulomenos*; preliminary consideration by a board of magistrates; debate in a decision-making assembly, and a vote taken in that assembly.'[22] Political initiative came from the individual citizen, working alone, and was deliberated upon by the citizens collectively, who then made up their minds free from social restraints such as family ties, friendships, local influence or wealth.[23] In this, the ancient direct democracy differed completely from modern representative democracy:

> For ninety-nine per cent of the citizens in a contemporary democracy institutionalized political participation is restricted to voting every second year or so; and alongside the nation's political institutions there is a complicated network of semi-private and private institutions which tend to absorb the citizens' time and interest more than political institutions. Also, public opinion is formed by the media and not any longer in the parliaments. Thus the focus of interest tends to shift from political institutions to *the network of private or semi-private organisations that dominate and control society*: the party organisations, the unions, the corporations, the media and all the various kinds of organisations which, in a political context, we tend to call pressure groups. By contrast, ancient Athens had no guilds and trade companies (as at least the medieval city had), no unions, no media, and no political parties that can reasonably be compared to modern political parties (. . .) We have evidence of private and semi-private religious organisations and of informal groups of political leaders (. . .). But apart from that the sources give no information about important social organisations alongside the political institutions.[24]

Unlike modern politics, which is heavily embedded in society and in which political institutions see only part of the political process, ancient Greek politics,

---

[21] Hansen 1989; Sealey 1987: 148; Rahe 1984. Hence the stress in recent debates on Hellenistic democracy on the integrity of citizens and exclusion of foreigners: Grieb 2008: 355–8; Carlsson 2010: 289–91.

[22] Hansen 1991: 287.

[23] Hansen 1989: 111.

[24] Hansen 1989: 110 (my emphasis).

according to Hansen, were completely detached from society and the restraints and hierarchies it entailed. A clear and clean process governed by formal rules in which only the citizens participated free from social restraints. As a corollary, it has been argued that the reach of civic institutions, such as law and legal status, did not extend very far into society either.[25]

As an empirical statement, this view of Classical Athenian democracy certainly may (or may not) be valid (though this is not the place to examine it),[26] but adopted as a model on which to examine other ancient democracies, it potentially bars from our view a large section of ancient society whose importance, or lack of importance as Hansen would have it, should be argued rather than assumed. As recently pointed out by Christian Mann, pointing to the existence of democratic institutions simply cannot make the evidence of the influence of the wealthy go away.[27] On the other hand, the continued 'vitality' of democratic institutions helps sharpen the question: if democratic political institutions continued to repel the outsized influence of the wealthy few and denied them any power beyond that of ordinary citizens – through 'sovereign' assemblies and people's courts, which held magistrates accountable – how do we account for the pronounced presence of the same wealthy individuals in those same institutions?

In Rhodes, as we will see in the following chapter, a relatively small group of wealthy individuals managed to secure for themselves a privileged, and 'non-institutional', position in Rhodian politics through their regular appointment to political office. Furthermore, this 'magisterial elite', as we shall call them, managed to pass on power to their successors and to reproduce their hold on the Rhodian state through generations, often earning them the title of aristocracy.[28] This requires an explanation.

DISAGGREGATING THE *POLIS*

While ancient historians have been busy reinforcing the institutional separation of ancient democratic politics from ancient society, political scientists have been moving in a decidedly different direction. Dissatisfied with a tradition which held the state to be a unitary and autonomous entity, some political scientists in the late 1980s and early 1990s began to challenge both aspects, in

---

[25] As in Vlassopoulos's (2007) 'free spaces' or Gottesman's (2014) 'The Street'. On the latter, see the review by Harris (2012–13).

[26] Following the publication of Hansen 1989, a number of studies have been dedicated to the study of Athenian social institutions: Lambert 1993; Jones 1999; Ismard 2010.

[27] Mann 2012: 14.

[28] Gabrielsen 1997: 15–17; Rostovtzeff 1941: 685–7.

a project sometimes referred to as the 'disaggregation of the state', by focus-
ing their analysis on how certain parts of the state interacted with more or less
organised groups in society in the formulation and pursuit of specific policies.[29]
According to these political scientists, various organisations, both inside and
outside the state, established so-called 'policy networks' consisting of government agencies, political parties, media outlets, advocacy groups, business
organisations and companies. Though often confined to the level of individual
policies, some studies have been able to detect certain structural patterns in the
way such policy networks function and consequently speak more broadly to
the distribution of power in state and society.[30]

From the perspective of the ancient historian concerned with the study of
politics in an ancient democracy, this approach points a useful way forwards.
First of all, and in line with current scholarly consensus, it proceeds from the
assumption that formal political institutions had a vital role to play in shaping
democratic politics. At the same time, however, and by expanding the analysis to include organisations outside the institutions of the state, it avoids the
constitutional reductionism characteristic of much recent scholarship, which
potentially bars from our view certain social institutions which influence political outcomes. In other words, it provides not only an invitation to the ancient
historian to reconsider whether politics could in fact always be so neatly confined to the state, but also a basic model on which to view the workings of an
ancient democracy.

But before we proceed along these lines, it is necessary to state with some
precision what we are looking for in terms of (1) policy, (2) organisations, both
public and private, and (3) networks that tied these organisations together in
a common pursuit.

Policy

Much of the impetus for political scientists researching policy networks has
been the desire to explain better the processes by which public policies were

---

[29] Coleman and Skogstad 1990. Occasionally, this disaggregation of the state goes so far as to abandon all organisation, identifying individual state agents, i.e. ministers, secretaries and other civil
servants (and the networks of which they formed part), as the unit of analysis, resulting in a 'stateless state' (Rhodes, R. 2011). The approach has been almost completely ignored in the debate over
whether whether the ancient Greek *polis* (or, again, at least Classical Athens) was a stateless or
state-based community. As pointed out by Anderson (2009: 5–8) most participants in the debate,
regardless of their stance, have proceeded from the simple binary speration between state and
society. The shortcomings of the completely autonomous state as a model for the ancient Greek
polis can perhaps be seen in the 'compromise' position, that the *polis* was some kind of fusion of
state and society (e.g. Ober 1993: 129; Manville 1994: 24; cf. Anderson 2009: 5–8).

[30] E.g. Coleman 1990. Cf. Peters 1998: 1, 11–12.

formulated, advocated and eventually decided. Needless to say, modern political scientists pursuing this approach are able to draw on much more extensive and detailed evidence than that which is usually afforded the ancient historian, sometimes with the additional advantage of being able to create even more evidence.[31] In the case of Hellenistic Rhodes, the nature of our evidence severely complicates any search for the potential workings of any network of organisations precisely because policies, conventionally understood, are very hard to come by. The almost complete lack of inscribed decisions, whether laws or decrees, of the Rhodian council and assembly considerably hampers any study of virtually any measure adopted by the assembly. What we do have evidence of, however, is the regular election of members of a relatively small circle of individuals to Rhodian political and religious office.[32] As will be argued in detail as we survey Rhodian democratic institutions in Chapter 2, Rhodian magistrates took a leading role in formulating and advocating policy, and it is therefore justified to look upon placement in political office as proxy for policy or even a policy in and of itself.

Organisations

As Hansen reminds us, any search is of course not likely to yield evidence for mass media, trade unions or political parties in the modern sense. But what we can look for is the 'network of private or semi-private organisations that dominate and control society'. In doing so we may take a cue from Aristotle. In a widely cited passage in Book 3 of the *Politics*, Aristotle famously defined the *polis* as 'the community of citizens around a constitution' (*koinonia politon politeias*).[33] The passage is usually taken to reinforce the idea that politics in ancient Greece was indeed confined to an independent sphere reserved for the citizen and cordoned off from the rest of society by a set of explicitly political institutions (the *politeia*, or 'constitution'). But this is not the only definition of *polis* to be found in the Aristotelian corpus. Elsewhere, in the *Nichomachean Ethics*, Aristotle identifies a different set of organisations as the fundamental institutions of the *polis*:

> But all the associations are parts as it were of the *polis*. Travellers for instance associate together for some advantage, namely to procure some

---

[31] For his study of *Everyday Life in the British Government* (Rhodes, R. 2011), for instance, Rod Rhodes spent considerable time shadowing and interviewing members of the British civil service.

[32] Gabrielsen 1997. Grieb (2008: 399–44), though highly sceptical of 'aristocratisation' before the mid-second century, nevertheless concedes the outsize influence of the wealthy for the later period. For a critique of this divide, see Boyxen 2018: 49–57.

[33] Arist. *Pol.* 1276b1. cf. Jones 1999: 27–30; Hansen 1998: 88–9.

of their necessary supplies. But the *polis* association too, it is believed, was originally formed, and continues to be maintained, for the advantage of its members: the aim of lawgivers is the good of the community, and justice is sometimes defined as that which is to the common advantage. Thus the other associations aim at some advantage; for example sailors combine to seek the profits of seafaring in the way of trade or the like, comrades in arms the gains of warfare, their aim being either plunder, or victory over the enemy or the capture of a city; and similarly the members of a *phyle* or a deme (and some associations appear to be formed for the sake of pleasure, for example *thiasotai* and *eranistai*, which are formed for sacrifice and social intercourse, but all these associations seem to be subordinate to the *polis*, which aims not at a temporary advantage but at covering the whole of life) combine to perform sacrifices and hold festivals in connection with them, thereby both paying honour to the gods and providing pleasant holidays for themselves (. . .) All these associations then appear to be parts of the association of the *polis*.[34]

αἱ δὲ κοινωνίαι πᾶσαι μορίοις ἐοίκασι τῆς πολιτικῆς· συμπορεύονται γὰρ ἐπί τινι συμφέροντι, καὶ ποριζόμενοί τι τῶν εἰς τὸν βίον· καὶ ἡ πολιτικὴ δὲ κοινωνία τοῦ συμφέροντος χάριν δοκεῖ καὶ ἐξ ἀρχῆς συνελθεῖν καὶ διαμένειν· τούτου γὰρ καὶ οἱ νομοθέται στοχάζονται, καὶ δίκαιόν φασιν εἶναι τὸ κοινῇ συμφέρον. αἱ μὲν οὖν ἄλλαι κοινωνίαι κατὰ μέρη τοῦ συμφέροντος ἐφίενται, οἷον πλωτῆρες μὲν τοῦ κατὰ τὸν πλοῦν πρὸς ἐργασίαν χρημάτων ἤ τι τοιοῦτον, συστρατιῶται δὲ τοῦ κατὰ τὸν πόλεμον, εἴτε χρημάτων εἴτε νίκης ἢ πόλεως ὀρεγόμενοι, ὁμοίως δὲ καὶ φυλέται καὶ δημόται [ἔνιαι δὲ τῶν κοινωνιῶν δι᾽ ἡδονὴν δοκοῦσι γίνεσθαι, θιασωτῶν καὶ ἐρανιστῶν· αὗται γὰρ θυσίας ἕνεκα καὶ συνουσίας. πᾶσαι δ᾽ αὗται ὑπὸ τὴν πολιτικὴν ἐοίκασιν εἶναι· οὐ γὰρ τοῦ παρόντος συμφέροντος ἡ πολιτικὴ ἐφίεται, ἀλλ᾽ εἰς ἅπαντα τὸν βίον] . . . θυσίας τε ποιοῦντες καὶ περὶ ταύτας συνόδους, τιμάς τε ἀπονέμοντες τοῖς θεοῖς, καὶ αὑτοῖς ἀναπαύσεις πορίζοντες μεθ᾽ ἡδονῆς. (. . .) μάλιστα γὰρ ἐν τούτοις ἐσχόλαζον τοῖς καιροῖς. πᾶσαι δὴ φαίνονται αἱ κοινωνίαι μόρια τῆς πολιτικῆς εἶναι.

This is an altogether different conception of the *polis*. The *polis* is still a *koinonia*, but the components that go to make up the *koinonia* are very different. In the first we find only the citizens, who combine to form the *polis*, but in this second definition the concept of the citizen has given way to a focus on the social organisations that go to make up the *polis*: (1) more or less organised groups of merchants and soldiers, (2) the so-called religious

---

[34] Arist. *Eth. Nic.* 8.9.4–6 (1160a8–29) Translation adapted from Rackham 1926.

associations of *thiasōtai* and *eranistai* and finally (3) the public subdivisions, the demes and the *phylai*, together constituting an association of associations or a 'corporate *polis*'. In contrast with the definition in Book 3 of the *Politics*, the vision of the *polis* sketched here has usually been understood as describing society, or more precisely that part of society which was strictly non-political, and together the two are believed to illustrate the dual nature of the *polis* as both a state and a city (a duality which translations of *polis* into 'city-state', 'Stadtstaat' or 'cité-état' attempt to capture). But at least one group of organisations included in Aristotle's list of associations, namely the public associations of the demes and the *phylai*, straddled the divide (and so, depending on the status of their membership, did the private associations).

Public associations

Among those organisations which formed part of Aristotle's corporate *polis* were the *phylai* and the demes. From the examples supplied by Aristotle, we may guess that he was thinking of Athens in particular, but the distribution of the citizenry into a series of discrete associations, some of which (like the Athenian *phylai*) were themselves further subdivided by other associations, is a well-known feature of *poleis* throughout the Greek world.[35] Such associations formed part of the state by virtue of being open only to citizens and, crucially, by defining citizenship itself in that every citizen was a member of one or more of these associations.[36] The guarding of the citizenship, however, is only one of several state functions attested for public associations. In Athens, to take the best-known instance, public associations had a crucial role to play in the manning of the council, certain boards of magistrates and the courts, as well as in military organisation.[37] Similar functions are well attested outside Athens, as amply documented by Nicholas Jones's 1987 survey of public associations. Such 'constitutional' functions connected public associations directly to the political institutions of the *polis* and are regularly included in analyses of political institutions.[38] Moreover, in the case of Classical Athens the public subdivisions, the *phylai,* demes and the *gene,* have also been the subject of specialised studies.[39]

In addition to their 'constitutional' functions, public associations were also associations in their own right, with their own rules and procedures for collective decision-making, their own officers, properties, finances and cultic commitments

---

[35] Jones 1987.

[36] This exclusivism, coupled with a universalism that required all citizens to be members, is listed by Jones (1987: 1) as the defining characteristic of the 'public organisation'.

[37] Hansen 1991: 103–6; Whitehead 1986: 255–90.

[38] Grieb 2008: 36–42 (Athens), 147–53 (Kos), 206–9 (Miletos), 273–6 (Rhodes).

[39] Ismard 2010; Jones 1999; Lambert 1993; Whitehead 1986.

(though they might sometimes be difficult to disentangle completely from those of the state),[40] and their own opinions about who did and did not merit their special recognition.[41] Compared with the 'constitutional' functions of the public subdivisions, the associational aspects of public associations have been largely ignored.[42]

This is especially important when we turn to Hellenistic Rhodes, where the three major divisions of the citizenry, the *phylai* Lindia, Ialysia and Kameris, as the formerly independent *poleis* Lindos, Ialysos and Kamiros, predated the establishment of the joint Rhodian state. In several ways the *phylai* were reluctant to give up their *polis* identities and at least one, the Lindians, refused to accept on equal terms those new citizens which the federal Rhodian state assigned them, and successfully defended themselves against this measure.[43] When, late in the period with which we are concerned, the Kamireans chose to expand eligibility to the eponymous priesthood of their *polis* and *phyla*, the initiative as well as the sanction came from the Kamireans themselves.

Private associations

To Aristotle's corporate *polis* there also belonged private associations such as *thiasotai* and *eranistai*. Rhodes was famously the 'land of the *eranoi*' or private associations. About 200 have been epigraphically attested throughout the period with which we are concerned.[44] The turn of the nineteenth and twentieth century saw a remarkably antiquarian interest in private associations and in various aspects of their internal organisation.[45] More recent studies of private associations have aimed at situating the association phenomenon in a wider context, particularly within the field of Hellenistic religion and migration, but have largely avoided the issue of politics.[46] When occasionally political historians touch upon the issue, private associations are relegated to the social, non-political sphere.[47] Their cultic and social activities (and much attention has been given to funerary arrangements) are found to be non-political or even anti-political to the extent that their blossoming in late-fourth-century Athens

---

[40] Whitehead 1986: 255–60.
[41] Jones 1987: 3–4. For an overview of the 'private', i.e. not state-mandated, functions of public associations across the Greek *poleis*, see Jones's (1987: 396–403) appendix III.
[42] There have been a few attempts at 'disaggregating' Classical Athens: Ismard 2010 and especially Jones 1999. See also van Bremen 2013 for a non-Athenian, non-Classical case study.
[43] Gabrielsen 2000: 192–5. For Lindian unwillingness to allow outsiders to stand for election, see Chapter 4.
[44] See Chapter 5.
[45] Poland 1909; Ziebarth 1896; Foucart 1873.
[46] Trümper 2006; Harland 2003; Baslez 2001; 1998; Pakkanen 1996; Cotter 1996; Rauh 1993.
[47] Hansen 1989: 110

has been regarded as related to the end of politics and the *polis* (in the sense of 'state'). In fact, according to Nicholas Jones, private associations are even a sign of the decline of the *polis*:

> As the slow decline of the classical associations gathered steam, the two processes, one of atrophy, the other of growth, did become intertwined. The erstwhile domination of the 'public associations' (especially the deme and the quasi-public phratry) had artificially suppressed the need for true voluntary associations. Self-evidently, the demise of these groups will, in the absence of any corrective action by the central government, have given rise to a corresponding demand for new associations of appropriate type.[48]

On this interpretation public and private associations competed for the attention of the Athenian citizens in an associational zero-sum game, and one that eventually ended in the near-annihilation of the public associations. In Hellenistic Rhodes, as will be argued in Chapter 4, the democratic *polis*, as well as its subdivisions, were still very much alive and kicking, in spite of the presence of great numbers of private associations.

Outside Athens and in later periods the relationship between associations and the political elites of the cities they inhabited has also received some attention. Onno van Nijf has analysed the evidence for professional associations in the Roman East and pointed to their integration into civic life, including public processions and banquets, and their connections with established civic and imperial elites. The main outcome of this exchange was the creation of what Verboven has called 'the associative order', a process of stratification which allowed members of private associations to stake a claim for a privileged position in society outside of the elite.[49] Though some aspects of these studies will be relevant to the present study, the political backdrop for interaction between private associations and elites in Hellenistic Rhodes is fundamentally different. Even if at a glance (and we shall have that glance in a moment) the Rhodian political elite may share a number of traits with the Roman elites of later centuries, above all their wealth, membership in the magisterial elite still depended upon time and again securing a majority of the assembly to vote for a decree or a candidate.

Recently, however, historians of the Hellenistic world have begun to investigate the various points at which private associations interacted not just with the societies which they inhabited but also with the state, which in some cases

---

[48] Jones 1999: 305.
[49] Verboven 2007. Van Nijf (1997: 131–240, esp. 134) follows Ostrow (1990) in naming this process '*ordo*-making'.

led to cooperation between the state and private associations and on occasion to what were once wholly private organisations being co-opted by the state.[50] Among the former and of particular importance for this study, Vincent Gabrielsen noted the extensive bonds that existed between private associations in Rhodes, many of them formed by military personnel, and members of the Rhodian military and political elite, as well as their importance for trade.[51] In the course of the present study we will revisit the question, but also take a step further and ask whether private associations had a direct impact on Rhodian politics and in particular on the establishment of the Rhodian magisterial elite.

Families

Though it was not explicitly included in the corporate *polis*, Aristotle elsewhere pointed to the *oikos* as a constituent member of society, and for good reasons.[52] As a unit of reproduction, the *oikos* was central to the maintenance of a citizen population to man the political institutions, and the public associations, indeed the whole state, depended on it for its continued existence. But as a unit of production it was equally central to the distribution of wealth in society. Since – as we will see in a moment – wealth was a defining characteristic of the Rhodian magisterial elite, it will be important to trace the origins of their wealth, especially how material benefits were passed on from one member of the *oikos* to the other, allowing members of fairly small number of families to not only achieve political success, but to do so repeatedly over several generations.

Networks

According to Clyde Mitchell, one of the founding fathers of the field, a social networks analysis may be split into two levels of analysis. One is the morphological level, which consists in mapping the relational ties, 'the medium', between social agents through which resources, 'the message', may flow. Adherents of the morphological level of analysis, both within and outside the field of ancient history, often lament the unwillingness of other scholars to apply quantitative methods to their analysis, which, so these adherents claim,

---

[50] Gabrielsen and Thomsen 2015. For the intriguing case of the partial institutional merger of the Ionian-Hellespontine branch of the Dionysiac *technitai* and the *polis* of Teos, see Le Guen 2001: I 243–50; Aneziri 2003: 387–91. For private associations turned into tax groups, see Thompson 2015 (Ptolemaic Egypt) and Thomsen 2018 (late Hellenistic Lindos).

[51] Gabrielsen 1997: 123–9; 2001.

[52] Arist. *Pol.* 1253b1–14. Cf. Roy 1999; Hansen 1997: 10–12.

reduces social networks analysis to a 'trendy substitute label for traditional prosopographical methods' or a 'metaphor'.[53] However, many of the analytical concepts associated with this level of analysis, such as 'density' (the number of ties shared by agents) and 'degree centrality' (one agent's number of direct ties relative to those of other agents in the network), presuppose that the total (or near total) number of ties and agents within a network is ascertainable.[54] The method was developed by sociologists and anthropologists, who can draw their evidence from questionnaire surveys or field observations.[55] The historian, however, is not so fortunate and the ancient historian perhaps even less so. The fragmentary nature of our evidence poses considerable challenges to morphological analysis.

The concept of the social network, nevertheless, has heuristic value. That is, we may inform our analysis of attested social ties with the assumption that they form part of a larger network, the morphology of which we cannot hope to recover in full. In fact, the problem we face because of the state of our evidence is very similar to one faced by every network analyst, namely that of network boundaries. 'It is in the nature of networks to spread out, rather than being neatly contained', as the sociologist Bonnie Erickson put it, and the setting of any boundaries potentially cuts off structurally significant actors from the network under study.[56] In principle, a social network is 'infinite', meaning that it potentially includes every person on the planet (although, strictly speaking, this is still finite). In other words, no social network is ever complete even under the best of conditions.

The second, 'interactional' level of analysis examines the properties of individual ties. Mitchell points to a number of criteria through which ties may be analysed, first of all frequency and durability. These criteria are primarily interesting because of their ability to shape Mitchell's third criterion. This criterion is 'intensity' or the degree to which an individual is prepared to honour obligations implied in a tie between agents.[57] If intensity is weighted against the risk of the other agents not reciprocating, it turns into trust, a concept which has received much attention within the social sciences in recent years. In most cases the real object of interest is what is sometimes called 'generalized trust' or 'generalized social capital', by which is meant a shared propensity to engage in social (including economic) transactions with any member of society without prior knowledge of their characteristics or affiliations. Generalised trust is considered a public good which 'lubricates social life', to use Putnam's

[53] Ruffini 2008: 16; Reader 1964: 22; Mitchell 1969: 1–7.
[54] Mitchell 1969: 12–20.
[55] Mitchell 1969: 30–6.
[56] Erickson 1997: 151; Mitchell 1969: 12–15
[57] Mitchell 1969: 20–36.

expression, and drives down the transaction costs in economic exchange.[58] The sources of 'generalised trust' are usually sought in relationships of 'particularised trust', such as those that develop between neighbours or members of voluntary associations,[59] but as has been pointed out recently, the mechanisms by which 'particularised trust' is transformed into 'generalised trust' remain obscure and the assumption of a causal relationship between the two remains to be proven.[60] For our purposes we will limit ourselves to the more tangible 'particularised trust' and trace its potential for access to certain resources.

Networks are not static. Relationships may cease to exist and new ones may be formed, or the content of a relationship may change over time. A central question for the present study must therefore be how the relationship between two social actors influences the possibility of 'recruitment' of new ties to the network of each or both. A classic illustration in the literature is that of the customer who wishes to buy a used car, but is afraid to be had by the dealer and so seeks advice from a trusted friend who has recently bought a car from the same dealer.[61] The fact that one social actor (A) trusts another social actor (B) may influence a third's (C) decision to trust B if C considers A to be trustworthy. Seen from the perspective of B, earning the trust of A makes C a potential connection.[62] However, in order for trust to be propagated through the network, it must be externalised. If C is unaware of A's trust in B, then it is not likely to influence C's decision to form a relationship with B. This will become crucial for our interpretation of the honorific monuments which make up a fairly large portion of our evidence. Broadly speaking these monuments, usually a statue on an inscribed base, but occasionally honorific decrees, give evidence of a sort of transaction between an association (the state, a subdivision of the state or a private association) and an individual: the honorand performs a service for the association, which in turn reciprocates with an appropriate expression of gratitude. 'Appropriate' invariably means a public declaration of trust in or endorsement of the character of honorand in the hope that the spectator will be persuaded, thereby creating a good reputation.[63] The propagation of trust is, however, not unidirectional, as can be seen from the blatantly unsubtle hortatory clause usually appended to the decision

---

[58] Putnam 2000: 20–2; Fukuyama 1995. For a study of impersonal or generalised trust in the ancient Greek world, see Johnstone 2011.

[59] Putnam (2000: 402–14) recommends greater participation in voluntary associations, churches and neighborhood activities as a means of generating social capital (cf. Coleman 1990). To Fukuyama (1995: 3–57), however, social capital (including trust) is culturally rooted.

[60] Ogilvie 2004: 5; Stolle and Hooghe 2003: 234–40.

[61] Buskens 2002: 3

[62] Buskens 2002: 15–22.

[63] Buskens 2002: 3.

to erect an honorific decree: 'in order that those who seek honour (*hoi philoti-moumenoi*) will be many, knowing that the *thiasotai* know how to recompense with due thanks'.[64]

THE POLITICS OF ASSOCIATION IN HELLENISTIC RHODES

The aim of this study is to contribute to the understanding of ancient Greek democracy, in particular its variety, through a close examination of a specific case, that of Hellenistic Rhodes. In particular, the aim is to investigate how various groups in Rhodian society (some of them caught halfway between state and society) were mobilised by a few individuals in the pursuit of securing a stable base for their participation in politics, a participation which seems to have excluded the average citizen.

We will begin (Chapter 2) by surveying the political institutions of the Rhodian state and by drawing an outline of the magisterial elite whose members habitually acted as the political, military and religious agents of the Rhodian state. The remaining chapters will trace the social foundations of this privileged magisterial elite through three distinct networks: the family, public subdivisions and private associations. Chapter 3 traces the importance of family connections for access to the key resources of wealth and political experience. In Chapter 4 we turn to the public subdivisions of the three old *poleis* and their demes to examine their connections with individual members of the magisterial elite. Chapter 5 introduces the private associations, with a particular focus on the role of religion in building and maintaining connections between members, while Chapter 6 discusses the exploitation of associations by the magisterial elite. In Chapter 7, the issue of the relationship between private associations and the *polis* as a whole is discussed and the question of the existence of a Rhodian civil society is raised. Chapter 8 sums up the results of the study.

---

[64] *IG* II² 1261.53–5: ὅπως ἂν ὦσι πολλοὶ οἱ φιλοτιμούμε | νοι, εἰδότες ὅτι ἐπίστανται χάριτας ἀ | ποδιδόναι οἱ θιασῶται. Translation adapted from Kloppenborg and Ascough 2011: 61. Cf. Sickinger 2009.

CHAPTER 2

Rhodian Democracy

In 408/7 BCE, in the midst of the Peloponnesian War, the three independent *poleis* of the island of Rhodes, namely Ialysos, Kamiros and Lindos, joined together in a common island-wide state.[1] Several, indeed most, aspects of the formation of the new Rhodian state elude us. The dearth of epigraphic sources from the first century of the new unified state makes it difficult to piece together the functions or even existence of most political institutions, and the constant shifts in government between democrats and oligarchs make it near impossible to generalise from the few scraps of literary evidence we do have.[2] Following the expulsion of the Macedonian garrison in 322 BCE, however, the Rhodian state embarked on a long period of relative political stability that lasted well into the Imperial period.[3] From the beginning of this period, though slowly at first, epigraphic evidence combined with a few literary texts allows us to piece together a picture of political institutions in the federal state as well as in the constituent *poleis* of Lindos and Kamiros (and to a lesser extent Ialysos).[4]

POLITICAL INSTITUTIONS

Following the synoikism a new city, the city of Rhodes, or simply the *asty* as it was known locally, was founded on the island's northern promontory and intended to be the seat of the new federal Rhodian state's religious and

---

[1] Diod. 13.75.1. Gabrielsen 2000; Berthold 1984: 22 with n. 12.
[2] On the fourth century see Gabrielsen 2000; Berthold 1984: 19–37.
[3] Berthold 1984: 213–32; Schmitt 1957: 173–92; van Gelder 1900: 157–77.
[4] Grieb 2008: 264–311; Gabrielsen 2000 (cf. 1997: 24–31); Berthold 1984: 19–37.

political institutions.[5] As part of this process of integration, the three formerly independent *poleis* took on the roles of *phylai* in the new joint Rhodian state under the names Lindia, Kamiris and Ialysia. As such they served as the first set of civic subdivisions, which competed against each other at a number of state festivals celebrated in the *asty*, that is, the city of Rhodes. The *phylai* remained, however, centred on the three cities, which persisted both as towns and as important centres of cult and local administration.[6]

Council, assembly and courts

Collective decision-making in the federal Rhodian state was in the hands of the council (*boula*) and the people (*ho damos* or *ho sympas damos*) which met in assembly (*ekklesia*).[7] The normal procedure seems to have gone through the council, who heard proposals on a wide variety of matters. These ranged from petitions from private associations and civic subdivisions for permission to erect their own decrees in small public sanctuaries over matters of sanctuary management, and public honours, to decisions on foreign politics and war.[8] Rhodian councils sat for only six months, in either a winter or a summer term, and though we do not know the number of councillors or how they were selected, we may guess from Cicero's remarks on the rotation of both nobles and commoners through the Rhodian *boula* that councillors were selected by lot (the whole operation seemed utterly foreign to Cicero).[9] Its meetings were open to outsiders, who could also address the council, and Polybios

---

[5] The dates of establishment of the *asty* as well as the federal Rhodian institutions are a matter of some controversy. Gabrielsen (2000: 187–90, 192–5) stresses that the evidence for most institutions is of a later date and that certain and undeniable indications of *polis*-ness after 408/7 BCE could suggest that the process of political and physical synoikism was slower than traditionally imagined. An important crux in this connection is the dating of a list of Halios priests (*SEG* 12: 360), the beginning of which was set by Morricone (1949–51: 351–80) to 408/7 BCE, but questioned by Gabrielsen (2000: 187 with n. 49), who prefers a later date. The recent contribution to the debate by Badoud (2015: 162–3) lends support to Morricone's dating, but either view requires that some and not other priests are regarded as homonyms of more securely attested individuals.

[6] Jones 1987: 243–4.

[7] Gabrielsen 2000: 190–1; 1997; Berthold 1984: 39; van Gelder 1900: 234–5.

[8] Petitions for the setting up of decrees: *IG* XII.1 890; 922; 1032; *Lindos II* p. 1009. Management of the Asklapeion: *SER* 1. Honorific decrees: e.g. *IG* XII.1 56 (for honours enacted by the *boula* alone, see below). Foreign policy: Pol. 25.5.1–5; 28.17.13; 29.10.1–6; 30.21.1–5. War: Diod. 20.94.5.

[9] *IG* XII.1 53; *Annuario* 2 (1916) 142 no. 11; *Lindos II* 420. Cic. *Rep.* 1.31.47; 3.35.48. Grieb 2008: 291; Gabrielsen 1997: 26–7; van Gelder 1900: 243–5. For the Rhodian sacred and civil calendars, see Badoud 2015: 11–35.

relates how discussions could be somewhat heated.[10] After reaching a decision the *boula* passed on decrees to the Rhodian assembly (the *damos* or *sympas damos*) for ratification.[11] Here any issue was once again debated, whereupon the assembled Rhodians voted by a show of hands and decided by majority.[12] The assembly met perhaps once a month in the theatre of Dionysos in the *asty* and had the final say on all matters.[13]

It has been suggested that the assembly lacked the power of initiation and was reduced to rubber-stamping or rejecting *probouleumata*, prepared by the council.[14] This, however, is unlikely for two reasons. First of all, decrees of the Rhodian state are enacted in two ways. In most cases the enacting bodies are the *boula* and the *damos*, but in some the *damos* acts alone. The most likely explanation for the two types of enacting formulae is that they reflected two different procedures for decision-making. The first has a *probouleuma* enacted by the *boula* and subsequently debated and ratified (with or without amendment) by the *ekklesia*, while the other represented motions made directly before the *ekklesia* and without prior deliberation in the *boula*.[15]

Secondly, a passage in Livy's account of Rhodian attempts to appease the Romans after the battle of Pydna in 167 BCE suggests that the assembly was indeed able to make a snap decision in a single meeting without awaiting the opinion of the *boula*. A group of 'leading Rhodians' (*principes Rhodiorum*) managed to intercept the Egypt-bound Roman embassy of Gaius Popillius and Gaius Decimus and persuaded them to appear, not before the council as one would expect for ambassadors, but directly before the assembly (*contio*), perhaps even an irregular assembly since it took place the day after the ambassadors' arrival in Rhodes.[16] At the very same meeting, the Rhodians voted to prosecute those who had spoken against the Romans – a decree, according to Livy, more or less suggested by Gaius Decimus in his speech before the assembly and therefore not the result of a *probouleuma*. If Livy can be believed on the course of events on that day, the Rhodian council was completely bypassed.

Incidentally, inscriptions also preserve enactments by the *boula* alone. Though these are always honorific, the existence of honorific decrees passed

---

[10] Pol. 29.11.1–6. At the meeting of the council to hear the envoys of Genthios, the main political figures, Deinon, Polyaratos and *the hoi peri Theaideton*, were all present and debated the Rhodian response, causing tumult.

[11] Gabrielsen 2000: 190–1.

[12] Pol. 29.10.1–6. Gabrielsen 2000: 191.

[13] Gabrielsen 1997: 27; van Gelder 1900: 246.

[14] Berthold 1984: 39 with n. 4.

[15] Gabrielsen 1997: 27; Rhodes with Lewis 1997: 272–3.

[16] Livy 45.10.4–15. Livy is not explicit about where the deliberation took place, but references to 'the people (*populus*)' and 'the commoners (*multitudo*)' (45.10.10–12) clearly suggest the assembly. For the reception of foreign envoys by the council, see Grieb 2008: 289–90.

by both *boula* and *damos* suggests that the council was permitted to pass its own resolutions, but also that this privilege did not extend to any other matter.[17] On the strength of an unpublished decree,[18] it has recently been suggested that the Rhodian *boula*, following the Roman victory at Pydna, was endowed with greater independence and that this greater independence marked a profoundly 'aristocratic' turn in Rhodian political history.[19] The provision in question, that 'if this decree lacks anything, the *boula* is empowered to pass an additional decree',[20] however, finds a close parallel in a couple of Athenian decrees from the middle of the fourth century, by which the Athenian assembly left an open-ing for certain minor matters to be handled by the *boule* without subsequent ratification by the assembly – presumably to avoid burdening an increasingly busy assembly with trivial matters.[21] Rather than attesting to a dramatic change in powers, the passage in fact proves exactly the contrary: that the Rhodian *boula* could make independent decisions only when expressly permitted by the assembly and only to the extent that it did not contradict the assembly.

The people's court (the *dikasteria*) was in charge of justice, and like those of its Classical Athenian counterpart its judges were selected by lot through the use of an allotment machine (*kleroterion*) operated by a specially appointed

[17] Van Gelder 1900: 243. *Tit. Cam.* 78 (late second or early first century BCE); *IG* XII.1 53 (after second century BCE); *AD* 18 A (1963) 1 no. 1 (50–1 BCE); *Cl. Rhodos* 2 (1932) 206 no. 41 (first century BCE); *REG* 16 (1903) 184 A (first century BCE, two cases); *Lindos II* 384d–e (9 BCE); 392 (10 CE); *AD* 18 A (1963) 3 no. 2 (mid-first century CE); *Lindos II* 421 (c. 25–30 CE); *PdP* 4 (1949) 81 no. 2 (Imperial); *Tit. Cam.* 88 (undated); *SER* 32 (undated); *NSill* 26 (undated); *MDAI(A)* 25 (1900) 107 no. 106 (dated by editor to c. 200 BCE, but this seems unlikely: honours voted by all three *poleis* only appear in private monuments in the late first century BCE (cf. *AD* 18 A (1963) 1 no. 1; *Lindos II* 392; 393) and the Lysistratos son of Hagesandros mentioned in l. 7 is probably the same person mention in *Lindos II* 440, dated to 50–70 CE). On the limited independent power of the Athenian *boule* see Hansen 1991: 255–6.
[18] Papachristodoulou 1986 (cf. 1990).
[19] Grieb (2008: 339, following Wiemer 2002: 334 with nn. 35–8) points to this 'institutional change' as paving the way for Gabrielsen's (1997) 'naval aristocracy', whose influence prior to 167 BCE Grieb otherwise denies (2008: 316–20). In further support Grieb (2008: 340 with n. 444) cites the prominent place given to the *grammateus boulas* – directly following the *prytaneis* – in late dedications by Rhodian magistrates dated to the first centuries BCE and CE (*NSill* 20; *MDAI(A)* 20 [1895] 5 no. 1). The same order, however, can be found in a similar dedication dating to the period 188–166 BCE (*IG* XII.1 49, cited, but not dated, by Grieb) as well as in one dated precisely by its *grammateus boulas*, the grandfather of a famous Stoic philosopher, to about 210 BCE (*Cl. Rhodos* 2 [1932] 198 no. 30: for the date, see Badoud 2015: 102, 299). The change in prominence, in other words, does not exist and dedications made by Rhodian magistrates from the late third to the first century suggest rather profound continuities.
[20] [εἰ δέ τινός] κα ποτιδέῃ τόδε τὸ ψάφισμα κυρία ἔστω ἁ βουλὰ ποτιψαφιζομένα, as reported by Wiemer (2002: 334 n. 35) citing personal correspondence with Daniel Kah.
[21] *IG* II² 127.34–5 (356/5 BCE); *IG* II³ 1 404.7–9 (c. 345–320 BCE); Hansen 1991: 256; Rhodes 1972: 82 n. 3; Harris 2016b: 79.

magistrate (*klarotas dikastan*).[22] According to Aristotle, in the late fourth century BCE, judges, like magistrates, council members and assembly-goers, were paid by the state. Occasional reference to the waiving of pay by magistrates in the second and first centuries BCE suggests that this principle was maintained throughout the period with which we are concerned.[23]

The citizens of each of the three old cities continued to meet in assembly (*ekklesia*) to deliberate and vote on various matters relating their own affairs.[24] Matters of religion feature prominently in our evidence, including the financial aspects of sanctuaries, priesthoods and festivals, but the cities' infrastructure (such as the maintenance of city walls) was also among the items on these assemblies' agendas. After the synoikism, foreign relations seem to have been ceded to the federal assembly (though the Ialysians certainly, and the Lindians possibly, continued for at least some years to appoint their own foreign *proxenoi*) and legal disputes between citizens, and perhaps between the cities themselves, seem to have been handled through the federal *dikasteria*, as no trace of the local administration of justice can be found.[25]

The importance of religious matters was further underscored by the renaming of the cities' local councils as *mastroi*. At Lindos the *mastroi* numbered fifty-one members and these probably served a term of one year.[26] The *mastroi* had a probouleutic function vis-à-vis the assemblies, and most attested decisions of Ialysos, Lindos and Kamiros were issued in the name of both *mastroi* and assemblies.

Magistrates

The day-to-day running of the Rhodian state was in the hands of an impressive corps of magistrates. The most important were the five *prytaneis*, the *tamiai*

---

[22] *IG* XII.1 55.3; *NSill* 18.7; *Annuario* n.s. 1–2 (1939/40) 151 no. 7.8. Gabrielsen 2000: 191; van Gelder 1900: 258. For the six bronze *pinakes* found in Rhodes, see Fraser 1972.

[23] Arist. *Pol.* 1304b27–8. *Lindos II* 224.II.35 (148 BCE); *Cl. Rhodos* 2 (1932) 190 no. 19.14 (early first century BCE); *NSill* 18.4 (early first century BCE); *MDAI(A)* 11 (1886) 202 no. 1.4 (c. 80 BCE). Gabrielsen 2000: 191.

[24] *Lindos II* 419 (22 CE).

[25] Arist. *Pol.* 1304b29–30; [Dem.] 56.47. Gabrielsen 2000: 191; cf. 1997: 28.

[26] The basis of election of the *mastroi* is held to have been different in Kamiros and Lindos. On the strength of *Tit. Cam.* 109 (a decree of the Kamireans dated to the end of the fourth century) it is widely believed that Kamirean *mastroi* were elected by the *ktoinai* (Gabrielsen 2000: 193–4; van Gelder 1900: 222–4: on the *ktoina*, see Chapter 4), but it is in fact not entirely clear if the *mastroi* in question are to be identified with the councillors of the same name. At Lindos, a list of *mastroi* for the year 27 BCE is preserved on a statue base (*Lindos II* 378.141–207) organised by deme, suggesting that deme membership was the basis of selection of *mastroi* there. A similar, but only partially preserved, list from 43 BCE (*Lindos II* 346.89–147) shows considerably different quotas for each deme attested compared with those of 27 BCE. Conventionally this is interpreted as evidence of a reform of the quotas, but other possibilities surely exist.

and the ten *stratagoi* – the last usually elected on the basis of the three *phylai*, which could, however, be disregarded in favour of election from the entire citizenry.[27] Apart from these the Rhodians elected an array of magistrates charged with various duties, among them not a few responsible for securing the defence of the state. Most of these have come down to us merely as titles and for that reason a full review of Rhodian magistrates and their various tasks and areas of responsibility is not possible. Some general points, however, may be offered.

Some magistrates, the *stratagoi* and the military *epistatai* are known to have been elected (by show of hands, *cheirotonia*), but the method of appointment is only rarely mentioned and only to specify the authority (e.g. *toi cheirotonethetes hypo tou damou*) or re-election (e.g. *epicheirotonethenta to deuteron*).[28] Given the ability, however, of certain individuals to secure multiple offices, it may be supposed that most other offices were also elected. This was certainly the case in Lindos, and for Kamiros we can be certain that the *damiourgos* was elected, while multiple, and perhaps consecutive, terms in other offices suggest that election was the norm.[29] The only direct evidence for appointment by lot relates to an unspecified priesthood in the *asty*.[30] Tenure seems to have varied and the *prytaneis*, the chief magistrates of the Rhodian state, were elected for only six months.[31] The shortness of the term was perhaps an effort to restrain somewhat what was probably a powerful position (see below). In contrast, the nauarch was apparently appointed for the duration of whatever task he was assigned by the assembly.[32] In Lindos and Kamiros magistrates, including

---

[27] Dmitriev 1999.

[28] 'elected by the *damos*': *Lindos II* 215; 247; 249; 253; 272; 293; 347. Re-elected: *Cl. Rhodos* 2 (1932) 188 no. 18; *NSill* 18.

[29] Lindos: *IG* XII.1 761.38–43 (Bresson 1988; Thomsen 2018); Kamiros: *Tit. Cam.* 3.Dc.56–7. Xenombrotos son of Ktesias was *hypogrammateus* in c. 198 and c. 197 BCE (*Tit. Cam.* 45.41; 46.II.23); Ariston son of Epikrates was *hierokaryx* for four (consecutive?) years after c. 193 (*Tit. Cam.* 46.II.26; 47.29; 48.12; 49.1); Erasilas son of Sosistratos was *hierokaryx* for four (consecutive?) years leading up to c. 183 BCE (*Tit. Cam.* 47.30; 48.13; 49.2; 50.42).

[30] *ARW* 27 (1929) 349.15–6 (late second or early first century BCE). Fraser (1972: 121 with n. 56) argues that the selection by lot must have extended to all priesthoods (in the *asty*). However, the exact context of the decree is obscure. It calls for the creation of a register of 'the priests (οἱ μὲν ἱερεῖς, l. 11)', but which priests is not specified and it is not immediately clear whether the plural is meant to refer to different priesthoods or simply the succession of priests in the same priesthood. The latter seems a priori most likely and the instruction to include in every entry the name of the priest of Halios, for dating (ἀνα | γραφόντω τὰ ὀνό | ματα τὰ αὐτῶν | πατριαστὶ καὶ δάμο[υ] | καὶ τὸν ἱερῆ τοῦ Ἁλίου | ἐφ' οὗ ἔλαχε·, l. 11–16), would suggest that this priesthood was exempted and therefore lends support to this interpretation.

[31] Pol. 27.7.2–3. Grieb 2008: 292; Berthold 1984: 39; van Gelder 1900: 265–6. On the prytany year, see Badoud 2015: 16–18.

[32] Grieb 2008: 296–9; Berthold 1984: 39; van Gelder 1900: 249–50.

priests, seem to follow the eponymous priest or magistrate and must have had year-long tenure.[33]

Polybios' narrative of events in Rhodes in the time leading up to and during Rome's Third Macedonian War (171–168 BCE) allows a closer look at the interaction between one board of Rhodian magistrates and the council and assembly. Every six months the Rhodian assembly elected five *prytaneis*.[34] The five made up a board under the leadership of a 'chief-*prytanis*', for instance *hoi prytaneis syn Meneklei toi Archagora*.[35] The *prytaneis* seem to have had a hand in coordinating between the *boula* and the assembly and to have presided over the meetings of both bodies. Polybios may be taken to suggest that *prytaneis* presided over the meetings of the assembly.[36] Furthermore, the *prytaneis* occupied an important junction in the foreign relations of the Rhodians. They received foreign envoys and introduced them before the *boula* and the assembly, and whenever the assembly decided to send envoys to some foreign power it was apparently left up the *prytaneis* to appoint the envoys.[37]

As presidents of the Rhodian assembly, the *prytaneis* did not limit themselves to drawing up the agenda and overseeing the debates, but engaged directly in the debates, often as champions of specific policies. In 171 BCE, as war between the Romans and Perseus had drawn very near, Polybios places the *prytanis* Hagesilochos in the Rhodian assembly, not (or at least not only) as the president, but arguing for the decision to ready forty Rhodian ships to assist the Romans if war should come.[38] His successor in that office, Stratokles, presided over the assembly when war had come and Rhodian commitment to supporting Rome with ships was waning. Listening to the debate, Polybios relates how Stratokles was stirred into action:

[33] E.g. *Lindos II* 224 (Lindos, 148 BCE) or *Tit. Cam.* 38 (Kamiros, 223 BCE)

[34] Pol. 27.7.2. In line 1 of *NSill* 20 Maiuri restores [πρυτ]α[νε]ύ[σας πρ]άτα[ν] | ἑξάμηνον | τὰν ἐπ' ἱερέως Ἀγλωχάρτου | καὶ ἐπ' ἱερέως Φαινίλα. Although the restoration fits well with Polybios, the fragmentary condition of line 1 warns against placing confidence in the restoration. Since the top of the stone is completely broken, Maiuri's suggestion that only one line (above line 1) containing a name is missing cannot be confirmed, as there is no possibility of even approximating the original height. Against the restoration stands the fact that the division of the year into a 'first' and 'second' ἑξάμηνος is epigraphically unattested and depends entirely on Pol. 27.7.2, while the Rhodian council, which also sat for six months, was identified as that of either the winter period (χειμερινὰν ἑξάμηνον, *Lindos II* 707) or the summer period (τὰν θερινὰν ἑξάμηνον, *Annuario* 2 (1916) 142 no. 11).

[35] *MDAI(A)* 20 (1895) 386 no. 5.1

[36] The *prytaneis* shared a *hypogrammateus*, or under-secretary, with the *boula*: IG XII.1 49.I.11; *Cl. Rhodos* 2 (1932) 198 no. 31.11–2; *MDAI(A)* 20 (1895) 382 no. 4.11. The *prytaneis* are also found forming a *koinon* with the *grammateus boulas*: *Annuario* n.s. 1–2 (1939/40) 151 no. 7.10–1; SEG 33: 644.12–15.

[37] *I. Magnesia* 55.22–3; Pol. 15.23.3–4; 25.5.1; 27.4.4; 29.11.1–2. Wiemer 2002: 21; Berthold 1984: 39; O'Neil 1981: 471.

[38] Pol. 27.3.1–5 (Livy 42.45.1–7).

Upon this Stratokles the *prytanis* got up, and after saying many things against Perseus and in favour of the Romans, exhorted the many to ratify the decree relating to the dispatch of the ships.[39]

ἐφ᾽ οἷς Στρατοκλῆς ὁ πρύτανις ἐπαναστὰς καὶ πολλὰ μὲν κατὰ τοῦ Περσέως εἰπών, πολλὰ δὲ περὶ Ῥωμαίων ἐπ᾽ ἀγαθῷ, παρώρμησε τοὺς πολλοὺς εἰς τὸ κυρῶσαι τὸ ψήφισμα τὸ περὶ τῆς ἐξαποστολῆς τῶν πλοίων.

The glimpse into the debates of the Rhodian assembly is suggestive. The matter under discussion in both cases concerned foreign relations – an area of politics which usually fell under the *prytaneis*. In both cases the assembly debated the Rhodian response to a Roman request made through discussion or correspondence with the *prytaneis*.

In both instances the *prytaneis* were arguing for decrees already proposed. Evidence from other levels of the Rhodian state suggests that it was common practice for magistrates to propose legislation even in the old *poleis*, which, like the federal state, had probouleutic bodies (the *mastroi*). In the *ktoina* of the Potidaioi on the island of Karpathos a motion was introduced by the *hierothytai* (*hierothytan gnoma*).[40] Similarly, in Lindos many decisions were made at the suggestion of the *epistatai*, the Lindian officials whose duties corresponded roughly to those of the *prytaneis* at the federal level, as early as the late fourth century BCE and recurring at regular intervals through to the early first century CE.[41] Furthermore, in Kamiros a decree dated to the Roman period was enacted at the initiative of the magistrates (*archontes*).[42] The picture which emerges is one of heavily engaged magistrates, who weighed in on all phases of the decision-making process.

At Lindos and Kamiros, boards of three *epistatai* seem to have performed tasks similar to those of the federal *prytaneis*. Their close association with the secretaries of the *mastroi* (and at Lindos with the auditors) suggests that the *epistatai* presided over meetings and perhaps drew up the agenda of the *mastroi*, and the *epistatai* were not infrequently behind the decrees passed by the *mastroi* and assemblies.[43]

Institutionally speaking, the Rhodian state comes off as thoroughly democratic with a 'sovereign' assembly, people's courts, specialised magistrates and state pay for all. Although magistrates may have weighed in on the decision-making process, the shortness of their terms display a clear commitment to

---

[39] Pol. 27.7.12–14. Translation adapted from Paton 2012.

[40] *Lindos II* p. 1009.2.

[41] *IG* XII.1 761 (late fourth century BCE); *Lindos II* 233 (129 BCE); *RIPR* 22 (100–66 BCE); *Lindos II* 419 (22 CE); *IG* XII.1 762 (23 CE). Blinkenberg 1941: 24–5.

[42] *Tit. Cam.* 112.1.

[43] Dedications of the *epistatai*: *Lindos II* 190 (Lindos, c. 170 BCE); proposals by *epistatai* (*epistatan gnoma*).

the democratic idea of ruling and being ruled in turn.[44] Nevertheless, practically every student or commentator, from Strabo onwards, has expressed some reservations about the democratic nature of the Rhodian state or noted its 'aristocratic' veneer.[45] These reservations invariably revolve around the pronounced tendency for a few individuals, who seemingly preferred ruling to being ruled, to run for civic and religious office time and again. Their success in winning priesthoods and magistracies, and more importantly how this success was achieved within the framework of a democratic state, is the subject of this study, and it is to them we turn next.

CIVIC CAREERS

The preceding section traced an outline of Rhodian political institutions and reviewed the evidence for an extensive and politically involved executive branch. In this section we will begin to add flesh and blood to the bare bones of the institutions. The following takes the form of a prosopographic survey of priests and officers attested in epigraphy.

The chance survival of two dedications made by federal officers in two years between c. 188 and c. 166 BCE may illustrate the difficulties with piecing together civic careers:

col. I

[πρυτάνιες]·
1   [– – – – – –]αρ[– – –]
[ὁ δεῖνα] . Ἁγησιστράτου
[καθ' ὑ]οθεσίαν δὲ Ἐξακέστου
[. . . .]στρατος Δαμοκλεῦς
5   [. . .]σίλοχος Παυσία
[κα]θ' ὑοθεσίαν δὲ Ἀνδρωνίδα
[Πυθ]όδοτος Πυθοδότου
γραμματεὺς βουλᾶς·
[Θεύ]προπος Θευφάνευς
10   [κ]αθ' ὑοθεσίαν δὲ Θευφάνευς
ὑπογραμματεὺς
βουλᾶι καὶ πρυτάνεσι·
[Ἀρι]σταγόρας Ἀρισταγόρα
τοῦ Ἀρισταγόρα
vacat

---

[44] Arist. *Pol.* 1317b1.
[45] Strabo 14.2.5. Berthold 1984: 39; Rostovtzeff 1941: 687; Van Gelder 1900: 246. Cf. Gabrielsen (1997: 24–31), who rightly stresses Rhodian democratic institutions.

15 στραταγοί·
    [Πο]λυκρέων Δαμοφίλου
    [. . .]οκράτης Πύθωνος
    [. . .]αγόρας Πολυκλεῦς
    [. .]Ισανδρος Τιμοκράτευς
20 [Πει]σιάναξ Ἀπολλοδότου
    [κα]θ᾽ υοθεσίαν δὲ Γόργωνος
    [. . . .]ραγόρας Κλείνου
    [. . . . .]σιος Παναιτίου
    [. . . . .]στος Ἀλεξάνδρου
25 [ἐ]πὶ τὰν χώραν·
    [. . . .]ρίδας Δαμοκράτευς
    [εἰ]ς τὸ πέραν·
    [. . . .]χος Θαρσυβίου
    γραμματεύς·
30 [. . . .]ς Διοκλεῦς
col. II
    [ταμίαι]·
31 Ἀναξίκλει[τος – –]
    Δωρόθεος Νικαίου
    Νικοκράτης Παυσίων[ος]
    Ἐμμενίδας Παυσία
35 Μένιππος Οὐλιάδου
    Νικόμαχος Ἐξακέστου
    καθ᾽ υοθεσίαν δὲ Εὐφράστου
    Μενεκράτης Μενεκράτ[ευς]
    γραμματεύς·
40 Τηλέμναστος Ἀνδραγ[όρα]
    καθ᾽ υοθεσίαν δὲ Ἀρχιτ[– –]
    ἐπίσκοποι·
    Σωσικράτης Πλεισ[τ – –]
    Δεινόμαχος Σίμω[νος]
45 Αἰνήσιος Ἀναξικ[ρ]ά[τευς]
    Τελέστωρ Θευφά[νευς]
    Τρίτυλλος Ἀναξαγ[όρα]
    γραμματεύς·
    Ἐπιμένων Κλήνακτ[ος]
50 ἐπιμεληταὶ τῶν ξέ[νων]·
    Ἀριστομβροτίδας Ἀριστο[– –]
    Εὔφαντος Παυσανίου
    Σωκράτης Νυμφίωνος
    Ἀντίπατρος Ἡρακλε[. . . .]

55   Φίλτατος Φιλτάτου
      καθ᾽ υοθεσίαν δὲ Θαρσιπό[νου]
      γραμματεύς·
      Σιμίας Χαρμοκλεῦς
      ἀγεμὼν ἐπὶ Καύνου·
60   Φιλιστίδας Ἀρχιπόλιος
      ἀγεμὼν ἐπὶ Καρίας·
      Θευγένης Πιστοκράτε[υς]
      ἀγεμὼν ἐπὶ Λυκίας·
      Διοκλῆς Θευπρόπου
65   θεοῖς.

IG XII.1 49 (Fig. 2.1) was set up in honour of a *prytanis* who served some time, but not long, after c. 188 BCE, by fellow officers, including the *grammateus boulas*, the *hypogrammateus boulas kai prytanesi*, the ten *stratagoi*, the *tamiai*, the *episkopoi*, the *epimeletai ton xenon* and the *hagemones* of Kaunos, Caria and Lycia – a total of forty more-or-less-preserved names. By chance, part of a similar inscription also survives, preserving the names of eighteen officers of a different, though roughly contemporary, year (*MDAI(A)* 20 [1895] 382 no. 4). Of these eighteen, four can also be found in *IG* XII.1 49: (1) Peisianax son of Apollodotos and adopted son of Gorgon – one of the *prytaneis* – appears as *stratagos* in *IG* XII.1 49.20–1; the *stratagoi* (2) Nikokrates son of Pausion and (3) Menippos son of Ouliades are both found among the *tamiai* in *IG* XII.1 49.33 and 35; and finally (4) Theugenes son of Pistokrates the *stratagos* of the Peraia is named as *hagemon* of Caria in *IG* XII.1 49.62.

This overlap of officers between two years within a twenty-year period provides a first indication that civic office in Rhodes was the reserve of a relatively small group of people. The suspicion is confirmed by the evidence for individual 'careers' preserved in private monuments. The career of Eudamos son of Dexicharis provides a case in point. In the early second century BCE Eudamos held a number of different offices which were recorded on the base of the statue which his ward Gorgon son of Timokles and adopted son of Diokles set up, perhaps in or somewhere in the area of the Rhodian gymnasium where the base was found:[46]

<hr>

[46] *Cl. Rhodos* 2 (1932) 192 no. 20. The date assigned by the editor, 'principio del I sec. A. C.', based on epigraphic criteria, must give way to an earlier date since the sculptor, Demetrios son of Diomedon of Rhodes, also executed statues for the priest of Athana Lindia of 182 (*Lindos II* 167) and 154 (*Lindos II* 217) and at some point cooperated with Theon of Antioch (*Lindos II* 205), who was active in the same period as well as a member of the *Asklapiastai Nikasioneioi Olympiastai* and mentioned in their list of benefactors dated to the first half of the second century (*IG* XII.1 127.B.12–13; for the date see Maillot 2005 no. 24 with commentary). As for the original placement of Eudamos' statue in the area of, or perhaps in, the gymnasium below the Rhodian acropolis where it was found in 1929, it is perhaps supported by the unusual fact that Eudamos' term as gymnasiarch is mentioned first. In spite of Eudamos' military credentials he is probably not the *nauarchos* who commanded the Rhodian fleet at Side and Myonnesos in 190 (Livy 37.22.5–25.3; App. *Syr.* 22).

Figure 2.1 *IG* XII.1 49. Joint dedication by federal Rhodian magistrates (Ephorate of Antiquities of the Dodecanese – © Hellenic Ministry of Culture and Sports (N.3028/2002)).

Eudamos son of Dexicharis. Gorgon son of Timokles and adopted son of Diokles (dedicated this) for Eudamos who was his guardian and who was gymnasiarch of his *phyle* and trierarch and *hagemon* of Caria and *tamias* and *stratagos* of the Peraia and *prytanis*, to the gods. Demetrios son of Diomedon of Rhodes made (it).

> Εὔδαμος Δεξιχάριος
> Γόργων Τιμοκλεῦς
> καθ᾽ ὑοθεσίαν δὲ Διοκλεῦς
> ὑπὲρ Εὐδάμου
> 5   ἐπιτροπεύ[σ]αντος αὐτοῦ
> καὶ γυμνασι[αρ]χήσαντος φυλᾶς
> καὶ τριηραρχήσαντος
> καὶ γενομένου ἀγεμόνος ἐπὶ Καρίας
> καὶ ταμιεύσ[α]ντος
> 10 καὶ στραταγήσαντος ἐν τῶι πέραν
> καὶ πρυτανεύσαντ[ο]ς
>   θε[οῖς].
> Δημήτριος Δ[ιομέδοντο]ς Ῥόδιος ἐ[π]οίησε.

Over the years Eudamos had held the important offices of *hagemon* of Caria, *tamias*, *stratagos* of the Peraia as well as the prytany, a civic feat which his ward Gorgon had thought fit not only to commemorate, but also to emulate. Gorgon's own statue, which stood next to Eudamos', records his own terms of office as *tamias*, *stratagos* of the Peraia and *prytanis*.[47] Several such careers are attested in private monuments. Nikagoras son of Pamphilidas and adopted son of Nikagoras, a Lindian, could boast of having served four terms as *stratagos* of the Peraia, during which he was able to expand Rhodian territory considerably.[48] Damokritos son of Damokritos had also served a term as *stratagos* of the Peraia, but was also at one point *stratagos* of the island. Pasiphon son of Pasiphon held the same two offices in the first century (he was elected twice as the *stratagos* of the Peraia), but could add those of *grammateus boulas* and *tamias* of the Great Haleia, the quadrennial festival of Halios.[49] Entimos son of Timokleidas and adopted son of Ainesidamos had served as *stratagos* as well as *hagemon* of the *chora* and *astynomos*.[50] Ploutarchos son of Heliodoros, according to an inscription carved on the base of a statue dedicated by the

---

[47] *Cl. Rhodos* 2 (1932) 194 no. 22.
[48] *IG* XII.1 1036; *Lindos II*, 151 (Fraser and Bean 1954: 99 with n. 1; Berthold 1984: 138; Wiemer 2002: 184).
[49] *Cl. Rhodos* 2 (1931) 188 no. 18.16–22 (early first century BCE). Badoud 2015: 298.
[50] Damokritos: *Tit. Cam.* 72. Entimos: *IG* XII.1 44.

Aphrodisiastai Soteriastai, had served as *agonothetas*, *tamias*, *stratagos*, officer of the law courts, *epimeletas ton xenon* and *prytanis*,[51] but pride of place among such careers belongs to Polykles, whose monument was set up somewhere in the *asty* in the years following the First Mithridatic War, in which Polykles had been part of the military leadership. Apart from his many military commands, which included commands of Rhodian warships and culminated in his election as *stratagos* of the Peraia and his service as advisor (*symboulos*) to the nauarch Damagoras, Polykles had on numerous occasions been gymnasiarch as well as president of the courts, *grammateus boulas* and *prytanis*.[52]

The same tendency can be observed at the *polis* level, where local priesthoods played an important part in shaping individual careers. Nikomedes son of Neikostratos, for instance, a Kamirean citizen, held no fewer than three different priesthoods (of Pythian Apollo, Dionysos and Asklapios) as well as serving a term as *hieropoios* at some point in the first century.[53] Similarly, at Lindos in the early second century Timapolis son of Xenophon held the priesthoods of Athana Lindia and Zeus Polieus (in c. 193 BCE), Pythian Apollo, Artemis Kekoia and Poseidon, and was also *archierothytas*.[54] Many seem to have divided their time between civic and religious offices. In Kamiros, Philokrates son of Philostephanos seems to have begun his public career as one of Kamiros' twelve *hieropoioi* in c. 207 BCE, a career which reached its peak with his election as *damiourgos* twenty-one years later. During those years Philokrates held the office of *agonothetas*, the magistrate in charge of *polis* festivals who was also responsible for public announcements at these games.[55] Later he served as *grammateus mastron* or secretary of the Kamirean council before being elected as one of Kamiros' three *epistatai* in about 199.[56] Similarly, in Lindos Hagesianax son of Telesikrates, who served as *hierotamias*, also served a term as *epistatas* in an unknown year around 170 BCE, while Damon son of Kleumbrotos, who was *grammateus mastron* in that year, went on to be elected priest of Athana Lindia for the year 148 BCE.[57]

---

[51] *Annuario* n.s. 1–2 (1939/40) 151 no. 7.

[52] *NSill* 18. For Damagoras (son of Euphranor), see Kontorini 1993.

[53] *Tit. Cam.* 56b.

[54] *Lindos II* 158.

[55] *Tit. Cam.* 110. Duties of the *agonothetas*: *Tit. Cam.* 106. The *polis* of Kamiros celebrated at least two festivals at regular intervals, the Dionysia and the Panathenaia. In the *asty*, which elected several such magistrates, each responsible for one festival (*IG* XII.1 6), the name of the *agonothetas* forms part of the dating formula of games (*BCH* 99 [1975] 97).

[56] *Tit. Cam.* 110 with *TRI* 21. For the career of Philokrates, see Badoud 2015: 104–6. Cf. Gabrielsen 1997: 134–6.

[57] Hagesianax son of Telesikrates: *Lindos II* 190 (*epistatas*); 172 (*hierotamias*). Damon son of Kleumbrotos: *Lindos II* 190 (*grammateus mastron*); *Lindos II* 1 s.v. 148 (priest of Athana Lindia).

From the evidence so far surveyed one might get the impression that we are dealing with three separate magisterial elites: one in the *asty* and another two in Lindos and Kamiros. To be sure, private monuments in Lindos and Kamiros focus mainly (though not exclusively) on local offices and priest-hoods, but the chance discovery of monuments belonging to the same individuals found locally as well as in the city of Rhodes provides evidence that many members of the local elites had careers at the federal level as well. An inscribed base of a statue for Eupolemos son of Eupolemos (and adopted son of Timokrates) recovered on the Lindian acropolis attests his tenure of the priest-hood of Athana Lindia and Zeus Polieus (86 BCE), and we might have thought that Eupolemos had limited himself to pursue the service of this goddess only.[58] But the chance discovery, in the city of Rhodes, of another inscribed base for a statue of Eupolemos allows us to see that the priesthood of Athana Lindia was but one of many offices and priesthoods which he had occupied in the course of what we might term a 'career': *tamias* (during the festival of Halios), wartime *stratagos* (presumably during the war against Mithridates), *prytanis* and *prophatas*. The last office, furthermore, is attested also in a partially preserved list of *propha-tai* covering a period of only fifteen years including, incidentally, the year (89 BCE) Eupolemos served.[59] The fact that Eupolemos' term as *prophatas* predated his priesthood in Lindos, yet was not mentioned on the base of his statue there, clearly demonstrates two things: (1) that the makers of the monuments which make up so much of our evidence were sensitive to particular traditions and expectations shaped in no small part by specific institutions (in this case the sanctuary and priesthood of Athana Lindia) and cannot be read as up-to-date curricula vitae; and (2), by extension, that in the context of the Rhodian *asty*, even if the precise context cannot be ascertained, Eupolemos' tenure of the eponymous priesthood in Lindos was deemed worthy of mention.

Nevertheless, several federal Rhodian magistrates can be shown to have held civic or religious office in one of the three old *poleis*. A number of Rhodian *stratagoi*, in addition to Eupolemos son of Eupolemos, can be shown to have held at least one civic or religious office at the *polis* level. (1) Menekrates son of Nauphilos, who was *damiourgos* in Kamiros in c. 204, can be found in a list of Rhodian *stratagoi* (*Cl. Rhodos* 2 (1932), 198 no. 31) along with (2) Boulanax son of Damonax, who was *hierothytas* in Lindos c. 182. (3) Damagetos son of Kleukrates, *stratagos ek panton en toi astei* sometime in the second century, had also served a term as *grammateus mastron* in Kamiros.[60] That same office was also held by (4) an unknown fellow townsman from the deme of Silyrioi, who was

---

[58] *Lindos* II 293b (86 BCE). The statue was built into a family monument (*Lindos* II 293a–c), which included statues of Eupolemos' father and older brother (Ma 2013: 223; Thomsen forthcoming c).

[59] *SEG* 39: 759; *SER* 5.8 (Badoud 2015: 112–18).

[60] Menekrates: *Tit. Cam.* 3.Eb.33; *Cl. Rhodos* 2 (1932) 198 no. 31. Boulanax: *Lindos* II 167; *Cl. Rhodos* 2 (1932) 198 no. 31. Damagetos: *Tit. Cam.* 78a; *Tit. Cam.* 90.

also *hieropoios* in Kamiros as well as *stratagos ek panton tas choras tas in tai nassoi.*[61] Finally, (5) Damagetos son of Kleukrates, who was *grammateus mastron* in Kamiros sometime in the early second century, had also served a term as *stratagos.*[62] From Lindos (6) Nikagoras son of Pamphilidas and adopted son of Nikagoras, the successful *stratagos* of the Peraia, had served as one of Lindos' *hierothytai* before winning the office of *stratagos* of the Peraia four times.[63] Another *stratagos*, (7) Andrias son of Autokrates, had held the priesthood of Athana Lindia in 56 BCE,[64] and (8) Kallikrates son of Kallikrates, who served as *stratagos* with Timokrates (the son of Polycharmos?) around 160 BCE, is probably to be identified as the *epistatas* of Lindos in 159 BCE.[65]

A joint dedication by the *prytaneis* and their secretaries of an unknown year in the late third or early second century names two *prytaneis* who were also at some point (9) priest of Athana Lindia (probably in 197 BCE) and (10) priest of Apollo in Kamiros c. 201 BCE.[66] (The under-secretary of the *prytaneis* and the secretary of the *boula* were both also at some point priests of Athana Lindia.)[67]

The picture that emerges from this review of individual careers is one of a relatively small group of individuals who had somehow managed to monopolise political, military and religious office in both Lindos and Kamiros (and Ialysos, for which evidence is virtually non-existent, may be supposed to have been no different), and at the federal level.

Cursus and competition

Election for office or priesthood did not presuppose any previous tenure.[68] Nor was there any formal age requirement for any particular office or priest-

---

[61] *Tit. Cam.* 78 (= *IG* XII.1 701). One more local office should be included: Hiller von Gaertringen's restoration [ἱεροθυτήσ?]αντος ἐν Καμείρωι (l. 6) was rightly questioned by Pugliese Carratelli since the office is unattested in Kamiros (though two late inscriptions, *Tit. Cam.* 112, Roman period, and *Tit. Cam.* 86, undated, do mention a *hierothyteion* in Kamiros).

[62] *Tit. Cam.* 90.II.22–3; 78a.

[63] *IG* XII.1 1036; *Lindos II* 102; 151; 152(?).

[64] *Lindos II* 322 (and *Lindos II* 1).

[65] *SER* 22.9; *Lindos II* 212.

[66] Archinomos son of Archyllos: *Lindos II*, 150 (for the date see *Lindos II*, 1 v.s. 197); *Cl. Rhodos* 2 (1932) 198 no. 31. Hagesidamos son of Ainesidamos: *Cl. Rhodos* 2 (1932) 198 no. 31; *Tit. Cam.* 46.

[67] Panaitos son of Nikagoras, adopted son of Euphranoridas, *grammateus boulas* (*Cl. Rhodos* 2 (1932) 198 no. 31) and priest of Athana Lindia in c. 223 (*Lindos II* 1 v.s. 223) and of Poseidon Hippios in c. 225 (*Lindiaka VI* 18.109). For his family, including the Stoic philosopher, see Gabrielsen 1997: 132 and Blinkenberg 1941: 45–6. Onasandros son of Euphanes, *hypogrammateus boulai kai prytanesi* (*Cl. Rhodos* 2 (1932) 198 no. 31) and priest of Athana Lindia in 165 (*Lindos II* 1 v.s. 165) and of Dionysos (*Lindos II* 199).

[68] Grieb 2008: 318. The one exception to this rule was the priesthood of Artemis Kekoia at Lindos, which was held by former priests of Athana Lindia and Zeus Polieus in the second year after vacating that priesthood.

hood, although a minimum age for holding office in general may be safely assumed. Nevertheless, it is clear that some offices and priesthoods were usually held in sequence and some at particular stages in the magisterial career. Kamirean *damiourgoi*, for instance, can each be shown to have entered public life as one of Kamiros' twelve *hieropoioi*. On average, twenty-five years passed between their term as *hieropoios* and that of *damiourgos*. This considerable time span (in one case forty-one years elapsed)[69] suggests that Kamirean *hieropoioi* must on average have been fairly young. Some, like Theudoros son of Onasandros, who was *hieropoios* in c. 239 BCE, served a term as priest (Theudoros was priest of Athana Polias and Zeus Polieus in about 224 BCE) before being elected as *damiourgos*, but none can be shown to have held a priesthood after their term as *damiourgos* or a term as *hieropoios* after a priesthood.[70] Local political offices, such as *epistatas*, *mastros* or *grammateus*, cannot easily be placed in *cursus*, but it seems that these too usually followed a term as *hieropoios* and were capped by election as *damiourgos*. Philokrates son of Philostephanos began his career as *hieropoios* in c. 207 BCE before serving terms as *agonothetas*, *grammateus mastron* and *epistatas*, the last in 199 BCE. Finally, in 186 BCE, he was elected *damiourgos*.[71]

A similar pattern may be observed in Lindos, where appointment to the board of *hierothytai* marked the typical first step in a priestly 'career'. Like their Kamirean counterparts, Lindian *hierothytai* on average reached the eponymous priesthood of Athana Lindia twenty-five years after their first election, but again individual careers differ considerably.[72] As in Kamiros, there were several priesthoods through which the priestly elite would pass on the way to the priesthood of Athana Lindia. A number of priests of Athana Lindia can be found in the list of priests of Poseidon Hippios or in priestly dedications, always holding the latter office first.[73] While the priesthood of Athana Lindia was the most prestigious, a priestly career in Lindos seems to have culminated with the priesthood of Artemis Kekoia, which by the first century was held by a former priest of Athana Lindia in the second year after the end of his service to Athana.[74]

---

[69] Theudoros son of Onasandros, on whom see below.

[70] *TRI* 9b.II.58 (= *Tit. Cam.* 5.II.60); *Tit. Cam.* 35.5. Aristombrotidas son of Aristombrotidas was apparently never *hieropoios*, but served as priest of Athana Polias before being elected *damiourgos* for 170 BCE (*Tit. Cam.* 84). The priesthood of Halios, the eponymous priesthood of the federal Rhodian state, was apparently held only after those at Lindos and Kamiros (Badoud 2015: 154–7).

[71] See above (p. 31 with n. 56).

[72] *Lindos II* 1 with Blinkenberg's comments: priests of the years (year as *hierothytas* is given in parentheses) 151 (182); 141 (148); 136 (149); 87 (121); 78 (121); 76 (86); 74 (98); 62 (89); 61 (85); 48 (86); 45 (69); 39 (65); 29 (42); 28 (55); 20 (42); 1 (27).

[73] Badoud 2015: 84–6. Cf. Fraser 1953: 42–3.

[74] Blinkenberg 1941: 92. Cf. Badoud 2015: 46–7.

Private monuments presenting careers at the federal level invariably mention terms as *stratagos* before the prytany,[75] and terms as *tamias* before those of *stratagos*.[76] That this pattern of presentation reflects the chronological order of offices gains some support from the two joint dedications of federal magistrates mentioned earlier (*IG* XII.1 49 and *MDAI(A)* 20 (1895) 382 no. 4). The order of magistrates in the two lists is identical, beginning with the *prytaneis* and the secretaries of the *boula* and *prytaneis*, followed by the *stratagoi* and their secretary. (Here *MDAI(A)* 20 (1895) 382 no. 4 breaks off, the second column being lost, but it presumably followed the same order as *IG* XII.1 49, in which the *tamiai* are mentioned first, being followed by their secretary, the *epimeletai ton xenon* and the *hagemones*.) As mentioned above, a number of individuals figure in both lists, all of whom had moved up the *cursus* from *IG* XII.1 49 to *MDAI(A)* 20 (1895) 382 no. 4, seemingly confirming the pattern suggested by private monuments. No other office can be placed into this pattern, which at any rate was not strictly adhered to, since in two cases *tamiai* seem to have skipped a term as *stratagoi* on their way to the prytany.[77]

The fragmentary state of the evidence makes it difficult to ascertain whether federal office usually rested on prior local service. The numerous private monuments which mention offices and priesthoods on both local and federal levels provide insight into individual careers, but the order in which offices are listed need not be chronological. Eupolemos' monument, introduced above, first lists all the federal magistracies he held and – we may, by now, strongly suspect – in chronological order: *tamias*, *stratagos*, *prytanis*, *prophatas*. Then his priesthood of Athana Lindia and of Artemis Kekoia is mentioned, closely followed by the honours bestowed on him by the Lindians, before Eupolemos' liturgies complete the list. As it happens, there is good reason to think that Eupolemos' term as *prophatas* followed only after he had been priest of Athana in Lindos.[78]

The demand for political and religious office is difficult to quantify. Our evidence tells only of elections won, and no statue or dedication was ever set up in celebration of defeat. One might observe that the number of the most important federal magistracies (ten *tamiai*, ten *stratagoi* and two sets of five *prytaneis* a year) would promise easy advancement for those who managed to secure election to the board of *tamiai*. Mutiple terms as *stratagos* were allowed and popular *stratagoi* might crowd others out. It should be added that the decision to elect

[75] *IG* XII.1 56; *Lindos* II 222; *Cl. Rhodos* 2 (1932) 192 no. 20; 194 no. 22; *NSill* 18; 21; *SER* 15; *Annuario* n.s. 1–2 (1939/40) 151 no. 7; *SEG* 39:759; *RIPR* 3. The one exception is *SEG* 41:661, dated to the third century CE.

[76] *Cl. Rhodos* 2 (1932) 188 no. 18; 192 no. 20; 194 no. 22; *NSill* 21; *Annuario* n.s. 1–2 (1939/40) 136 no. 3; 151 no. 7; 155 no. 16; *SEG* 39:759.

[77] *AD* 18 A (1963) 1 no. 1; *Cl. Rhodos* 2 (1932) 193 no. 21. Hiller van Gaertringen 1895: 384.

[78] For dates in Eupolemos' career, see Badoud 2015: 129–30.

sometimes 'by *phylai*' and sometimes 'from all' also affected the chance of election, and that not everyone was satisfied with passing through the *stratagia* on their way up from *tamias* to *prytanis*. In Lindos and Kamiros, where our view is less impaired, the availability of priesthoods narrowed with every step towards the pinnacle. Each year the Kamireans elected twelve *hieropoioi* and the Lindians fifteen *hierothytai*, usually among the young and ambitious, but offered only ten and twelve annual priesthoods respectively. In fact the pantheon of Lindos, and with it the availability of priesthoods, had been gradually expanded through the third century, a process which presumably was driven as much by private ambition as by piety (see Chapter 4). The most prestigious priesthoods, the eponymous priesthoods in both Lindos and Kamiros, were of course limited to only a single occupant per year, and as a consequence on average only one in twelve Kamirean *hieropoioi* and one in fifteen Lindian *hierothytai* would see their careers climb all the way to the top. Furthermore, in both cities (and perhaps in Ialysos too), elections for the eponymous priesthood were held in accordance with a so-called 'triennial rule' which limited a candidate's eligibility to every third year, resulting in a relatively narrow window of opportunity and not insignificant competition.

OUT OF OFFICE

In the previous section we noted the active participation by magistrates in the Rhodian assembly. It is perhaps, therefore, hardly surprising that we find several members of the magisterial elite among those who took an active part in politics by either bringing proposals or speaking for or against such proposals in the assemblies on both *polis* and federal level.

We obviously do not possess the minutes of the meetings of the assembly, nor do we have individual speeches or even very many extant decrees from any level of government. Yet what evidence remains does point to active participation in the assembly by members of the magisterial class. The scanty bits of evidence for the Rhodian *boulomenoi* come from two different sources: a number of decrees preserving the names of those who proposed them and the accounts of particular debates of the Rhodian assembly written by Polybios.

We begin with the decrees. (1) From second-century Kamiros, the mover of the decree in honour of Philokrates was one Nauphilos son of Menekrates, the later *damiourgos* of 158 BCE.[79] (2) In Lindos, Hagesitimos son of Timachidas, who brought the decree which ordered the compilation of the famous Lindian *anagraphe* before the Lindian council and assembly in 99 BCE, was one

---

[79] *Tit. Cam.* 110.1–2; 53.1–2. Nauphilos' father Menekrates son of Nauphilos also served as *damiourgos* in 204 and as *stratagos* (*Tit. Cam.* 3.Eb.33; *Cl. Rhodos* 2 (1932) 198 no. 31.II.5).

of the Lindian *hierothytai* of 148 BCE.[80] (3) Similarly, a Lindian decree of 22 CE concerning several aspects of sanctuary finance was moved by Hippias the son of Hippias (and grandson of Hippias), who was elected leader of the board of Lindian *epistatai* the year after.[81] (4) In 129 BCE the Rhodian *boula* and assembly granted the association of the *Euthalidai* permission to set up an honorific decree for one of their members in a public sanctuary. The petition, which must have taken the form of a formal decree, was introduced by Euphranor son of Dardanos, a member of the association, but also the Lindian priest of Sarapis in 148.[82] The prescript of a fifth decree belonging to the 170s or 180s BCE has been found in what was once Seleukeia-on-the-Kalykadnos.[83] The mover of the decree, Epinikos son of Eukles of the Ialysian deme of the Kryasseis, cannot be identified, but the general lack of evidence from Ialysos makes it impossible to assess the significance of the silence.

Next, Polybios offers occasional glances into debates of the Rhodian assembly in the first half of the second century, reporting the names of what he believed were the most prominent voices in the debates. Two of them are Hagesilochos son of Hagesias and Stratokles, whom we met earlier as the *prytaneis* who made their voices and opinions heard in the assembly both during and after their tenure. Among their friends and collaborators Polybios lists Astymedes, the priest of Athana Lindia in 154 BCE and later of Halios, and his father Theaidetos, both of whom were sent to Rome as ambassadors, and Philophron, another Rhodian envoy. Finally, a certain Rhodophon is mentioned by Polybios. This Rhodophon, who cannot be identified in the epigraphic record, is very probably the same man mentioned by Athenaeus and described by him as *politeuomenos*.[84]

According to Berthold, however, these represented an establishment challenged by a popular party led by Deinon and Polyaratos, who stood outside the magisterial elite. Specifically, Berthold places emphasis on the fact that the two are not known to have held any office.[85] But the silence of Polybios on this issue cannot be given this much weight. Polybios does not provide career information on any of the people involved in his narrative; Hagesilochos and Stratokles are known to have held the office of *prytanis* only because they acted as such during the heated discussions in the Rhodian assembly, and the fact that Polybios does not mention a prytany of Deinon or Polyaratos (or

---

[80] *Lindos II* 224.I.16.

[81] *Lindos II* 419; 420.

[82] *IG* XII.1 890; *Lindos II* 224.7 (Euphranor's son or father was chosen *epistatas* of Lindos by the Rhodians in the same year.)

[83] *TRI* 16.

[84] Athen. 10.444d; Berthold 1984: 183 with n. 8

[85] Berthold 1984: 186–7.

any other leader) does not constitute evidence that they never held this or any other office. Similarly, their absence in the epigraphic record cannot be pushed very far. Their opponents, Hagesilochos or Stratokles, cannot be found in the epigraphic record, nor can any of the remaining members of the group of which they were part, with the exception of Astymedes son of Theaidetos. Berthold's case for the outsider politicians rests essentially on the silence of the evidence, a silence which is hardly surprising and at any rate dependent on downplaying or even dismissing Livy's remark that Deinon and Polyaratos were 'first citizens (*principibus civitatis*)', supplemented by Polybios, who relates that the sons of Pankrates, the tyrant of Kibyra, had been educated in the house of Polyaratos, suggesting the latter shared at least one attribute with the magisterial class, to which we will turn immediately, namely wealth.[86] Finally, a fragment of Polybios concerning a debate of the Rhodian *boula* might suggest that not only both Deinon and Polyaratos, but also Theaidetos, were members of that body.[87]

WEALTH AND THE MAGISTRATE

So far the civic and religious magistracies on both the federal and *polis* levels of the Rhodian state have been shown to be dominated by the members of a relatively small circle of individuals, who not only managed time and again to place themselves in the most important offices, but were also heavily engaged in shaping Rhodian foreign policy in the assembly, in or out of office.

Occasional references in inscriptions to the waiving of pay for office have already been mentioned and provide a first clue as to the wealth of incumbents of military office. Apart from these, indications of the wealth of officeholders may come from three other sources. One (1) is the private monuments, often statues, set up by the priests and magistrates or their families upon their leaving office or in recognition of their civic careers; another (2) is the performance of costly liturgies such as the *trierarchia* or the *choragia*; and finally, (3) there is representation in a number of public subscriptions by the *poleis* of Kamiros and Lindos as well as from the federal Rhodian state, which preserves the names of contributors to some public project.

---

[86] Livy 44.23.10; Pol. 30.9.13–19. However, Polybios adds that the pair had lost their fortunes and fallen, first into debt, and later into the pocket of Perseus. Polybios futhermore indicates that Polyaratos was on friendly terms with King Ptolemy Philometor (30.9.1–2).
[87] Pol. 29.10.1–6.

Private monuments

Sometime between c. 282 and 262 BCE Pausanias son of Agathagetos was priest of Athana Lindia. To mark the event his sons commissioned and set up a bronze statue of their father on the Lindian acropolis, perhaps in the propylaion where its base was later found. Judging from the marks on the base, the statue was near life-size and presented a male figure (probably Pausanias himself) in a walking posture, supported by a stick or a spear. When Pausanias' son Polydoros ended his term of the same priesthood in c. 217 BCE he too dedicated a statue.[88] Each statue must have set the brothers back several thousand drachmas. When the demesmen of the Kamirean Bybassioi in the Peraia decreed the setting up of a statue (of unknown material) and an honorific decree in the third or second century, the expected cost was 2,100 drachmas. The figure (if perhaps a little low) compares to evidence of statue cost from elsewhere. In the late fourth century the Athenian assembly conferred the title of *proxenos* on Asklapiades of Byzantion and honoured him with a bronze statue worth 3,000 drachmas, a figure also mentioned by Diogenes Laertius.[89]

One of the more conspicuous monuments on the Lindian acropolis will surely have been that of Polykles son of Polykrates, who held a number of priesthoods in the closing years of the fourth century. His monument consisted of six statues of himself, his mother, his father and two wives (who were also sisters), mounted on a six-and-a-half-metrelong marble base.[90] Surely this was a testament to Polykles' devotion to his family, but also to the size of his wealth. But Polykles' commitment to showcasing his civic-religious career stretched even further, as did his personal finances. The statue base of a second monument survives on the Lindian acropolis, consisting of at least three larger than life-size statues of the gods which he had served as priest, each dedicated by Polykles in his capacity as priest of Zeus Polieus, Athana Lindia and Pythian Apollo.[91]

Though Polykles' monuments may have belonged to an impressive, but small group of large monuments, they would have been surrounded by hundreds of other monuments like those of Pausanias, his son Polydoros, and innumerable other priests and officers. Over the course of time the Lindian

---

[88] *Lindos II*, 83 with Blinkenberg's comments. Badoud (2015: 228) now places Pausanias' priesthood in the interval between the priest lists' fragments C and D (282–262 BCE). *Lindos II* 104 (Badoud 2015: 58–60).
[89] *RIPR* 45; *IG* II² 555; Smith 1988: 16 with n. 21; Gauthier 2000: 48 with n. 31; Ma 2013: 264–5.
[90] *Lindos II* 56 with Blinkenberg's comments.
[91] *Lindos II* 57.

acropolis was covered with monuments commemorating not only the priests of Athana Lindia, but other priesthoods and civic offices also.[92]

Liturgies

Apart from their own considerable cost, the private monuments of priests and magistrates occasionally mention costly liturgies. A certain Timapolis son of Euphragoras, for instance, was priest of Pythian Apollo in Lindos, but also put his no doubt considerable private funds to use on behalf of the *polis* as *choragos* or sponsor of one of the many state festivals.[93] Festival expenses included processions and sacrifices for the gods as well as competitions of Pyrrhic, tragic and comic choruses, and though direct evidence is lacking, it may be presumed to have been a costly affair; figures from Classical Athens range from 1,500 to 5,000 drachmas.[94] Among the known *choragoi* we find some of the leading members of the magisterial elite, such as Pasiphon son of Pasiphon, a Lindian who served as *tamias*, *stratagos* and *grammateus boulas*, and who sponsored a chorus in the *asty*; and Onasandros son of Euphanes, priest of Athana Lindia in 165 BCE, *hypogrammateus* of the Rhodian *boula* and *prytaneis*, whose chorus won at an unknown Lindian festival.[95]

---

[92] In the second and first centuries BCE alone no fewer than sixty-one priests of Athana Lindia were commemorated with private monuments on the Lindian acropolis (*Lindos II* 141; 147; 148; 150; 155; 157; 158; 159; 165; 168; 194; 197a; 197b; 197c; 197d; 197e; 198; 199; 203; 214; 217; 219; 225a; 225b; 227; 231a; 232; 244a; 245; 246; 248; 250; 251; 253; 257; 260; 264; 283; 284; 285; 286; 287; 288; 293b; 293c; 299a; 299b; 300a; 300c; 308a; 308b; 311; 313; 314; 317; 320; 321; 322; 351; 352; 353; 360) and a further eight were related to those commemorated with a private monument (of the years 157, 155, 153, 118, 107, 89, 61 and 59).

[93] *IG* XII.1 836 (138 BCE).

[94] Davies 1971: xxi; Wilson 2000: 89–90.

[95] Pasiphon: *Cl. Rhodos* 2 (1932) 188 no. 18. Onasandros: *Lindos II* 199. Lindian *choragoi* for processions and sacrifices: *IG* XII.1 762. Pyrrhic choruses: *Lindos II* 131d; *Cl. Rhodos* 2 (1932) 188 no. 18. Tragic choruses: *Tit. Cam.* 63; *SER* 20; *Annuario* n.s. 1–2 (1939/40) 155 no. 16. Satyr choruses: *Tit. Cam.* 63. Comic choruses: *NSill* 21; *Lindos II* 199; *SER* 20. Magistrates as *choragoi*: *IG* XII.1 68 (priest of Dionysos); 70 (*agonothetas*); 836 (priest of Apollo, *archierothytas*, *hierothytas* and *epistatas*); 838 (priest, *hierotamias* and *hierothytas*); *Lindos II*, 179f. (*agonothetas*); 299 (priest of Athana Lindia and *epistates*); 236 (*agonothetas*); 245 (priest of Athana Lindia, priest of Artemis Kekoia, priest of Halios and *hierothytas*); 264 (priest of Athana Lindia, priest of Pythian Apollo, priest of Artemis Kekoia?, *archierothytas*, *epistatas*?); 300 (priest of Athana Lindia, priest of Pythian Apollo, priest of Artemis Kekoia, *archierothytas*?); *Tit. Cam.* 63 (*stratagos*, *tamias*, *phylarchos*); *Cl. Rhodos* 2 (1932) 195 no. 23 (*prytanis*, *episkopos*, *tamias* and trierach); *NSill* 18 (see pp. 125–7); 21 (*tamias*, *stratagos*, *prytanis*, *agonothetas*?, trierarch, *damiourgos* in Kamiros); *SER* 18 (trierarch and *phylarchos*); *Annuario* n.s. 1–2 (1939/40) 155 no. 16 (*tamias*, *stratagos* and trierarch); *Hermes* 36 (1901) 440 no. 1 (trierarch); *SEG* 39: 759 (*tamias*, *stratagos*, *prytanis*, *prophatas*, priest of Athana Lindia, priest of Artemis Kekoia, *phylarchos*, trierarch, *epimeletes ton hippon*).

In Classical Athens a trierarch was (as the name implies) the commander of a special type of warship, the three-banked warship or trireme. He was, however, also a taxpayer selected from among the wealthiest citizens and charged with putting a state-owned ship in fighting order. Rhodian trierarchs, at least occasionally, took to the sea with their warships, but frequent reference to a specialist captain, the *epiplous*, suggests that in Rhodes the meaning of *trierarchos* had shifted further towards the meaning 'sponsor of a warship'. As a consequence, the word was also used of the sponsor/captains of other types of vessels including the far larger quinqueremes and smaller aphract vessels.[96] One such smaller vessel was sponsored by Entimos son of Timokleidas and adopted son of Ainesidamos, who was *stratagos*, *hagemon* and *astynomos* sometime in the first century.[97] Damagoras son of Euphranor, the celebrated *nauarchos* who commanded the Rhodian contingents in the war against Mithridates, also sponsored a warship, most probably a quadrireme.[98] Again, figures from Classical Athens may give an impression of the cost involved: 4,000 to 6,000 drachmas, but to this must be added that the Rhodian system differed from the Athenian in that some trierarchs brought their own vessel, a costly private investment at risk of being lost completely in the service of the state.[99]

Epidoseis

Not a few public subscriptions, or *epidoseis*, from the *asty* as well as the *poleis* of Lindos and Kamiros, have survived to this day.[100] From Kamiros is preserved a handful of *epidoseis* from roughly the century between 250 and 150 BCE. In each a number of wealthy citizens pledged to donate a sum of money to a specific public project. *Tit. Cam.* 158 preserves one such list dated to the second half of the third century BCE, in which the Kamireans called upon their wealthy citizens to contribute funds for the construction of a stoa and a number of cisterns, presumably on the Kamirean acropolis.

The list preserves (or partially preserves) the names of fifteen contributors (including the deme of the Loxidai) who gave between 100 and 3,000 drachmas occasionally on behalf of themselves as well as one or two family members. Several contributors are known to have held office in Kamiros or are related to officeholders (see Table 2.1).[101]

---

[96] On the meaning of *epiplous*, see Segre 1936: 231–3; Gabrielsen 1997: 101 with n. 96.

[97] *IG* XII.1 44.

[98] *Lindos* II 303.5. Though only the first name appears, the date of the inscription (90–70) fits Damagoras son of Eupranor. See also *NSill* 18.14; *IG* XII.1 41; 46.157. For the family of Damagoras, see *SEG* 43: 527 with Kontorini 1993.

[99] Davies 1971: xxi–xxii; Gabrielsen 1997: 103–5.

[100] The Rhodian *epidoseis* are collected by Migeotte 1992.

[101] Migeotte 1992: 127 with n. 81.

Table 2.1 Officeholders in Kamirean *epidoseis*.

1. *Tit. Cam.* 158 (Kamiros, about 230 BCE)		
Line	**Name**	**Contribution (drachmas)**	**Office or relation to officeholder**
10	[Λυ]κάων Σμινδυρίδα	3,000 and 1,000 on behalf of sons	*Hieropoios* c. 259 BCE (*Tit. Cam.* 24.5); *damiourgos* c. 236 BCE (*Tit. Cam.* 3.Ea.51)
11	[Σω]σικράτης Σωκράτευς	1,000	*Damiourgos* c. 231 BCE (*Tit. Cam.* 3.Eb.3)
12	[Οὐλί]ας Μνασιτίμου	500	*Damiourgos* c. 227 BCE (*Tit. Cam.* 3.Eb.7)
14	[Ἀστ]υκράτης Ἀστυκράτευ[ς]	1,500	*Hieropoios* c. 246 BCE (*Tit. Cam.* 32.10); adoptive father of NN *hieropoios* c. 235 BCE (*Tit. Cam.* 35.1–2)
16	[Ἐκ]φευξις Φιληράτου	2,000	*Agonothetas* c. 255 BCE (*Tit. Cam.* 29.14)
17	[. .]νοκλῆς Μνασιτίμου	500	Brother of *Tit. Cam.* 158.12
24	[Κλει]σίμαχος Εὐκλείδα	100	Priest of Athana c. 233 BCE (*Tit. Cam.* 5.II.61)
29	[Β]είτυλος Εὐκλείδα	300	Brother of *Tit. Cam.* 158.24
31	[Ο]ὐλίας Ξενοκλεῦς	500	Son of *Tit. Cam.* 158.17; nephew of *Tit. Cam.* 158.12

2. *Tit. Cam.* 159 (about 170 BCE)		
9	Κριτόβουλος Ἀριστομβροτίδα	100	Brother of *Tit. Cam.* 159.13
13	[Ἀριστομβ]ροτίδας Ἀριστομβροτίδα	–	Priest of Athana *and damiourgos* 171 BCE (*Tit. Cam.* 84); *epimeletes ton xenon* (*IG* XII.1 49.II.51)

3. *Tit. Cam.* 159b (Kamiros, about 180 BCE)		
Line	**Name**	**Contribution (drachmas)**	**+Office or relation to officeholder**
3	[Ἀ]ριστομαχίδας Α[— — —]	–	Probably to be identified with Ἀριστομαχίδας Ἀριστομάχου priest of Dionysos and the Muses c. 219 BCE (*Tit. Cam.* 40.II.9) and priest of the Dioskouroi (*Annuario* 8/9 (1925/26) 320 no. 3);

			his father was priest of Pythian Apollo c. 251 BCE (*Tit. Cam.* 31.19) and a son Ἀπολλωνίδας Ἀριστομαχίδα was priest of Asklapios c. 187 BCE (*Tit. Cam.* 50.33)
4	[Αἰ]νέτων Ναυσίπ[που]	–	*Damiourgos* c. 168 (*Tit. Cam.* 3.Ec.34) and *hieropoios* c. 187 BCE (*Tit. Cam.* 50.5)
6	[Θεύ]δωρος Μεν [— — — —]	–	Possibly a son of Μενέστρατος Ἀριστέως καθ' ὑοθεσίαν δὲ Θευδώρου who was *hieropoios* c. 227 BCE (*Tit. Cam.* 38.1.6)

4. *Tit. Cam. Supp.* 220 no. 157b (Kamiros, about 170 BCE)

Line	Name	Contribution (drachmas)	Office or relation to officeholder
3	Ἀρ[ισ]τομβροτ[ί]δας Ἀριστομ[βρ]ο[τί]δα	30 and 10	Same as *Tit. Cam.* 159.13
6	Κριτόβουλος [Ἀριστομβροτ]ίδα	–	Same as *Tit. Cam.* 159.9
	Ναύσιππος [Κριτ] ο[βούλ]ου	–	Son of *Tit. Cam.* 159.9; nephew of *Tit. Cam.* 159.13
A.I.19	Ξενόμβροτος Ῥοδίππου	10	*Hypogrammateus* c. 198 and c. 197 BCE (*Tit. Cam.* 45.41; 46.II.23)
A.I.26	Κλεώνυ[μος Δαμο?] κράτευς	10	Son of priest of Aphrodite c. 208 BCE (*Tit. Cam.* 43.II.10)
A.II.13	Στρατοκλῆς Ἐρ[ατοκλεῦς]	–	Probably *hieropoios* of c. 214 BCE and son of [Ἐρ]ατοκλῆς Στρατο[κλεῦς] the *damiourgos* of same year (*Tit. Cam.* 41.1–3); father of Ἐρατοκλῆς Στρατοκλεῦς *hieropoios* c. 196–190 BCE (*Tit. Cam.* 47.9)
A.II.17	Ἀρίστων Ἐπ[ικράτευς]	–	*Hierokaryx* for four (consecutive?) years after c. 197 BCE (*Tit. Cam.* 46.II.26; 47.29; 48.12; 49.1)
A.II.18	Ἐρασίλας Σω[σιστράτου]	–	*Hierokaryx* for four (consecutive?) years leading up to c. 187 BCE (*Tit. Cam.* 47.30; 48.13; 49.2; 50.42)
B.III.10–11	Εὔκλειτος Εὐκ[λεῦ]ς	30	*Damiourgos* c. 144 BCE (*Tit. Cam.* 3) and related to several Kamirean priests and magistrates (see below)

B.III.15–16	Τιμαγό[ρας] Τιμαγόρα	–	Damiourgos c. 139 BCE (Tit. Cam. 3.Ed.3)
B.III.17–18	Ἀρίστων Ῥοδοπε[ίθευ]ς	–	Hieropoios c. 198 BCE (Tit. Cam. 45.8)
B.III.20–1	[Πυθ]όδωρος Ἀπολλ[οδώρ]ου	–	Hieropoios c. 198 BCE (Tit. Cam. 45.11)
B.III.25–6	[Π]α[σί]χαρις Ἀρχιδά-μου	30	Probably son of Ἀρχίδαμος Πασιχάριος damiourgos c. 200 (Tit. Cam. 3.Eb.37)
B.III.26–8	Ἀλκέτας [Δα]μωφέλευς καθ᾽ ὑ(οθεσίαν) [δὲ] Τιμασιθέου	10	Brother of Δαμοκλῆ[ς] [Δ]αμωφέλευς κ[αθ᾽ ὑ(οθεσίαν) δὲ] Τιμασιθέου (see below).
B.III.29–31	Δαμοκλῆ[ς] [Δ]αμωφέλευς κ[αθ᾽ ὑ(οθεσίαν) δὲ] Τιμασιθέου	10	Priest of Sarapios c. 187 BCE (Tit. Cam. 50.30)
B.III.33	[Δ]αμοκλ<ῆ>ς Ἀλκέτα	5	Nephew of Tit. Cam. Supp. 220 no. 157b.B.III.29–31
B.III.34–5	Τιμ[ασ]ίθεος Ἀλκέτα	5	Nephew of Tit. Cam. Supp. 220 no. 157b.B.III.29–31
B.III.36–7	Εὐκλείδας Ἀλκέτα	5	Nephew of Tit. Cam. Supp. 220 no. 157b.B.III.29–31
B.III.38–9	Σιμίων Ἀγλουδ[άμ]ου	10	Hieropoios c. 187 BCE (Tit. Cam. 50.7); brother (or son) of Ἀγλούδαμος Ἀγλου[δάμου] hieropoios c. 196–190 BCE (Tit. Cam. 47.4)

One Lykaon, son of Smindyridas, who also gave the largest contribution (a staggering 3,000 drachmas) on his own behalf and a further 1,000 on behalf of his two sons, heads the list of individual contributors. Lykaon had begun his public career as one of Kamiros' twelve annually elected *hieropoioi* in c. 259 BCE before becoming *damiourgos* in c. 236 BCE.[102] Of the thirteen remaining contributors, eight more either served in various religious offices or were related to officeholders (see Table 2.1) giving more than three-quarters of the total sums collected. The same picture emerges from other Kamirean *epidoseis*. In *Tit. Cam.* 159, a subscription for funds to celebrate the Panathenaia festival (see below), the names of only two contributors survive: a priest and *damiourgos* and his brother (who gave 100 drachmas). *Tit. Cam.* 159b, also badly damaged, preserves parts of only five names, three of which may nevertheless be identified as officeholders or their relatives. The longest surviving *epidosis*

---

[102] *Tit. Cam.* 158.10; *hieropoios*: *Tit. Cam.* 24.5; *damiourgos Tit. Cam.* 3.Ea.51.

from Kamiros, *Tit. Cam. Supp.* 220 no. 157b, preserves the names of nineteen
citizens who are known to have held office or were related to officeholders.
Curiously, contributions here are quite modest, ranging from 5 to 30 drachmas. This might suggest that not all officeholders came from wealthy families,
were it not for the fact that one of the contributors was the same priest and
damiourgos who contributed to the deme of Arioi (*Tit. Cam.* 159) and whose
family dedicated a statue in his honour.[103] A more likely explanation, suggested
by Migeotte, is that the small size of contributions reflects the relatively modest need of the Kamireans which this particular *epidosis* was meant to meet.[104]
Together the four Kamirean *epidoseis* contain approximately sixty-five contributors, of whom nineteen can be demonstrated to have held office at some
point. If we add relatives of officeholders, their proportion of all contributors rises to above half. Though none of the remaining contributors held the
office of *damiourgos*, the Kamireans offered a great variety of civic and religious
offices whose annually elected custodians are only occasionally known to us.
Accordingly, the list of Kamirean magistrates who contributed to *epidoseis* can
only be considered a minimum.

The sources of wealth

'You cannot have money, any more than anything else, without taking pains
to have it', said Aristotle of the Liberal Man.[105] The source of this wealth was
land. On the eastern shore of what was once the Ialysian *chora*, a couple of miles
south of present-day Archangelos, remains have been found of a large rectangular *peribolos* surrounding a small tower. The site, littered with coarse sherds,
has been identified as a fortified agricultural facility or *pyrgos kai oikia*. Similar
compounds, often with clear traces of farming activity, have been identified in
other parts of the Greek world,[106] among them at Lardos some 10 miles further south in what was once Lindian territory and at Loryma in the Rhodian
Peraia, in which the remains of an olive press are preserved in situ. Though
of similar design, the facility south of Archangelos stands out for its size (the
foundations of the tower measure 13 by 16 m, more than double the size of its
Attic counterparts), suggesting that it served a rather large estate. Furthermore,
traces of several ceramics workshops have been identified in rural parts of the
island and the Peraia, suggesting that large parts of the agricultural production
of Rhodes were aimed directly at overseas markets.

---

[103] *Tit. Cam. Supp.* 220, no. 157b.3, 6; *Tit. Cam.* 159.9, 13; 84.
[104] Migeotte 1992: 132.
[105] Arist. *Eth. Nic.* 4.1.21 (1120b17–20).
[106] Young 1956; Papachristodoulou 1989: 135–7; Gabrielsen 1997: 105–7.

Rhodian amphorae have been discovered in every corner of the Medi-terranean and far beyond, especially in areas famous for grain, such as Sic-ily and the Black Sea, but above all in Egypt, the proverbial 'bread basket' of the Mediterranean. Remains of Rhodian amphorae have been found here in impressive quantities, but most remarkable is the Rhodian share of the Egyptian wine market suggested by the relative numbers of Rhodian amphorae to those of others famous wine-producing communities.[107]

Curiously, given its share in the archaeological evidence, in Egypt Rhodian wine is hardly ever encountered in the extensive written sources. This appar-ent discrepancy has been interpreted to the effect that Rhodian wines, the containers of which have been found in so great numbers, were of a relatively low quality compared with those of other islands in the Aegean – a sort of 'vin de table', consumed in great quantities, but hardly worth mentioning.[108]

This would require an acute awareness of markets and demands on behalf of the producers, as well as a certain standardisation of the product, a process which must have begun at the largest estates and therefore with the Rhodian elite.[109]

The attraction of Alexandria, however, was not only the Egyptians' taste for cheap Rhodian wine, but the massive amounts of grain for export produced on the banks of the Nile. Here we find the Rhodian magisterial elite once again. Agathokles son of Hagemon was of a wealthy Kamirean family, and his father is probably to be identified with Hagemon son of Agathokles who was elected *hieropoios* in Kamiros in 253 BCE.[110] Sometime around the turn of the third and second centuries he led a grain ship into the harbour of Ephesos. Once unloaded the grain was taken to the city's agora and sold to the citizens. In response, and on the suggestion of one Dion son of Diopeithos, the citizens of Ephesos voted to enrol Agathokles as a citizen of Ephesos (*I. Ephesos* 1455):

---

[107] Rauh 1999; Lund 1999.

[108] Kruit and Worp 2000.

[109] Lawall 2011. An example of standardisation of production, presumably aimed at ensuring a standardised quality of wine, can be found from Amos in the Rhodian Peraia. Three inscribed leases (*TRI* 69, 70 and 71) instruct the tenants of farmland owned by the demesmen of the Amioi on the planting of vines and fig trees (Salviat 1993).

[110] *Tit. Cam.* 30.4. Bresson 1980. It is worth mentioning, though the connection must remain highly conjectural, that the Italian excavations in Kalavarda, in what was once Kamirean ter-ritory (Porro 1916), included remains of seven amphorae carrying the mark of the 'fabricant' Ἀγαθοκλεῦς, dated to the turn of the third and second centuries by a handle found in Paphos on Cyprus (*Paphos V* App. I no. 50) dating from Archokrates' term as priest of Halios in 205 BCE (Badoud 2015: 256 s.v. 205; cf. Finkielsztejn 2001: 113–14). Amphorae carrying the mark of Ἀγαθοκλεῦς have been found in large numbers across the Mediterranean world, particu-larly at Pergamon (*I. Pergamon* II 767–73) and along the sea route to Egypt, in Cyprus and Palestine, and in Egypt itself, but also in considerable numbers in Sicily.

Resolved by the council and assembly; Dion son of Diopeithos said: Since Agathokles son of Hagemon of Rhodes has brought in 14,000 *hekteis* of grain of which 1/6 was wheat into the city, and having heard that grain was being sold in the agora for more than six drachmas (per *hektis*?), he was persuaded by the *agoranomos* and wishing to please the people he sold all the grain at a fairer price. It was decided by the council and assembly to give Agathokles of Rhodes citizenship on the same and equal terms both to him and his descendants, and the Essens [priests of Artemis] shall assign him a tribe and a *chiliastys* by lot, and the *neopoiai* shall inscribe this in the sanctuary of Artemis where the rest of the citizenships are inscribed in order that all may know that the people give thanks to those who are benevolent to them. Tribe Bembine, *Chiliastys* Aigotos were selected.

1   [ἔδο]ξεν τῆι βουλῆι [κ]αὶ τῶι δήμωι· Δί[ω]ν Διοπείθους εἶπεν· ἐπειδὴ Ἀγαθοκλῆς
    [Ἀ]γήμονος Ῥόδιος σῖτον εἰσαγαγὼν εἰς τὴμ πόλιν πυρῶν ἐκτεῖς μυρίους
    τετρακισχιλίους, καὶ καταλαβὼν τὸν σῖτον τὸν ἐν τῆι ἀγορᾶι πωλούμε-
    νομ πλέονος δραχμῶν ἔχς, πεισθεὶς ὑπὸ τοῦ ἀγορανόμου καὶ βουλόμενος
5   χαρίζεσθαι τῶι δήμωι ἐπώλησε τὸν σῖτομ πάντα εὐωνότερον τοῦ ἐν τῆι ἀγορᾶι πωλουμένου· δεδόχθαι τῆι βουλῆι καὶ τῶι δήμωι, δοῦναι Ἀγαθοκλεῖ
    Ῥοδίωι πολιτείαν ἐφ᾽ ἴσηι καὶ ὁμοίαι καὶ αὐτῶι καὶ ἐκγ[ό]νοις, ἐπικληρῶσαι δὲ
    αὐτὸν τοὺς ἐσσῆνας εἰς φυλὴγ καὶ χιλιαστὺγ καὶ ἀναγράψαι αὐτῶι ταῦ-
    τα τοὺς νεωποίας εἰς τὸ ἱερὸν τῆς Ἀρτέμιδος οὗ καὶ τὰς λοιπὰς πολιτείας
10 ἀναγράφουσιν, ὅπως ἄπα<ν>τες εἰδῶσιν ὅτι ὁ δῆμος ἐπίσταται χάριτας ἀπο-
    διδόναι τοῖς εὐεργετοῦσιν αὐτόν. ἔλαχε φυλὴμ Βεμβίνης, χιλιαστὺν Αἰγώτεος.

Around the same time Agathokles was honoured by the citizens of Arkesine on the island of Amorgos, this time with the titles of *proxenos* and *euergetes*.[111] The Arkesinian decree is silent about the reason for honouring Agathokles,

---

[111]   *IG* XII.7 9.

but it seems reasonable to assume that his services to this city were also related to the grain trade.

Throughout the Hellenistic period the Rhodians pursued a policy of close cooperation with the Ptolemies to ensure easy access to this – for Rhodes – so vital market. This of course was of general benefit to the state, since it ensured the steady flow of merchants through the harbours of Rhodes, a traffic which at its height, according to one member of the magisterial elite, yielded an annual income of 1,000,000 drachmas from the harbour toll collected at Rhodes.[112] But the case of Agathokles son of Hagemon suggests that it also served the narrower interest of the landed Rhodian elite, for whom Egypt was a primary export market for their own agricultural products, as well as an indispensable business partner in the import of grain to Rhodes and the Greek cities of the Aegean and on the coast of Asia Minor.

---

[112] Pol. 30.31.12. Gabrielsen 1997: 71–4.

CHAPTER 3

The *Oikos*

O ver the years, the Lindian acropolis came to include a large collection of life-size bronze statues depicting the succession of eponymous priests of Athana Lindia, embodying the passage of time and the continuity of the city's most important cultic institution and by extension the community itself.[1] Many of these statues were set up by proud family members of the priests they portrayed, and over time a good number were incorporated into larger monuments uniting family members, underscoring the presence and importance of another institution: the family.[2]

Among these statues was one set up by Lysistratos son of Pythagoras and adopted son of Euratos, in commemoration of his tenure of the priesthood in Lindos (in 162 BCE), terms as *prytanis*, *agonothetas* and *grammateus* of the *boula* in the *asty*, as well as two victories in the *choragia*. At some later point the statue was detached from its original base and incorporated into a new multiple-statue monument for Lysistratos, his brothers and their father.[3] The epigram carved on the base of the statue and later transferred to the family monument situated Lysistratos' success squarely within that of his father and brothers (*Lindos II* 197f.1–4):

> Before, our father burned sacrifices on the altar to you, Pallas, as is the custom, within your sacred dwellings, and then we three brothers-in-blood

---

[1] E.g. *Lindos II* 53 (Peisiphon son of Peisistratos, c. 320 BCE); 105 (Aristeus son of Thymandros, c. 238 BCE); 217 (Astymedes son of Theaidetos, 154 BCE); 238 (Aristonomos son of Kallisthenes, 95 BCE); 417 (Melanthios son of Zenon and adopted son of Iason, 20 CE). Thomsen forthcoming b.

[2] Ma 2013: 223–4; Griesbach 2016; Thomsen forthcoming b.

[3] Ma 2013: 239. Cf. Blinkenberg 1941: 461–9; Dyggve 1960: 302; Griesbach 2016.

did, to whom alone you granted this, you who inhabit the sacred rock of Lindos.

πρὶμ μέν τοι γενέτας ἐπιβώμια θ[ύ]ματα, Παλλάς,
ὡς θέμις, εὐιέρων ἐντὸς ἔλαμψ[ε δ]όμων,
τρισσοὶ δ' ἁμὲς ἔπειτα συναίμον[ες] οἷς τόδε μούνοις
ὤπασας ἃ Λίνδου σεμνὸν ἔχεις σ[κ]όπελον.

Lysistratos' boastful (but also, at the time,[4] truthful) claim concerning the uniqueness of his and his brothers' achievement, in as much as it belonged to all of them equally, is a clear indication that the honour which election for the priesthood brought with it belonged as much to the family as to the individual priest.

Indeed, at Lindos running for religious office was often a family undertaking. When the Lindians in 99 BCE elected Andron son of Xenomenes and adopted son of Archinos, priest of Athana Lindia for the coming year, they also saw fit to elect his three sons hierothytai for the same year. In fact, several more examples suggest that the Lindians often preferred to stock their college of hierothytai with the sons of the eponymous priest.[5] At Kamiros too, joint dedications by the eponymous damiourgos and the twelve hieropoioi who served with him dating to the third century give evidence that young members of the magisterial elite often began their careers in the very same year in which their fathers reached the pinnacle of theirs. In seven out of thirty cases in which the names of the damiourgos and hieropoioi can be read or convincingly restored, the hieropoios heading the list is also the son of the damiourgos.[6]

Though the many joint dedications at Kamiros suggest that damiourgos and hieropoioi worked closely together in tending to the relationship with the divine, it is not immediately clear what benefit the Kamireans expected from the election of fathers and sons in the same year.[7] There are, however, several examples of fathers and sons acting together from various other levels of the Rhodian state. At Tymnos – a Kamirean deme or ktoina in the Peraia – a decree was enacted while a certain Kleinias son of Epigonos was hierothytas. The proposer of the decree was one Epigonos son of Kleinias, no doubt a

---

[4] The sons of Astykrates son of Astykrates, priest of the year 87 BCE, followed their father in 60, 54 and 51 BCE, respectively (see Blinkenberg's comments on Lindos II 1 s.v. 87).

[5] Lindos II 282.46–8. See also Lindos II 324, base of a statue for Thrasylochos son of Thrasylochos, the priest of 55 BCE, dedicated by, among others, the year's fifteen hierothytai, who included not only two of the priest's sons, but also two of his nephews (Blinkenberg 1941: 138). Cf. Lindos II 378b (27 BCE); IG XII.1 844 (69 BCE).

[6] Tit. Cam. 18; 22; 27; 29; 32; 41; 52. On the Kamirean hieropoioi and Lindian hierothytai, see Dignas 2003. Cf. Smith 1972.

[7] For the prestige of the Kamirean hieropoioi, see Dignas 2003.

son or father of the *hierothytas*.[8] In Lindos, in the year 99 BCE, the ageing Hagesitimos son of Timachidas, who proposed compiling the list of notable dedications in the sanctuary and the epiphanies of Athana Lindia, made sure his decree also called for the election of his own son, Timachidas, as one of the two men charged with producing the *anagraphe*.[9] Even in the *asty* fathers and sons worked together. Theaidetos had made a name for himself as a *politeumenos* and many-times ambassador in the years following the treaty of Apamea, but by the time the Third Macedonian War was drawing nearer, his group of political allies had come to include also his son Astymedes, whom Polybios lists among those who favoured sending ships to aid the Roman fleet at the Hellespont.[10]

In both Lindos and Kamiros (and presumably in Ialysos too) some families managed to successfully reproduce their social and civic position over several generations. Consider, for instance, the family of Eukleitos son of Eukles (Fig. 3.1). In the waning years of the fourth century BCE Eukleitos held the priesthood of Athana Polias at Kamiros - a position which ranked second in prestige only to the eponymous magistracy of *damiourgos*.[11] For this office Eukleitos managed to secure election at some point during the following two decades.[12] A generation later, in c. 264 BCE, his son, Eukles son of Eukleitos (I), entered the same office.[13] No trace is left of Eukles' children, but it may be supposed that he had at least one son named in accordance with the family tradition, for in c. 197 a Eukles son of Eukleitos (II) served as one of Kamiros' three *epistatai*.[14] When his son, Eukleitos son of Eukles (III), won election as *damiourgos* in about 144 BCE he did so as a member of a successful family which had managed to remain part of Kamiros' civic and religious elite for more than a century and a half.

[8] *RIPR* 102.1–3 (first century BCE). For the contents of the decree, see below, p. 66.
[9] *Lindos II* 2.A.1–12. Hagesitimos is on record as *hierothytas* in 148 (*Lindos II* 224.I.16). His son is known, apart from his role in compiling the *anagraphe*, to have fought in the Mithridatic war (*Lindos II* 292) and to have served as *prophatas* in the *asty* in 87 (*TRI* 2 no. 6).
[10] In 27.7.3 (with Walbank's (1979) comments ad loc.) Polybios associates Astymedes with Agathagetos and Rhodophon, who are later associated with Theaidetos and Philophron (28.2.3), whose collaboration went back at least to the years following the peace of Apamaea (22.5.2).
[11] *Tit. Cam.* 5 (l. 35). The priesthood of Athana, alone among the Kamirean priesthoods, is included in lists of religious magistrates (from the year c. 283 BCE onwards [*Tit.Cam.* 15], but with considerable gaps). When these lists from the mid-third century begin to include other priesthoods, the priest of Athana is invariably listed first while the relative order of other priesthoods varies (e.g. *Tit. Cam.* 27; 30). This undoubtedly reflects the prestige associated with this office, a conclusion which is further underlined by frequent reference to incumbency in private monuments of individuals who also held the office of *damiourgos* (e.g. *Tit. Cam.* 84).
[12] *Tit. Cam.* 10.
[13] *TRI* 8.A.20.
[14] *Tit. Cam.* 46.17. Eukles son of Eukles, who was priest of Poseidon c. 197 BCE and of Althaimenes c. 187 BCE, may be another son (*Tit. Cam.* 45; 50).

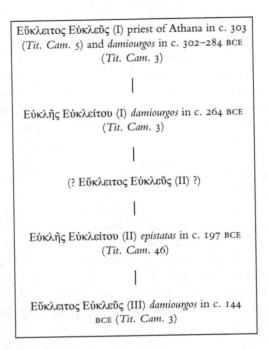

Εὔκλειτος Εὐκλεῦς (I) priest of Athana in c. 303
(*Tit. Cam.* 5) and *damiourgos* in c. 302–284 BCE
(*Tit. Cam.* 3)

|

Εὐκλῆς Εὐκλείτου (I) *damiourgos* in c. 264 BCE
(*Tit. Cam.* 3)

|

(? Εὔκλειτος Εὐκλεῦς (II) ?)

|

Εὐκλῆς Εὐκλείτου (II) *epistatas* in c. 197 BCE
(*Tit. Cam.* 46)

|

Εὔκλειτος Εὐκλεῦς (III) *damiourgos* in c. 144
BCE (*Tit. Cam.* 3)

Figure 3.1 Stemma of Eukleitos son of Eukles.

Similar family histories abound, but the story of Eukleitos' family also illustrates that a family's membership in the magisterial elite was tenuous. For
sixty-seven years during the second half of the third century there is no trace
of the family in the surviving records.[15] Even the uniquely successful family of
Lysistratos (six priests of Athana Lindia in four generations) could not reproduce its social and civic position indefinitely.[16] In fact, and somewhat ironi-
cally, neither Lysistratos nor his two brothers, for all their success, would see a
son replace them in the priesthood of Athana Lindia.[17]

[15] This lacuna may be caused by the state of the evidence, but it is at least certain that no member of the family held the office of *damiourgos* in this period; when a member of the family
resurfaces in the early second century it is in a minor office.

[16] Lysistratos' great-grandfather, Herakleitos son of Archokrates, is known to have held several
priesthoods (*Lindos II* 159) on his way to the priesthood of Athana Lindia in about 283 BCE.
Lysistratos' father, Pythagoras son of Archokrates, and his uncle, Kleagoras son of Timasarchos,
held the eponymous priesthood in 195 and 198, respectively. Badoud 2015: 288–9.

[17] A son of Archokrates, the oldest of the three, was honoured with a gold crown and a bronze
statue by the Lindians around the middle of the second century, but otherwise nothing is
known of their (natural) descendants. See Badoud's (2015: 288–9) stemma I. Cf. Blinkenberg
1941: 35–6.

A tally of Athana Lindia priests with officeholding forefathers in the second and first centuries BCE shows that out of 182 priests only 75, or 41 per cent, belonged to families with some demonstrable prior experience in public life at Lindos.[18] That number, of course, is a minimum, since the evidence for offices and priesthoods other than that of Athana Lindia comes almost exclusively from a handful of monuments listing officers of a single year, or private monuments recording the career of a single family or individual. Clearly, however, families faced difficulties in reproducing their social position over the generations.

PRESERVING THE *OIKOS*

'Let there be a single-born son to nourish the father's *oikos*', advised Hesiod, 'in this way wealth is increased in the halls.'[19] With equal or near-equal partition of the patrimony being the norm in the Greek world and presumably therefore also in Rhodes, more sons (and daughters) meant smaller shares of the estate for all at the time of succession.[20] Therefore Hesiod also thought it best that the single-born son, in turn, have only one son (as well as a long life over which to accumulate his wealth) in order to pass on the estate and the social position that came with it to the next generation. This, as Hesiod surely knew, was easier said than done, since the pursuit of the 'one-son-winning-strategy' was considerably hampered by demographics.[21] High rates of mortality, especially infant mortality, threatened every low-fertility household with extinction.[22]

As Hopkins and Burton pointed out in a seminal article on Roman consular families, precisely these basic demographic realities meant that perhaps as much as a third of families did not see a son live beyond the age of forty, the age at which a would-be Roman consul would begin to contemplate a run for that office. Another third of families, or slightly less, had two or more sons reach that age and so would see the family estate broken up, threatening to leave each son with a less than sufficient share to support a career in public life; similar challenges must have faced elite families in Rhodes.[23]

[18] *Lindos II* 1 with Blinkenberg's comments.
[19] Hes. *Op.* 376–7. Trans. Most 2018.
[20] Bresson 2016b. Cf. Harrison 1968: 130–2.
[21] Lysimachos son of Aristeidas, (himself one of at least five children) had two daughters, but apparently no sons to succeed him (*Cl. Rhodos* 2 (1931) 190 no. 19).
[22] For a recent overview of fertility and mortality in the ancient Greek world, see Bresson 2016a: 41–9.
[23] Hopkins and Burton 1983: 73–4 with n. 54. Recently, Bresson (2016a: 41–51) has criticised the reliance on pre-industrial demographic models as being perhaps too pessimistic. Nevertheless, as Bresson admits, there can be little doubt that mortality, and especially infant mortally, was extremely high compared with modern rates.

Wealth, though the *sine qua non* for a position in the magisterial elite, was not the only resource to be propagated through family ties. As we have just seen, the patronage of an established member of the elite (for instance a father) was probably equally important. In the following we will investigate the role of the family in combating demographic challenges and securing access to (and the effective allocation of) two critical resources: wealth, in the form of inheritance and dowries, and support, in the form of patronage from established members of the magisterial elite.

Marriage

In about 313 BCE, Polykles son of Polykrates was priest of Athana Lindia. Years earlier, however, when it was time for Polykles to marry, he chose a daughter of a certain Archonidas for his wife. When she died, Polykles decided to remarry and chose another daughter of Archonidas, a sister of his late wife. When eventually Polykles decided to erect a monument for himself and his family (the occasion seems to have been his tenure as priest of Athana Lindia) on the Lindian acropolis, both wives, Antigona and Gorgia, were portrayed in bronze statues along with Polykles himself and his parents.[24]

Polykles' choice in wives offers initial insight into the importance of family to the magisterial elite. First of all, the fact that Polykles married two women of the same family suggests that marriage was not only a union of two individuals, but also a union of two *oikoi*.[25] We know nothing else about Polykles' father-in-law, Archonidas, and are therefore not in a position to speculate on Polykles' reasons for preferring wives from this family.

In other cases, however, we are better informed. The marriage between Pasiphon son of Pasiphon and Hagemo daughter of Timaratos united two leading Lindian families of the late second and early first centuries. Pasiphon came from a line of priests of Athana Lindia, but directed his own ambitions towards offices and priesthoods in the *asty*, eventually capping his career with the eponymous priesthood of Halios in the 80s BCE. Hagemo's family had an equally distinguished history of officeholding, and the union extended both families' grip on the priesthoods at Lindos to the

---

[24] *Lindos II* 56.
[25] For the importance of existing relationships between grooms and fathers-in-law, see Vérilhac and Vial 1998: 220–1.

next generation, when his oldest son (perhaps by a different wife) won that of Athana Lindia in 52 BCE.[26]

For others, however, marrying into an established family seems to have facilitated a first entry into the magisterial elite. Elpikrates son of Elpikrates was undoubtedly a wealthy man, but so far as we can tell also a new arrival in the Lindian elite. He married Pasinikas daughter of Aristomachos, who unlike himself came from a well-established family (her father and brother? both advanced to the priesthood of Athana Lindia, in 157 BCE and 108 BCE, respectively). Elpikrates himself has left no record of office or priesthood, but his son by Pasinikas succeeded his maternal grandfather and uncle in the prestigious priesthood in 71 BCE.[27] Similar marriage alliances can be found among other members of the Rhodian elite around the turn of the second and first centuries. In Kamiros, Kritoboulos son of Aristombrotidas watched his brother, Aristombrotidas, rise to prominence and though clearly a wealthy man (who on several occasions participated in *epidoseis*; see Chapter 2) he is not known to have entered public life himself. Here we must obviously state our reservations due to the fragmentary nature of the evidence, but it is at least certain that he did not win the office of *damiourgos* as his brother did. But Kritoboulos married into a prestigious and politically active Kamirean family (again unlike his brother, who seems to have married his first cousin). His wife Nikaina daughter of Nausippos was probably the sister of Aineton son of Nausippos, a *hieropoios* of 183 and *damiourgos* of 164 BCE.[28] Their son,

---

[26] *Cl. Rhodos* 2 (1932) 188 no. 18. For Pasiphon's possible tenure as priest of Halios, see Badoud 2015: 196. Pasiphon's father (*IG* XII.1 840.5; *Lindos II* 1 s.v. 124; *TRI* 54) and great-grandfather (*Lindos II* 243; 244a–h; *TRI* 12) both served as priests of Athana Lindia, among other things. Cf. Badoud's (2015: 297–8) stemma VIII. Hagemo's brother (*Lindos II* 1 s.v. 74; 282.49; 297; 299b), father (*Lindos II* 1 s.v. 107; 258; 299a) and grandfather (*Lindos II* 1 s.v. 134; 230; 299a) all held the priesthood of Athana Lindia. Another brother, Aristeidas, had a son (Hagemo's nephew) elected to the priesthood in 68 (*Lindos II* 1 s.v. 68) The base for a statue of Pasiphon (*Cl. Rhodos* 2 [1932] 188 no. 18) lists his living relatives as dedicators. They included two sons, Pasiphon and Timaratos, named after their grandfathers. Neither of the two sons had apparently established his own family at the time. A third son, Nikasagoras (the later priest of 52 BCE), however, appears in the list with his wife and two children and was therefore presumably the oldest of Pasiphon's sons. His name, Nikasagoras, appears nowhere else in Pasiphon's or Hagemo's stemmata and he may therefore be a son from a previous marriage.

[27] *Lindos II* 252.II.150–6. Aristomachos son of Aischinas: priest of Poseidon in 182 (*Lindos II* 167.I.14), of Athana Lindia in 157 (*Lindos II* 1). Aischinas son of Aristomachos (and adopted son of Hagesis): priest of Athana Lindia in 108 (*Lindos II* 1; 257).

[28] *Tit. Cam.* 90; *Tit. Cam.* 3.Ec.34. Nausippos son of Nausippos and grandson of Aineton, the *epistatas tou peribolou*, is perhaps another brother (*Tit. Cam.* 90). Nikaina is listed as the daughter of a certain Nausippos of the deme of the Plarioi (*Tit. Cam. Supp.* 220, 157b.6–9: Κριτόβουλος [Ἀριστομβροτ]ίδα ['Ἄριος —']|καὶ ὑπὲρ τᾶ[ς] γυνα[ι]κὸ[ς Νικαίνας]|Ναυσίππου Π[λαρίας? καὶ τῶν υἱῶν]|Ἀριστομβρο[τί]δα [καὶ Ναυσίππου —']. Aineton son of Nausippos appears in *Tit. Cam.* 159b, an *epidosis*, under the heading Πλά[ριοι] (*Tit. Cam.* 159b.1).

Nausippos, won the damiourgy, probably around 130, a feat repeated in turn by his own son, Aristombrotidas.[29]

For members of families whose grip on power was perhaps beginning to slip, marriage alliances were a means of re-entry into the magisterial elite. Timokrates son of Eupolemos and adopted son of Hagemon (Fig. 3.2) had been *hierothytas* at Lindos and then priest of Athana Lindia in about 200 BCE and had three sons who lived to have children of their own. None of these three sons is known to have held any priesthood or office, and though we must again allow for the state of the evidence, it is at least possible that the three-way division of their patrimony had left none with an estate large enough to support a public career. In the next generation, however, members of the family began bringing the lines of descent back together. Timokrates' (III) son Hagemon, one of Timokrates' (I) grandsons, secured a marriage to Euagis, a daughter of Kleisithemis son of Eratophanes, at some point before reclaiming his family's membership in the magisterial elite as priest of Athana Lindia in 112 BCE. Timokrates' father-in-law, Kleisithemis, was a wealthy man and in a position to provide his daughter with a suitable dowry;[30] each of his two sons contributed 1,800 drachmas to

---

[29] *Tit. Cam.* 3.Da.35. Aristombrotidas son of Nausippos: *Tit. Cam.* 59a. SEG 42: 749 no. 4 preserves the name of another son, Kritoboulos son of Nausippos.

[30] Here and throughout I use the term 'dowry' as convenient shorthand for the share of their father's property (landed or otherwise) which daughters received from their fathers' estates, whether at the time of their marriage or upon their father's death. In Classical Athens women received a dowry (in some cases substantial dowries) of money or chattels which was added to their husbands' estate once children were born, but daughters did not inherit (Bresson 2016b: 29; Vérilac and Vial 1998: 142–3; cf. Harrison 1968: 45–60, 130–8). In Gortyn, women could not only inherit landed property, but also claim half the income from the land for themselves (Bresson 2016b: 18–27). In Sparta, and elsewhere, women inherited land and retained full rights to their property (Bresson 2016b: 50–9). That kindship endogamy is so well attested among the Rhodian elite is a clear indication that marriages entailed the tranfer of significant property from one *oikos* to another. The nature of this property (landed or otherwise) cannot easily be determined, and nor can whether the transfer was (as at Athens) in the form of a dowry or through a woman's claim on inheriting from her father or mother or both (for review of different senarios, ancient and anthropological evidence, see Bresson 2016b). The attestation, in Rhodes, of female adoptions (though very rare compared with Rhodian male adoption), even in cases where there were other legitimate children, could be taken to suggest that women did inherit. The evidence for Rhodian women's rights to dispose of money is ambiguous. They apparently needed the consent of their *kyrios* in order to contribute even trivial amounts to subscriptions (*Annuario* 1–2 [1939/40] 168 no. 21), seemingly echoing the law of Athens, quoted in Is. 10.10, that Athenian women needed the consent of their *kyrios* in any transaction above the value of a *medimnos* of barley (for the necessary qualification, see Schaps 1979: 52–8). Still, the fact that women appear as contributors at all clearly suggests that the money they promised was their own (Schaps 1979: 49). Occasionally, such contributions involved larger amounts, e.g. the combined 100 drachmas given by two citizen women (*SEG* 43.526.9–13) or the 200 drachmas given by Kleo of Phaselis (*Cl. Rhodos* 2 [1932] 177 no. 6.24–6). Schaps (1979: 48–52) collects similar instances from around the Greek world.

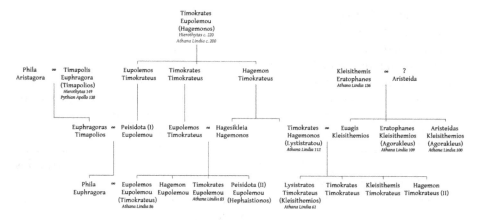

Figure 3.2 Stemma of the Timokratids (cf. Badoud 2015: 292–3; Blinkenberg 1941: 50).

an *epidosis* for an unknown purpose.[31] The marriage was doubly auspicious for Timokrates since it forged a connection with a politically important family. Not only had Kleisithemis himself been priest (in 136 BCE), but both his sons went on to win the priesthood (in 109 and 100 BCE). Accordingly, Timokrates and his four children dedicated a statue of Euagis on the Lindian acropolis – one of the few women to receive such a commemoration in a sanctuary dominated by the statues of priests of Athana Lindia.[32]

Marriage also facilitated entry into the magisterial elite for those who, though undoubtedly in possession of the resources, lacked the formal qualifications. At Lindos, access to the priesthoods and other offices was jealously guarded by those citizens who belonged to demes located on the island of Rhodes, at the expense not only of their fellow Rhodians of Ialysos and Kamiros, but also of those Lindians belonging to demes in the Peraia and on the island of Karpathos (see Chapter 4). As a demesman of the Karpathopolitai – a Lindian deme on Karpathos – Aristagoras was barred from standing for election at Lindos and therefore from pursuing an important means for achieving the status he presumably aspired to. The legal barriers erected by the Lindians of the island could, however, be breached through marriage. Aristagoras gave his daughter Phila in marriage to Timapolis, a Lindian from the island deme of the Kamyndioi, who among other things had served as *epistatas* and priest of Pythian Apollo at Lindos. Their son married into the family of Timokrates, which by then had come some of the way in re-establishing itself, and eventually Aristagoras' great-great-

---

[31] *Lindos II* 259.14–20.
[32] *Lindos II* 256. On the display of statues on the Lindian acropolis, see Ma 2013: 233–9; Griesbach 2016; Thomsen forthcoming b.

grandson was able to do what his Karpathian great-great-grandfather could not, namely ascend to a priesthood in Lindos.[33]

While marriage might serve to unite two different families, it could also bring together different branches of the same family, and kinship endogamy (marriages between uncles and nieces, first cousins) seems to have been fairly common.[34] Such a marriage would cause two diverging branches of a family to converge and ensure that estates partitioned in one generation were at least partially reunited in the next. The family of Timokrates son of Eupolemos and adopted son of Eupolemos again provides several examples. Timokrates' (I) grandson Eupolemos son of Timokrates married his cousin Hagesikleia daughter of Hagemon; she was another grandchild of Timokrates (I) and sister of Timokrates (III) whom we met above. In turn, one of their four children, Eupolemos (son of Eupolemos and adopted son of Timokrates, whose impressive career was treated in Chapter 2), married his second cousin, Phila, another great-grandchild of Timokrates (I) – Phila daughter of Euphragoras (and of Peisidota). Marrying the daughter of an uncle meant that the dowry was passed from one male member of the family directly to another, while marrying the daughter of an aunt meant that any dowry was temporarily deposited with another family before it was returned to the family.

As a result of these two marriages between cousins, Eupolemos son of Eupolemos and adopted son of Timokrates stood to inherit from his great-grandfather through three lines, rather than just one. In fact, as we will see in the next section, Eupolemos added a fourth line when he was adopted by his maternal uncle (and first cousin once removed) Timokrates son of Hagemon, who, apart from no doubt considerable wealth, had something more to offer, which was not to be found among Eupolemos' immediate ancestors: namely the experience of successful election for the priesthood of Athana Lindia.

---

[33] *Lindos II* 252, the Lindian *epidosis* which furnishes so much of the evidence for the leading Lindian families of the late second century, includes not a few female members of demes outside the twelve privileged island demes who had married into the Lindian elite: a daughter of Deinokrates of the Amioi (a Lindian deme of the Peraia) married Aristonymos son of Kallisthenes, the priest of Athana Lindia in 95 and later of Halios (*Lindos II* 252.120–3; 283; I s.v. 95).

[34] The Kamirean Aristombrotidas son of Aristombrotidas married Nikaina daughter of Kritoboulos, who was either his cousin or his niece (*Tit. Cam.* 84). Tryphaina, the daughter of Aristeidas son of Aristeidas (cf. *IG* XII.1 46.6–8), married her maternal uncle Melantas (*RIPR* 9). The stemmata analysed by Rice (1986) provide several examples of marriages between uncles and nieces (stemmata 5, 6, 7, 8). For kinship endogamy as an important means of preserving family estates in Classical Athens, see Cox 1998: 3–37.

Adoption

Rhodian inscriptions give evidence of a surprisingly high number of adoptions among the citizens.[35] Adoption was signalled – and is therefore intelligible to us – not by the exchange of one patronymic for another, but by adding the adoptive father's name to make up the rather cumbersome name phrase, which we have already come across several times: for instance, Neupolis son of Neupolis and adopted son of Chariton (Νεύπολις Νευπόλιος καθ' ὑοθεσίαν δὲ Χαρίτωνος) or Aristolochoas son of Aristodoros and adopted son of Philtias (Ἀριστόλοχος Ἀριστοδώρου καθ' ὑοθεσίαν δὲ Φιλτία).

Historians are in agreement that the frequency of adoptions clearly indicates that Rhodian adoption differed from what is known of adoption elsewhere in the Greek world.[36] Nevertheless, most explanations have proceeded from the assumption that adoption in Rhodes functioned much as in Athens and that the reason for its frequency should be found not in the institution itself, but in particular social and political circumstances – a view which was inspired in part by the rather sudden appearance in the epigraphic evidence of the adoption formula in the 260s BCE.[37] None of these explanations, however, is satisfactory. The idea that adoption was a means through which Rhodian aristocrats of the mid-third century revolted against a newly introduced deme system, which supposedly had broken up existing bonds of kinship, fails on a number of points; but most importantly, it cannot explain why adoption was still so widely practised several centuries later.[38] Similarly, the speculation that there existed a Rhodian law requiring all male citizens to have a certain number of children – for which there is neither evidence nor parallel – hardly makes sense of the observable practices.[39]

Unlike the case in Classical Athens, adoption at Rhodes was clearly not only aimed at securing the continuation of the *oikos*, since some adopters still

---

[35] Van Gelder 1900: 284. Cf. Smith 1967; Rice 1988. Poma (1972: 210–69) collects 493 cases to which more must now be added.

[36] Van Gelder 1900: 284; Poma 1972: 171; Rice 1988; Gabrielsen 1997: 112–20.

[37] Badoud (2015: 247–9) collects the earliest evidence, including variations in the formula, which by the turn of the third and second centuries gave way to the form quoted in the text here. Cf. Rice 1988: 138.

[38] Poma 1972: 203. For one thing, as noted by Rice (1988: 140), demotics are attested by the late fourth century (*Lindos II* 51). For another, many adopters and adoptees, including among the earliest cases, were closely related and belonged to the same deme.

[39] Rice (1988: 142–3), but without any indication of what that number ('x') might be. The explanation furthermore assumes either a remarkable degree of altruism on behalf of the great number of families which gave up sons for adoption or, as suggested by Rice, but without any evidence, that there would have been some form of compensation for families who thus sold their surplus sons to those with filial deficits.

had living natural sons.[40] Panaitios son of Nikagoras and grandfather of the famous Stoic philosopher had three sons (and two daughters), at least two of whom survived to have sons of their own (in addition to civic careers), but nevertheless Panaitios adopted an additional son from a leading Kamirean citizen, who in return adopted one of Panaitios' sons.[41] There are also cases of men being adopted by their own grandfathers, who, by definition, had already seen their line extended, not just by one, but by two generations (see below). Secondly, Rhodian adoptions were not equally distributed along the social ladder. Funerary inscriptions from the Rhodian necropolis belonging to citizen men, representing a broader section of the citizen population (though it is impossible to say how much broader) than that of the magisterial elite, have only few adoptees. Among 342 funerary inscriptions only 19 men (6 per cent) had been adopted.[42] Contrast that with the 15 per cent of adoptees among the Kamirean *damiourgoi*, 10 per cent among civic magistrates in the *asty*, or the staggering 42 per cent of adoptees among the priests of Athana Lindia in the second and first centuries.[43]

Against this, Gabrielsen has argued that adoption at Rhodes differed profoundly from its Athenian counterpart and that the peculiar name formula provides an initial clue about the institution: at Athens, the adoptee would give up membership of his natural father's household, as well as any claim on his natural patrimony, to become in every aspect the son of his adopter, and change one patronymicon for another to reflect his newly acquired status.[44] By contrast,

---

[40] Rubinstein 1993: 16–21; Harrison 1968: 82–9.

[41] For the family's stemma, see Badoud 2015: 299.

[42] Two of those nineteen adoptees attested in the small funerary epigraphy in the Rhodian necropolis are in fact known to us as quite wealthy: (1) Nikagoras son of Pamphilidas and adopted son of Nikagoras (*IG* XII.1 202) was *hierothytas* in Lindos in about 220 (*Lindos II* 102.24–5) and *stratagos* (*Lindos II* 151); (2) Euphranor son of Basileides and adopted son of Basileides (*IG* XII. 201) is mentioned in the family monument *AD* 18 A (1963) 12 no. 17 and in among those who contributed to a statue of a gymnasiarch (*IG* XII.1 46.213), both before his adoption.

[43] For Kamiros I count 151 *damiourgoi* between 200 and 1 BCE whose names can be read or reconstructed, including 23 adopted *damiourgoi*. Of these dedications by fellow magistrates from the city of Rhodes: adoptions *IG* XII.1 16 (undated, 1 in 6); 19 (undated, 1 in 10); 42 (first century, 2 in 17); 47 (first century, 1 in 21); 46 (first century, 42 in 433); 49 (second century, 7 in 40); 50 (first century, 2 in 24); *SER* 22 (second century, 2 in 16); *MDAI(A)* 20 (1895) 382 no. 4 (second century, 2 in 18). This list of priests of Athana Lindia in Lindos (*Lindos II* 1, with *TRI* 12) provides an extreme example. In the years between 200 and 1 BCE, for which we have the names of 192 priests, no fewer than 80 priests were adopted. Adoptions, of course played a role in circumventing the triennial rule, which guided the election of the priests of Athana Lindia (Gabrielsen 1997: 112–20).

[44] Rubinstein 1993: 45.

adopted Rhodians retained their natural patronymic, but added a second adoptive patronymic as part of the phrase 'and by adoption son (*kath' hyothesian de*) of x'. This signalling of a 'double sonship' was interpreted by Gabrielsen as an indication that adoption in Rhodes did not, as in Athens, entail the complete legal transfer of the adoptee from one *oikos* to another, but rather gave the adoptee a claim on inheriting from not one, but two fathers. The notion of a double sonship finds initial support in the fact that adopted Lindians, whose fathers belonged to different demes and *phylai*, apparently had a choice of standing for the priesthood of Athana Lindia as a member of either their natural or adoptive deme. At Lindos, a so-called triennial rule (see Chapter 4) limited eligibility for Athana Lindia's priesthood to once every three years by allowing only candidates from one of Lindos' three *phylai* – each consisting of four demes – to stand for election each year. Blinkenberg, who first identified the triennial rule, noticed that some adopted priests managed to circumvent the rule and were elected in years when their natural demesmen were ineligible.[45] At the same time other adopted priests, though adopted by members of demes belonging to a different *phyla*, were nevertheless elected in years belonging to their natural demesmen, suggesting that adopted Lindians had a choice of standing for election as members of either their native or adoptive deme and *phyla*.[46] Since deme membership was passed from father to son, Gabrielsen concluded, dual membership as the result of adoption should indicate that adoptees were in fact recognised as having two fathers – one natural and one adoptive.

If Gabrielsen is right that an adoptee held full membership in both his natural and his adoptive deme as a consequence of a 'double sonship', we should expect that the adoptee could (1) exercise his political rights in both natural and adoptive demes and (2) pass on either membership – or both – to his children. The first is amply demonstrated by the dozen or so adopted priests who held the priesthood of Athana Lindia in years when their natural demesmen were ineligible, and in the two cases in which priests who had been adopted into a deme belonging to a different *phyla* nevertheless won election for years belonging to their native deme and *phyla*.[47] The second requires that we trace inheritance of deme membership over several generations (Table 3.1).

[45] Blinkenberg 1941: 95–6.
[46] Gabrielsen 1997: 116–17. Gabrielsen (1997: 137) collects fourteen cases. Recently Badoud (2015: 41) has criticised the emphasis on adoption as a means to circumvent the triennial rule and in particular the cases produced by Blinkenberg (1941: 96) in support. Badoud is right to reject four of the five cases (years 143, 142, 118 and 71) – none of which is included in Gabrielsen's fourteen cases. The fifth case, that of Timokrates son of Hagnon and adopted son of Lysistratos, is rejected by Badoud since there is in his view not good evidence for Timokrates' deme affiliation prior to his adoption. Timokrates' sister Hagesikleia daughter of Hagemon, however, is directly attested as 'Klasia' (*Lindos II* 252.42–3), rendering Timokrates' native membership of Klasioi (Tribe C) certain.
[47] Gabrielsen 1997: 137–40 (see n. 46 above).

Table 3.1 Deme affiliation of Archokrates son of Archipolis and adopted son of Lysistratos and his descendants.

Name	Year	Natural deme (tribe)	Adoptive deme (tribe)	Source
Ἀρχοκράτης Ἀρχιπόλιος καθ' ὑοθεσίαν δὲ Λυσιστράτου	202	Lindopolitai (B)	(A)	*Lindos II* 118; 155; *Cl. Rhodos* 2 175 no. 4.
Μοιραγένης Ἀρχοκράτευς καθ' ὑοθεσίαν δὲ — — — — — Κατταβίου		Lindopolitai (B)	Kattabioi (A)	*Lindos II* 190; 624
Archokrates Moirageneus		Kattabioi (A)		
Μοιραγένης Ἀρχοκράτευς καθ' ὑοθεσίαν δὲ Λυσιστράτου	118	Kattabioi (**A**)	Lindopolitai? (B)	*IG* XII.1 827; 846; *Lindos II* 248

Archokrates son of Archipolis and adopted son of Lysistratos was by birth a member of the deme of the Lindopolitai, a deme that belonged to the Lindian Tribe B. He was elected priest of Athana Lindia for 202 BCE, a year of Tribe A in which the Lindopolitai were not eligible, and therefore on the strength of his membership in his adoptive deme.[48] His son, Moiragenes (I) son of Archokrates, nevertheless inherited his membership in his father's natural deme, the Lindopolitai.[49] But as the adopted son of an unknown man from the deme of the Kattabioi (belonging to Tribe A) he was apparently able to pass membership in this deme on to his son, Archokrates son of Moiragenes, who as far as we can tell remained unadopted. His son in turn, Moiragenes' (I) grandson and namesake, Moiragenes (II) son of Archokrates, was elected priest for 118, a year of Tribe A, and so undoubtedly on the strength of his membership in the Kattabioi.[50] Prior to his election, however, this Moiragenes (II) had himself been adopted by one Lysistratos son of Archokrates who belonged to a deme of Tribe B, most likely the Lindopolitai.[51] Though he named a son after his adoptive father

---

[48] *TRI* 13.dII.16–17 (priest of Poseidon Hippios, 221 BCE); *TRI* 12.H.6–7 (priest of Athana Lindia, 202 BCE); *Lindos II* 155 and *SEG* 39: 742 (priest of Halios, about 185 BCE) with Badoud 2015: 169–70; *Cl. Rhodos* 2 (1932) 175 no. 4.4–5 (Lindopolitas).

[49] *Lindos II* 190 (*epistatas* in Lindos about 170 BCE, prior to adoption); 624 (named as Kattabios and one other deme, most likely Lindopolitas).

[50] *IG* XII.1 827; *Lindos II* 1; 248 (priest of Athana Lindia, 118 BCE).

[51] For the family's stemma see now Badoud 2015: 288–9. Cf. Blinkenberg 1941: 36–7.

he nevertheless – and unlike his grandfather and namesake – passed on membership in his natural rather than adoptive deme to his son, who was elected priest of Athana Lindia in 82, again a year of Tribe A, and therefore undoubtedly as a demesman of the Kattabioi.

As is evident from this four-generation family history, adopted Rhodians were able to enter their children into the rolls of either their natural or adoptive deme (but apparently not in both). Crucially, this was the case regardless of whether the adoptees had been priest in a year of their native or adoptive deme or indeed whether they served as priests of Athana Lindia at all. The latter is especially important since it dispels any notion that the Rhodian law of adoption was shaped by that priesthood.[52] Nor need additional deme membership have been an important factor in most adoptions. On the contrary, in many cases men were adopted by their paternal grandfathers or uncles, who could offer to register their adoptive sons only with the deme to which they already belonged.[53] What they did offer, however, was an additional father. In these – and perhaps in all – cases, adoption must have served primarily to manipulate the traditional order of intestate succession by allowing a nephew, a brother or a grandson to inherit directly even in cases where the adopter had legitimate issue. Lysistratos son of Timokrates, for instance, was adopted by his maternal grandfather, Kleisithemis, the priest of Athana Lindia in 136 BCE (see Figure 3.1 above). Kleisithemis had two sons, who both ascended to the same priesthood (in 109 and 100 BCE) when Lysistratos was probably a young boy. Lysistratos and his brother Timokrates were both elected *hierothytai* in 85 BCE, but only Lysistratos had been adopted by their grandfather and, by 85 BCE, must have already inherited from his maternal grandfather. His brothers, however, would have inherited only from their natural father. Kleisithemis' reasons for privileging Lysistratos are obscure, but the effect was tangible: alone of four brothers, Lysistratos ascended to the priesthood of Athana Lindia, in 61 BCE. The adoption of Lysistratos by his maternal grandfather may have caused his natural father, Timokrates son of Hagemon and adopted son of Lysistratos, to rethink his own succession. At some point he adopted his nephew Eupolemos son of Eupolemos (Timokrates' sister Hagesikleia's son), whom we met above, and who went on to become priest of Athana Lindia in 86 BCE.

---

[52] Pugliese Carratelli 1953: 486; cf. 1949: 160; Fraser 1977: 46–7. *Contra* Gabrielsen 1997: 117–18.

[53] For instance, Euphraniskos son of Kallixeinos and adopted son of Nikasidamos, who was adopted by his paternal uncle (Badoud 2015: 294–5). In other cases onomastics strongly suggests a familial link. Rice (1988: 139) interprets twenty-seven cases in which adopter and adoptee had the same name as adoption by uncles, and eight cases in which natural and adoptive father shared a name as adoption by brothers (though, in both cases, grandfathers seem equally possible).

In adoption, it seems, the Rhodians had come up with a system that allowed greater flexibility in combating the problem of the division of the patrimony. To be sure, adoption might mean smaller shares, but it allowed those with plenty to direct resources where they might be expected to make the greatest impact.

In summing up the findings of the preceding sections it may be useful to call up the stemma of the Timokratid and Kleisithemid families (Figure 3.1) once again, but this time in the shape of a network. The ties, consisting of family lineage, natural and adopted, and marriage became the avenues through which two vital resources flow, namely wealth (in the form of inheritance and dowries) and patronage. It is impossible to assess the quality and quantity of those resources (what estate could be passed on, how it was divided between sons and the size of dowries, on the one hand; on the other, the extent of patronage), but nevertheless a picture emerges in which, excepting the two progenitors of the stemma (Timokrates I and Kleisithemis I), all but one priest shares a direct tie with another, older priest and family member, as a son, an adoptive son or a son-in-law.

Through a mixed strategy of marriage (both within the family and outside to members of other influential families) and adoption, the descendants of Timokrates managed to re-establish and reproduce themselves as one of the most influential *oikoi* in Lindos at the turn of the second and first centuries, supplying at least one priest of Athana Lindia in every generation for three generations (112, 86, 83 and 61). The marriage of Timokrates son of Hagemon and adopted son of Lysistratos to the daughter of Kleisithemis son of Eratophanes appears to have been critically important. The *oikoi*, however, were in fact joined completely in the next generation when Lysistratos, the son of Timokrates, became by adoption also the son of his maternal grandfather (Kleisithemis son of Eratophanes). As Lysistratos ran for, and eventually was elected, priest of Athana Lindia in 61 BCE, he succeeded no less than seven family members: his cousins (in 83 and 86), his maternal uncles and brothers by adoption (in 109 and 100), his father (in 112), his maternal grandfather (in 136) and his paternal great-grandfather (in c. 200).

CHAPTER 4

Public Associations

The deme was the fundamental unit of citizen organisation in Hellenistic Rhodes and all citizens belonged to one. Membership was hereditary and upon coming of age citizen men and women were entered onto the rolls of their father's deme.[1] From thereon out, deme membership was an integral part of citizen identity and expressed through the regular addition of a *demotikon* to a citizen's name. Hundreds of inscribed epitaphs, particularly from the necropolis outside the Rhodian *asty*, are evidence of the importance placed on membership even in non-political contexts.[2]

Each of the fifty-five demes (which are securely attested as such) was closely associated with a part of Rhodian territory either on the island itself, or on the mainland (the Peraia) or the constituent islands: the Thyssanountioi in Thyssanous on the Loryma peninsula, the Nettidai in Netteia, modern-day Apolakkia, on the south-western coast of Rhodes, and the Brasioi further

---

[1] A late-second-century *epidosis* from Lindos (*Lindos II* 252) preserves the names and donations of a number of prominent citizens who donated on behalf of themselves and their households. Each had his name inscribed with his demotic as was the case for adult dependants, i.e. wives and occasionally mothers (on feminine demotics, see below), while children who had not yet come of age were entered simply with their name. The implication seems to be that dependant children were not yet full members of their father's deme.

[2] Some 430 citizens' names with demotics are attested in funerary inscriptions from the Rhodian necropolis, including 84 women with feminine demotics (attested there and elsewhere for 40 out of 55 demes, with the remaining 15 demes belonging to those least well attested generally). Feminine demotics seem to imply some notion of female deme membership even if our limited evidence does not allow any insight into what that membership entailed. For the rarity of Athenian feminine demotics in the Classical period, see Whitehead 1986: 77–81 (cf. Vestergaard et al. 1992: 8–9).

north in Brasia, 'the most beautiful land' in the foothills of Mount Atabyros, to mention only a few of those whose geographic location is known with some precision.[3]

The demes held assemblies and elected a number of magistrates, and seem to have been responsible for the maintenance of sanctuaries and other matters of cult.[4] A mid-second-century decree of the demesmen of the Tymnioi on the mainland allows a glimpse into the smaller world of deme society. Their decree orders that a stoa in or near the deme's agora be made available to those who sacrifice to Zeus and Hera, along with certain furnishings to prepare the stoa for the event, but calls upon a magistrate, the *hierothytas*, the public slave (*damosios*) and any one of the demesmen to denounce any disorderly behaviour (specifically the burning of wood in the stoa and otherwise damaging the building) before another magistrate, the *hierotamias*. The latter, in the case of transgressions, would exact a fine to be paid to Apollo.[5] Other deme decrees confirm that many if not all demes were custodians of important sanctuaries, such as the sanctuary of Athana in Arkaseia, Asklapios in Thyssanous, and Apollon Kedreieos in Kedrea.[6]

In addition to their membership in demes all Rhodians seem to have been members of a parallel set of associations, the *ktoinai* (or *ptoinai*).[7] Like the demes they were associated with specific territories, which must have overlapped completely with those of the demes (though not necessarily with any one deme) and were assigned to one of the three old *poleis*. A Kamirean decree of the late fourth or early third century assumes that all (Kamirean) *ktoinai* had territories with several sanctuaries, and orders the Kamirean *ktoinatai* to congregate at their 'most revered sanctuary' and elect a *mastros* for each *ktoina* 'in accordance with the law of the Rhodians', who would come to Kamiros and

---

[3] Brasioi: an inscribed jug, *SEG* 43: 543 (Shear 1908), found at Monolithos declared that 'καλλίστα γᾶς hα Βρασία hως ἐμῖν δοκεῖ'. The ancient necropolis of nearby Siana was known locally as Prasos, when Kinch explored the area in the early twentieth century (Hiller von Gaertringen, *RE* Suppl. V [s.v. Rhodos] 747; cf. Papachristodoulou 1989: 76). Nettidai: two inscriptions mentioning Netteia (*IG* XII.1 890 and *Lindos II* 652) have been found, respectively in and east of Apolakkia. For general discussions of the location of the demes, see Fraser and Bean 1954 (the demes of the Peraia and islands); Bean and Cook 1957 (demes of the Peraia); Cook 1961 (demes of the Peraia); Papachristodoulou 1983 (cf. Bresson 1988: 145–6 [the demes of Lindos]); 1989 (the demes of Ialysos on the island).

[4] *RIPR* 44 (decree of the Bybassioi, mid-second century BCE); 102 (decree of the Tymnioi, second or first century BCE).

[5] *RIPR* 102.

[6] *Historia* 7 (1933) 577 no. 1 (Arkaseia, second century); *RIPR* 118 (Thyssanous, mid-second century); *RIPR* 3 (Kedrea, first quarter of second century).

[7] Gabrielsen (1997: 151–4) collects the evidence.

attend all the sacrifices there.[8] The fact that these elections were apparently mandated by the federal Rhodian assembly strongly suggests that *ktoinai* were found throughout Rhodian territory.[9] A catalogue of property owned by a private association of *eranistai* included a burial precinct located in Rhogkyon as well as 'another plot in the *ktoina*', adding further support for the association with a specific territory.[10] As it happens, the toponym, Rhogkyon, almost certainly gave its name to the Kamirean deme of the Rhogkidai, and it is possible that the *ktoinai* represent an older system of citizen organisation which was superseded – but not replaced – by the deme system.[11]

What little is known of the internal organisation and activities of the *ktoinai* mirrors that of demes. Like the demesmen, the *ktoinatai* met in *ekklesiai* to pass decrees and elect officers, styled *hierothytai* and *tamiai* like the officers of the demes.[12] On Karpathos the *ktoina* of the Potidaeis in Potidaion, which was also home to the deme of the Karpathopolitai, would invite the recipient of an honorific crown to dine in the *hierothyteion* – as did the demesmen of the neighbouring Arkaseis – and it may be that the Potidaioi shared this facility with the Karpathopolitai.[13] The only two confirmed members of the Potidaeis

---

[8] *Tit. Cam.* 109. Badoud 2011: 555–7, 561–3; Dignas 2003: 48–9; Gabrielsen 1997: 151; Pugliese Carratelli 1951: 83–8; 1949: 154–71; van Gelder 1900: 191–2, 222–5. See also the second-century decree of a private association in Syme in honour of a citizen who had come forwards with the funds for the repair of a sanctuary neglected by the *ktoinatai* (*IG* XII.3 1270.12–14, c. 155 [Badoud 2015: 239 no. 923]).

[9] According to an old view (Pugliese Carratelli 1942: 199–200; Papachristodoulou 1989: 56) the *ktoinai* in the course of the first century BCE drifted away from the state, accepted foreigners and became essentially private associations. Gabrielsen (1997: 123), rightly, stressed the continued contact with the demes and prefers to see the *ktoina* as public subdivisions open to foreigners. The evidence for foreigners in *ktoina* comes from two sources: (1) the name of a private association whose members were also members (*ktoinetai*) of the *ktoina* of the Matioi and which had Philokrates, a citizen of Ilion, as its benefactor (the *Matioi ktoinetai eranistai Philokrateioi*, *IG* XII. 1 157.9–10); and (2) a private monument from Syme (*IG* XII.3 6, quoted on p. 142) in which Euphrosynos of Idyma (or perhaps Sidyma) was honoured by two *ktoinai*. Neither, however, proves that Philokrates or Euphrosynos were actually members of the *ktoinai*. Honours do not necesarily imply membership and as a private association the *Matioi ktoinetai eranistai Philokrateioi* were free to accept any member, in spite of their name.

[10] *IG* XII.1 736. Gabrielsen 1997: 151–4.

[11] Gabrielsen 1997: 151–4. Van Gelder's suggestion (1900: 222) that the *ktoinai* were further subdivisions of the demes cannot be substantiated. Three late decrees and honorific monuments give evidence of collaboration or at least coordination between a deme and a *ktoina*, but one need only suppose an overlap of territory to explain the collaboration (Gabrielsen 1997: 152).

[12] *Ekklesia*: *IG* XII.3 1270.13. Magistrates: *Lindos II* p. 1007.2, 46. Gabrielsen (1997: 122, 152–4), following Blinkenberg (1941: 1008–9), adds an *epistatas*, but the reconstruction of *Lindos II* p. 1007.5–6 is far from secure.

[13] *Historia* 7 (1933) 577 no. 1.13.

(and indeed of any *ktoina*), were also demesmen of the Karpathopolitai, and a late dedication made jointly by the *damos* of the Karpathopolitai and the *ktoina* of the Potidaieis suggests close cooperation between the two groups.[14]

A third set of associations, the *patrai*, are attested in Kamiros, Lindos and the Rhodian *asty*.[15] Not much is known about the internal organisation of the *patrai*, but the name of a Lindian *patra* of the Dryitai, which it shared with a deme, suggests that it too belonged to an old system of public organisation, though evidently one which was still alive in the Hellenistic period. Around the turn of the third and second centuries, the *patriotai* of the Druitai passed a decree for a certain Eualkidas son of Aristolochos who had been *hierothytas*, and the voting of honours suggests a formal organisation modelled on that of the democratic *polis* (i.e. with a defined membership and elected magistrates); but since the base of the statue also mentions honours voted by the demesmen of the Lindian deme of the Lindopolitai, it is impossible to say whether Eualkidas had served the *patra*, the deme or even the Lindian *polis* in this capacity.[16] An enigmatic inscription from Kamiros lists a number of presumably Kamirean *patrai*, but the exact meaning of the list still puzzles historians. The latest attempt at breaking into the logic of the inscription identifies it as a list of participating *patrai* in religious celebrations.[17] Whatever the purpose and significance of inscribing this list of *patrai*, the fact that it was inscribed, and that it was set up in Kamiros, suggests that the *patrai* had some connection with the *polis*. Whether every Rhodian citizen (supposing that *patrai* were also found in Ialysos) were member of a *patra* is impossible to say. The evidence for *patrai* elsewhere in the Greek world, collected by Gabrielsen, suggests that *patrai* were public subdivisions and that membership was universal and state sanctioned.[18] This of course need not apply to Rhodes.

To be a member of a deme, a *ktoina* and perhaps a *patra* was tantamount to being a Rhodian citizen. But each set of associations was split in three and assigned to one of the three constituent *poleis*. The *ktoinai* on the island of Rhodes, if we are to identify their origins in the period preceding the creation of the federal Rhodian state, must have split along the borders between the

---

[14] *Lindos II* p. 1007.51–2; *IG* XII.1 978 (early second century CE). Cf. *RIPR* 132, a dedication by deme, *katoikeuntes* and the *ktoina* of the Sarapiastai (Thyssanous, 81–96 CE). Gabrielsen 1997: 151–2. The extent to which membership differed between deme and *ktoina* is, however, not at all clear.

[15] *Tit. Cam.* 1; *Lindos II* 146; *IG* XII.1 88; *MDAI(A)* 25 (1900) 109 no. 108 (possibly).

[16] *Lindos II* 146 (c. 200 BCE); *IG* XII.1 88 (copy found in the *asty*).

[17] Gabrielsen 1997: 147–9.

[18] Gabrielsen 1997: 141–5. Jones (1987: 246–7) doubts their relation to the *poleis*, and prefers to see them as private associations, mainly objecting to Andrewes's (1957) attempt to place the *patrai* in an indeed questionable hierarchy with the even more obscure (and late-attested) *synnomai*.

formerly independent states and so 'the Kamirean *ktoinai* on the island' must have all been located in the Kamiris, the *chora* of Kamiros. The same was true of the deme system, introduced only after Rhodian political unity had become a reality. In terms of civic organisation, the merger of Lindos, Kamiros and Ialysos into one state had never been fully implemented, as old territorial and organisational divisions persisted and remained centred on the three *poleis* of Lindos, Ialysos and Kamiros.

BEING LINDIAN

The late-fifth-century creation of new federal institutions centred on the newly established *asty* on the island's northern promontory was accompanied by similarly ambitious developments in the cultic life of the federal Rhodian state. Halios, the Sun god and mythical progenitor of the Rhodians as the grandfather of the heroes Lindos, Ialysos and Kamiros who settled the island, was an early focal point, with a sanctuary founded on the new Rhodian acropolis immediately or soon after the synoikism.[19] By the late second century BCE, the public Rhodian pantheon had been expanded and its divine members were serviced by annually elected priests.[20] By that time too, the cycle of festivals which the Rhodians put on, complete with choral and athletic contests, had grown to include among others the quadrennial (Great) Halieia, a Dionysia and Alexandria and an Epitaphia. The three old cities were directly involved as the *phylai* Lindia, Ialysia and Kamiris, and competed against each other in athletic and equestrian contests.[21]

Cultic life in the three old cities, however, did not stagnate as a result. On the contrary, the Lindians and Kamireans not only kept up worship of their ancestral gods, but added to their pantheons as well.[22] At the turn of the fourth and third centuries, when increasing epigraphic output at Lindos allows a closer look, the Lindians maintained a fairly modest pantheon includ-

---

[19] Papachristodoulou 1999: 27–44. Cf. Dignas 2003: 37–8.

[20] *Lindos II* 134 (dedication by Rhodian priests, late third century); cf. *Annuario* 8–9 (1925/6) 320 no. 3; *Annuario* 27–9 (1952) 351 (list of priests of Halios); *SER* 5 (list of *prophatai*, first century); *SER* 4 (list of priests of Asklapios, early first century CE).

[21] Parker 2009; Arnold 1936; van Gelder 1900: 294–8. *Cl. Rhodos* 2 (1932) 215 no. 55 (second or first century [Iacopi ad loc.], late third century [Badoud: 2015: 189–90]); *Tit. Cam.* 281 no. 21 (first half of second century); *Lindos II* 222 (mid-second century). Interestingly, the Rhodian festival liturgies, such as the tribal *gymnasiarchia*, *phylarchia* and *choregia* were apparently open to all citizens regardless of their tribal affiliation (*NSill* 19, statue base honouring a demesman of the Lindian Nettidai for, among other things, his *phylarchia* for the *phyla Ialysia*. Cf. *Tit. Cam.* 63, monument in honour of a *phylarchos* and *choragos* of the *phyla* Ialysia discovered in Kamiros).

[22] Dignas 2003. Cf. Parker 2009.

ing Poseidon Hippios, Pythian Apollon and Athana Lindia, the city's patron deity whose cult was managed by an eponymous priest also responsible for the cult of Zeus Polieus.[23] Over the next couple of centuries, however, that pantheon – and with it the opportunity for the Lindian elite to serve the gods and their community – was greatly expanded. By the early first century the Lindians also elected annual priests of Dionysos, Artemis, Sarapis, Lindos and the other heroes, and several of Apollo.[24]

Members of the Lindian magisterial elite took great advantage of their city's many priesthoods, embarking on what might be called careers in the service of the gods. The career of Aristokrates son of Pasichares and adopted son of Sosiphilos, commemorated by the inscription that accompanied his statue on the Lindian acropolis, seems to have been fairly typical. He entered public life as one of Lindos' ten *hierothytai* and served annual terms as *archierothytas* and priest of Pythian Apollo before, in 129 BCE, he was finally elected priest of Athana Lindia and Zeus Polieus.[25] From the known dates of entry into public life (a term as *hierothytas*) for a total of sixteen priests of Athana Lindia we know that such a career usually spanned two and a half decades, often punctuated by additional priesthoods or civic offices both locally and in the *asty*.[26] As we saw in Chapter 2, Lindian priests brought their fame and electoral success with them to the federal level, in many cases adding political office and priesthoods to their careers.

A list of priests of Poseidon Hippios, discovered at Loryma north of Lindos, allows us to track an early stage in the development of the expanded pantheon. The list records the names of four *hiereis statoi* or 'standing priests' who held the priesthood for some duration, perhaps for life, until one year, around 315

---

[23] It is not altogether clear when Athana Lindia and Zeus Polios began to share a priest. The fourth-century priest Gorgosthenes knew of dedications to Zeus Polios and Athana, at the time, Athana Polias (*Lindos II* 2 I, II, III), but was himself apparently only priest of Athana. Dedications by 'priests' to both deities are attested from the late fourth century (*Lindos II* 56), but similar dedications to Athana Lindia and Apollo also appear (*Lindos II* 61). In a joint dedication by Lindian priests of the early years of the third century (*Lindos II* 70, including the priest of Pythian Apollo, an *archierothytas* and ten *hierothytai*) Zeus Polios was left out. The first unequivocal reference to a joint priesthood belongs to the mid-third century (*Lindos II* 91).

[24] Dionysos: *Lindos II* 109 (c. 225). Sarapis: *Lindos II* 102 (c. 220). Lindos and the other heroes: *Lindos II* 282 (98). Apollon Olios: *Lindos II* 228 (138). For Artemis Kekoia, Apollon Karneios and Apollon es Kamyndon, see below.

[25] *Lindos II* 232. For the similar career (*hierothytas*, priest of Apollo, priest of Athana Lindia) of Mikythos son of Mikythos and adopted son of Euboulos, see *Lindos II* 251. Most careers, however, can only be partially recovered and must be pieced together from several inscriptions.

[26] *Lindos II* 1 with Blinkenberg's comments: priests of the years (year as *hierothytas* is given in parantheses) 151 (182); 141 (148); 136 (149); 87 (121); 78 (121); 76 (86); 74 (98); 62 (89); 61 (85); 48 (86); 45 (69); 39 (65); 29 (42); 28 (55); 20 (42); 1 (27). For civic offices, see above, pp. 31–3.

BCE, when 'the Lindians decided to elect them annually'.[27] This expansion of access to the priesthood seems to betray a high demand among the Lindian elite for the prestige it entailed, and the expansion of the number of annually elected priesthoods in both Lindos and Kamiros should probably therefore be seen as an attempt meet that demand.

The addition of the priesthood of Poseidon Hippios to the college of annually elected priests in Lindos is also indicative that the Lindians, in expanding their official pantheon, did so with an aim to further the integration of their territory and their citizens within it. By the middle of the third century the priesthood of Artemis Kekoia, whose sanctuary was located in the woodland interior of the island in what was probably the deme of the Ladarmioi, appears for the first time among the priesthoods previously held by a priest of Athana Lindia.[28] A list of Artemis's priests found at Kekoia and datable to the second quarter of the third century BCE – that is, a quarter of a century before the priesthood is attested in Lindos – seems to confirm that Artemis Kekoia at that time was not yet a stable part of the Lindian pantheon, since none of the priests named there had held, or went on to hold, the priesthood of Athana Lindia.[29] This, however, would soon change, and by the end of the century the priesthood of Artemis Kekoia had become closely associated with the priest of Athana Lindia and Zeus Polieus. The priesthood was added to the portfolio of the priests of Athana Lindia and Zeus Polieus, who went on to serve Artemis Kekoia in the second year (perhaps to allow for the successful rendering of accounts) after their terms in the eponymous priesthood had ended.[30] By the beginning of the first century the eponymous priest of Lindos bore the title of 'priest of Athana Lindia and Zeus Polieus and Artemis Kekoia' even though his service to the last deity still lay two years in the future.[31] Similarly, Apollon Karneios, whose priest had joined the college of Lindian *synhiereis* by the beginning of the first century, was closely identified with Loryma north of Lindos, where Poseidon Hippios also had his sanctuary.[32] Around that same time, a priest of Apollon es

---

[27] *Lindiaka VI* 18 with Badoud 2015: 86. For later examples of *hiereis statoi*, see Dignas 2003: 39.

[28] *Lindos II* 91. For the location of the Ladarmioi, see Bresson 1988: 145.

[29] *IG* XII.1 884. Hierokles son of Aristotimos, who would serve as *prytanis* around 260 (*Bulletin de la Société Archéologique d'Alexandrie* 32 [1933] 131; Badoud 2015: 47 n. 116), was probably the son of Aristotimos son of Hierokles, priest of Poseidon Hippios (*Lindiaka VI* 18.13.)

[30] Blinkenberg 1941: 92. Cf. Badoud 2015: 46–7.

[31] Late-third-century statue bases naming priests of 'Athana Lindia and Zeus Polieus and Artemis (in) Kekoia' (e.g. *Lindos II* 93b; 100; 101) are strongly suggestive of the system, documented from 98 BCE onwards (*Lindos II* 282, 98 BCE; 308, 65 BCE; 324, 55 BCE). Blinkenberg 1941: 92. Cf. Badoud 2015: 46–7.

[32] *Lindos II* 282, a dedication of a statue of Athana Lindia's priest for the year 98 BCE, records a priest of [Ἀπόλ]λωνο[ς] Καρνείου [τοῦ ἐς] Λώρυμα. The priesthood appears regularly in the ensuing century (*Lindos II* 294; 299c; 347; 349; 378) without, however, the topographical reference.

Kamyndon, whose sanctuary must have been in the deme of the Kamyndioi, was added to the college. The early history of these rural Lindian priesthoods has left no mark in the epigraphic material, but widespread evidence for local deme and *ktoina* cults with regional appeal – such as Poseidon at Potidaion on Karpathos or Zeus and Hera at Tymnos in the Peraia – makes it likely that some or even all of the rural priesthoods began as such locally managed cults before becoming Lindian cults. Regardless, their inclusion among the *synhiereis* represents both a continued expansion of the availability of priesthoods and a clear attempt at greater Lindian integration.

The greatest prize on the Lindian priestly *cursus* was the priesthood of Athana Lindia and Zeus Polieus, since the synoikism the eponymous magistrate of Lindos. The prestige associated with Athana Lindia and her agents, the priests, had not come about of itself, but was continuously maintained and expanded by the Lindians, who carefully maintained and emphasised its importance, not just for Lindos, but for the entire Rhodian state. The most powerful expression of this was the Lindian *anagraphe* commissioned by the Lindians at the suggestion of Hagesitimos son of Timachidas in 99 BCE.[33] Hagesitimos' motion called for the compilation of the most important entries in the sanctuary's inventory of dedications and a history of the epiphanies of the goddess.[34] In an effort to substantiate the claim, set out in the decree, 'that the sanctuary of Athana Lindia is both the oldest and most venerable', the completed list included forty-two items along with the names of the dedicator, the occasion for dedication and even a short bibliography for authority (Fig. 4.1).

The list of dedicators traces the history of the sanctuary back in time to the mythical foundation of the island of Rhodes: Kadmos, Minos, Herakles, his son Tlepolemos – the legendary king of the island and leader of the Rhodians in the Trojan War – as well as Helen and Menelaos had all made dedications to Athana.[35] In addition to these came dedications by Amasis of Egypt and Artaphernes, the Persian satrap, and finally those of important statesmen of the fourth and third centuries, beginning with Alexander himself and including several Ptolemies, Pyrrhos of Epiros and Philip V.[36]

The Lindian elite had been active in this public relations scheme for a long time. The fact that two of the main sources for the sanctuary inventory were letters written by Gorgosthenes and Hieroboulos, both priests of Athana in Lindia writing respectively to the Rhodian *boula* and the Lindian *mastroi*, suggests

[33] *Lindos II* 2.

[34] *Lindos II* 2.a.1–14. Dignas 2003: 44–5; Higbie 2003.

[35] *Lindos II* 2 iii–xi (cf. Strabo 14.2.6; Hom. *Il.* 2.653–6). Blinkenberg 1941: 149–200 (cf. 1912). Higbie 2003: 204–42.

[36] *Lindos II* 2 xxix, xxxii, xxxviii, xxxix–xlii. Higbie 2003: 65–8.

Figure 4.1 *Lindos II* 2. The Lindian *Anagraphe* (© National Museum of Denmark).

that the attempt to highlight the position of the sanctuary through its precious historic artefacts was not an idea born in 99 BCE, but a strategy employed continuously by the Lindians since the early years of the joint Rhodian state.[37] Furthermore, early in the second century BCE the college of *synhiereis* in the Rhodian *asty*, headed by the priest of Halios himself, had travelled to Lindos and set up a dedication on the acropolis there, in Athana Lindia's sanctuary.[38] A comparable dedication by Lindian priests on the Rhodian acropolis has yet to be found, and the symbolic significance would not have been lost on many. It is hardly a coincidence that this particular priest of Halios was also a former priest of Athana Lindia for the year c. 202 BCE.[39]

To the inventory of prestigious dedications the Lindians in 99 BCE appended a history of the goddess's epiphanies. Among other things it recounted how the goddess had saved Lindos from a Persian siege in the early fifth century by providing the citizens with drinking water, which she caused to rain down on the desperate Lindians.[40] Equally important, another epiphany told the story of how the goddess, acting through her priest, gave advice to the Rhodians on how best to resist the siege of Demetrios (305/4 BCE) in one of the key events in Rhodian history (*Lindos* II 2.95–107):

> When the city was being besieged by Demetrios, it seemed to Kallikles who had formerly been priest of Athana Lindia, but still lived in Lindos, that the goddess stood before him and ordered him to send word to Anaxipolis one of the *prytaneis* that he should write to King Ptolemy and call upon him to aid the city and she would grant victory and power, and that if he did not send word to the *prytanis* and if he (the *prytanis*) did not write to Ptolemy they would regret it.

> 95   πολιορκευμένας ὑπὸ Δημητρίου τᾶς πό-
> λιος ἔδοξε [Κα]λλικλῆς ὁ ἐεικὼς ἐκ τᾶς
> ἱερατείας τᾶς Ἀθάνας τᾶς Λινδίας ἔτι
> διατρίβω[ν] ἐν Λίνδωι ἐπιστᾶσαν αὐτῶι
> καθ᾽ ὕπνον τὰν θεὸν ποτιτάσσειν ἀπαγ-

---

[37] Blinkenberg dates the terms of both priests to the mid-fourth century. *Lindos* II 2 (B I) with Blinkenberg's comments.

[38] *Lindos* II 134.

[39] *Lindos* II 1; 118; 155; *NSER* 165 no. 16 (priest of Athana Lindia); *Lindiaka* VI 18.II.101 (priest of Poseidon in 231); *SEG* 39: 742 (dedication in Rhodes as priest of Halios). For the association of Archokrates, see Chapter 6.

[40] *Lindos* II 2 D.2–59.

100 γεῖλαι ἐνὶ τῶν πρυτανίων Ἀναξιπόλει,
     ὅπως γράψηι ποτὶ βασιλῆ Πτολεμα[ῖ]ον
     καὶ παρακαλῆ<ι> βοαθεῖν τᾶι πόλει ὡς [ἀ]γη-
     σευμένας αὐτᾶς καὶ νίκαν καὶ κράτος πα-
     ρασκευαξεύσας· εἰ δέ κα μήτ' αὐτὸς ἀπαγ-
105 γείληι ποτὶ τὸν πρύτανιν μήτε ἐκῆνος
     γράψηι τῶι Πτολεμαίωι, μεταμελησεῖν
     αὐτοῖς.

As epiphanies go this is surely not the most impressive, but the rest, as they say, is history. The Rhodians did ask Ptolemy (as instructed by the Athana's priest, the *anagraphe* would have us believe), but sent also to Cassander and Lysimachos for help, all of whom sent supplies.[41] Ptolemy, however, was the most eager contributor and was regarded as most important to the success of the city's defence.[42] With this story the Lindians retrospectively laid claim to what had turned out to be the winning, if perhaps somewhat obvious, strategy, and attached not only themselves and their goddess but also her priest directly to the salvation of the whole Rhodian state.[43]

To be a priest of Athana Lindia and Zeus Polieus, then, was to be at the head of an important Rhodian cultural institution with a deep history that was intertwined with that of the Rhodian state as a whole. To reach this pinnacle, members of the Lindian elite, in close parallel with their peers in Kamiros (and presumably also Ialysos), dedicated themselves to the service of the local gods, continuously proving and confirming their commitment to the community by going through a *cursus* of priesthoods and civic offices. Through annual elections the citizens of the three cities had the opportunity to weigh elite candidates against each other, and every successful election was therefore an expression of approval and support – a support that was of vital importance for members of the elite with their eyes fixed on the federal *polis* and politics.

Election for office or priesthoods was not the only means by which the Lindian, Kamireans and Ialysians could express their support for members of the elite. Each of the three constituent cities regularly passed honorific decrees for their most outstanding citizens.[44] Few extant decrees survive, often clouding our view of the kind of behaviour that merited such special recognition, but the survival of a Kamirean decree of one Philokrates son of Philostephanos from the first quarter of the second century (*Tit. Cam.* 110) illustrates the kind

[41] Diod. 22.96.1–3.
[42] As a sign of their gratitude the Rhodians deified Ptolemy (Diod. 22.100.1–5). Morelli 1959: 66–7.
[43] Dignas 2003: 44–5.
[44] See n. 49 below.

of career in public service that culminated in the voting of honours by the citizens of the constituent *poleis*. Philokrates had entered public life in Kamiros as one of the twelve *hieropoioi* in about 207 BCE and served in subsequent years as *agonothetas*, *grammateus mastron* and *epistatas* before winning the *damiourgia* in about 186 BCE. He was commended for his conduct in all of these offices and it was probably, as has been suggested, as *epistatas* that Philokrates had taken charge of the rebuilding of the city's defences, which had been thrown down by a devastating earthquake in 198 BCE. He had been active in the Kamirean assembly as the proposer of a particularly memorable financial measure that outsourced the maintenance of Kamiros' city walls and saved the city a great deal of money. Philokrates had also taken it upon himself to reorganise the public archives, which had for many years been in disorder, and had led an effort to prosecute on the Kamireans' behalf certain individuals who had encroached upon public lands along the border with Lindos.[45]

Philokrates' decree is unique, but the available evidence (fragmentary though it may be) can be pieced together to suggest that his varied record of public service was not unique. No decree survives for Aristombrotidas son of Aristombrotidas, a contemporary Kamirean who was the subject of another honorific decree around the same time, but several inscriptions document his tenure as priest of Athana and as *damiourgos* (as well as office on the federal level), and both he and his brother had contributed to subscriptions most likely connected with the devastation of Kamiros in the same earthquake.[46] A late-fourth-century BCE decree of the Lindians honoured a number of prominent citizens, among them a number of priests of Athana Lindia for their contribution in ensuring a positive outcome for their city in certain lawsuits, while another priest and recipient of Lindian honours, Astymedes son of Theaidetos of Polybian fame, had clearly distinguished himself as a politician.[47]

In Philokrates' case the crown was awarded only posthumously, but such delay in returning gratitude seems to have been rare, as most of the prizes commonly awarded along with a crown assume the honorand to be alive.[48] From Lindos in particular, numerous summaries of honorific decrees, preserved on

---

[45] *Tit. Cam.* 110 (cf. *Tit. Cam.* 44.14 and 45.35). For a detailed commentary including the dating of events in Philokrates' career, see Badoud 2015: 104–7, 369–72.

[46] *Tit. Cam.* 84 (statue base); 3.Ec.31 (list of *damiourgoi* [for the dating of the damiourgoi, see Badoud 2015: 101–7]); 159.13 (*epidosis*, early second century); *Tit. Cam. Supp.* 157b.3 (*epidosis*, early second century); *IG* XII. 49.II.51 (joint dedication of magistrates in the *asty*, after 188).

[47] *IG* XII.1 761 (see now Badoud 2015: 79 and below); *IG* XII.1 852/856 (base of statue for Astymedes with summary of honorific decree). For Astymedes' career in Rhodian and international politics, see Pol. 27.7; 30.4–5, 22; 31.6–7; 33.15 (cf. Blinkenberg 1941: 488–9; Badoud 2010: 127–8).

[48] In the case of the right to wear a crown (*stephanophoria*) at certain events the right is explicitly 'for life' (*SEG* 39: 759.12–13. Cf. Kontorinni 1983: 164).

the bases of statues which had been set up in partial fulfilment of decrees, provide an impression of their contents. The base of a statue of Athanodoros son
of Hagesandros and adopted son of Dionysios, the priest of Athana Lindia in
22 BCE, is a representative example (*IG* XII.1 847):[49]

> [The Lindians honoured] Athanodoros son of Hagesandros and adopted
> son of Dionysios with praise, a gold crown and a bronze statue, and
> granted him also the proclamation of this honour forever, and front
> seat at the games, and a meal in the Hierothyteion, and the privilege
> of wearing each year a crown at the festivals which the Lindians cel-
> ebrate, because of his piety towards the gods and the *eunoia* and *philo-
> doxia* which he continues to show towards the people of Lindos and the
> *sympas damos*.

        [Λίνδιοι ἐτίμασαν]
     I Ἀθανόδωρον Ἀγησάνδρου
            καθ᾽ υοθεσίαν δὲ Διονυσίου
        ἐπαίνωι, χρυσ[έ]ωι στεφάνωι
            καὶ   εἰκόνι   χαλκέαι – – –
     5 δεδώκαντι δὲ αὐτῶι καὶ ἀναγόρευσιν
        τᾶνδε τᾶν τιμᾶν εἰς τὸν ἀεὶ χρόνον
            καὶ προεδρίαν ἐν τοῖς ἀγῶσι
        καὶ σίτησιν ἐν ἱεροθυτείωι καὶ στεφαναφορίαν
        ἐν ταῖς παναγύρεσι καθ᾽ ἕκαστον ἐνιαυτὸν
    10 αἷς ἄγοντι Λίνδιοι – – – καὶ
            τᾶν τιμᾶν ἀναγορεύσει
        εὐσεβείας ἕνεκα τᾶς ποτὶ τοὺς θεοὺς
        καὶ ἀρετᾶς καὶ εὐνοίας καὶ φιλοδοξίας
        ἃν ἔχων διατελεῖ εἰς τὸ πλέθος τὸ Λινδίων
    15 καὶ εἰς τὸν σύνπαντα δᾶμον.

To be honoured, in other words, was hardly a one-off event. The memory of
the crowning would be kept alive through its continuous re-enactment every
time the Lindians gathered in celebration, with the honorand himself singled

---

[49] Similar honours include: *IG* XII.1 846 (honours for Moiragenes son of Archokrates and
adopted son of Lysistratos, priest of Athana Lindia 118 BCE); *Lindos II* 243 (honours for Pasiphon
son of Epilykos and adopted son of Damokles, priest of c. 187 BCE, *hierotamias* [244a], priest of
Halios [245]); 297 (honours for Aristeidas son of Timaratos, priest of Athana Lindia 74 BCE);
307 (honours for Nikotimos son of Timostratos, priest of Athana Lindia 65 BCE) and a relative
of the nauarch Damagoras [*SEG* 43: 527]); 379 (honours for Lapheides son of Hierokles, priest
of 25 BCE).

out through his wearing of an honorific crown and his conspicuous seating during the celebration of games such as the Sminthia, at which the Lindians put on choruses.⁵⁰ Finally, the honorand's central place in public memory was cemented by the erection of a life-size bronze statue on the Lindian acropolis.

On occasion, honorific decrees of the Lindians (like the one cited above) and the Kamireans invoke 'the whole (Rhodian) people' (*ho sympas damos*, l. 15) as a co-beneficiary of the honorand's enduring *areta* and *eunoia*. In doing so, the citizens of Lindos and Kamiros would seem to have taken the liberty of speaking on behalf of all Rhodian citizens, but there is evidence to suggest that the whole Rhodian people had in fact taken an active role in expressing their gratitude for the honorand.

In the early years of the third century BCE, the Kamireans voted to praise and crown one of their citizens, a certain Panaitios son of Simos. Though most of the decree has been lost, a fragment preserves provisions for the announcement of the crown, an event which, apart from the Kamireans, involved also 'the *damos*' (*Tit. Cam.* 106.3–12):

> When the *damos* has given (it), the *agonothetas* is to crown him and announce at the Dionysia, on the first day of the contest of the cyclic [i.e. dithyrambic] choruses, that 'the *koinon* of the Kamireans praises and crowns Panaitios son of Simos', relating the reasons why the Kamireans request that he who is named in this decree is to be crowned.

δό[ν]-
τος δὲ τοῦ δάμου, ὁ ἀγωνοθέτας στε-
5   φανωσάτω αὐτὸν καὶ ἀναγορευσά-
τω Διονυσίοις ἐν τῶι ἀγῶνι τῶν κυκλί-
ων τᾶι πράται ἀμέραι ὅτι Καμιρέων
τὸ κοινὸν ἐπαινεῖ καὶ στεφανοῖ Παναί-
τιον Σίμου, λέγων τὰς πράξεις ἐφ᾽ αἷς
10   αἰτεῦνται Καμιρεῖς στεφανῶσαι αὐτὸν τὰς ἐγ τῶιδε τῶι ψαφίσματι γε-
γραμμένας·⁵¹

---

⁵⁰ For the Sminthia festival and the choragic liturgy attached to it, see *IG* XII.1 762 with Thomsen 2018.

⁵¹ *Tit. Cam.* 106 (for the date, see Badoud 2015: 223 no. 441). For the process of petitioning the federal assembly, see Gabrielsen 1994b. Compare also *Tit. Cam.* 86, an undated statue base for Sylla son of Sylla of the Kasareis (in the Peraia), mentioning praise, a gold crown and a statue granted by the Kamireans and to be announced in a manner (and language) very similar to that described in Lindos.

Since the crowning of Panaitios was to take place only when 'the *damos* has given (it)', it seems possible that 'it' was in fact the crown itself. An honorific decree of the deme of the Brykountioi lends support to this interpretation. When the demesmen voted to honour a Samian doctor with a gold crown, they attached a provision to their decree, which called for the election of a demesman and instructed him 'to petition (αἰτησάσθω) the *sympas damos* (i.e. the federal assembly) for the giving (τὰν δόσιν) of the crown'.[52] Though a similar provision does not appear in the preserved part of the decree of the Kamireans, it concludes with a list of five citizens who had been 'elected', in close parallel with other decrees with provisions for petitioning the federal assembly.[53] That these five Kamireans had been elected to petition the federal assembly for a crown for Panaitios gains further support from the prescribed announcements. An *agonothetas*, associated with a contest of dithyrambic choruses, was to crown Panaitios and relate 'the reasons why the Kamireans had petitioned (αἰτεῦνται) to crown him who is written in this decree'. The direct reference to the petition (αἴτησις) in the instructions to the *agonothetas* announcement indicates that the *agonothetas* in question was the magistrate in charge of the federal Rhodian festival for Dionysos, and not his Kamirean counterpart.[54] The similarity with the Brykountian appeal to the federal assembly also helps identify 'the *damos*' which the Kamireans petition as the federal Rhodian assembly. Though often referred to by other bodies as the *sympas damos* (presumably to distinguish it from the deme), the federal assembly itself never used the expression, preferring instead simply 'the *damos*'.[55]

Together, the two decrees allow us to reconstruct the procedure. After passing an honorific decree, a civic subdivision, in this case the Kamireans, could submit a petition (αἴτησις) to the federal Rhodian assembly to have the crown proclaimed at the Dionysia in the *asty* and before the assembled people. Similar

[52] *IG* XII.1 1032.32–3 (c. 100 BCE); cf. *IG* XII.1 1033.28–33. For the date, see Badoud 2015: 239 no. 905.
[53] *Tit. Cam.* 106.19–23. Cf. *IG* XII.1 1033.31–2; 922.21–2; 890.27–8.
[54] The Rhodians each year elected a number of *agonothetai* (*NSill* 20.8, first century BCE) who presided over the games in the various festivals. An *agonothetas* is directly attested for the Great Erethimia (*BCH* 99 [1975] 97.a.2–3, third century BCE) and the Great Haleia (*Lindos II* 449.7–8, c. 100 CE; 465.h.7–8, late second century CE), and it seems a reasonable inference that an *agonothetas* was also in charge of the Dionysia, which included choral competitions (*IG* XII.1 762; 71; *NSill* 18.17–18; *SEG* 39: 759.17–18; *SER* 20. The restoration [Διονύσωι] in *SER* 7.3, however, has little to recommend it). The office of *agonothetas* in Kamiros is well attested from the early third century BCE onwards (e.g. *Tit. Cam.* 23.19–20) and was, presumably among other things, in charge of announcements at the Kamirean Panathenaia (*Tit. Cam.* 110.54–6). For the office and liturgy of *agonothetes* in the Hellenistic world, see Papakonstantinou 2016. Cf. Camia 2011.
[55] The use of *damos* as part of the phrase 'the *boula* and the *damos*': *NSill* 20.13; *IG* XII.1 383. 'The *damos*' as the federal assembly: *Cl. Rhodos* 2 (1932) 169 no. 1.1; *Lindos II* 209; 215; 224; *IG* XII.1 58; 91; 89; 833(?).

petitions for the permission to erect an inscribed decree in a public sanctuary suggest that such petitions could be presented either directly to the (sympas) damos or by way of the boula, and that they took the form of a proposal to crown the honorand and announce the honours – sometimes, as in the case of the Kamirean decree, with a particular time and venue prescribed.[56] As the Kamirean decree makes clear, however, the approval of the federal assembly did not mean that that body adopted the honorific decree as their own (the agonothetas was to proclaim that the Kamireans had crowned and praised Panaitios), but in granting 'the giving of the crown' at a pan-Rhodian festival, the assembly of course did to some extent endorse the Kamirean decision.[57]

What the citizens of Lindos, Kamiros (and presumably also Ialysos) offered their elite members was the opportunity for their service – and their fellow citizens' grateful response – to be broadcast before a wider Rhodian audience.

DEMES AGAINST DEMES

Lindian priesthoods – and in particular that of Athana Lindia and Zeus Polieus – were prized possessions of the Lindian elite and a means through which its members could reach for fame and prestige which resonated well beyond the borders of Lindia. This was not just a Lindian delusion; others too recognised their attractiveness and they wanted in.

As early as the late fourth century, the priesthoods along with other offices in Lindos were the subject of legal disputes (dikai) between the Lindians and certain outsiders. The apparent apple of discord was the restrictions on eligibility for office in Lindos, and measures had been taken to remove the elections for civic offices and priesthoods from Lindos (presumably to the asty).[58] Kamireans and Ialysians, jealous of Lindian priesthoods, might be suspected to be behind such measures, but the list of suspects must be expanded to include those Lindians – or perhaps, rather, nominal Lindians – who belonged to demes in the Peraia and on the islands of Karpathos.[59]

---

[56] Gabrielsen 1994b.

[57] For the Athenian Dionysia as a venue for the proclamation of honours by civic subdivisions, see Thomsen forthcoming a.

[58] IG XII.1 761 (see below). Thomsen 2018: 287; Badoud 2015: 75–82; Gabrielsen 1997: 132–3. Bresson 1988: 145–7.

[59] Both the Kamireans and (it would seem) the Ialysians similarly did not allow citizens of the other two poleis to stand for election or otherwise take part in their public affairs. The Kamireans, however, seems to have reversed this policy in about 12 BCE (Badoud 2015: 95, following Blinkenberg 1941: 400 contra Pugliese Carratelli 1956: 73). There is good evidence that both Kamiros and Ialysos allowed their fellow citizens of the Peraia and other islands to participate, Badoud 2015: 77.

Though members of the Lindian demes in the Peraia and on Karpathos were clearly full citizens of Rhodes and even regarded as members of the *phyla* Lindia, the twelve demes located on the island of Rhodes continued to bar them from civic and religious office in Lindos. A decree enacted by the *mastroi* and the Lindians, and erected in Physkos in the Peraia, demonstrates that the demesmen of the Physkioi were under Lindian jurisdiction and bound by the decisions of political institutions in Lindos, but draws a distinction between 'the Lindians and the Physkioi'.[60] Throughout the period with which we are concerned, not a single Lindian citizen from a deme in the Peraia or on Karpathos ever held an office or a priesthood in Lindos. Nor did the overseas demes send *mastroi* to Lindos, and it is likely therefore that the demesmen of Karpathos and the Peraia assigned to Lindos were not only barred from office, but altogether excluded from political participation in Lindos.[61]

In response to this challenge the twelve demes, which, at least later, referred to themselves as the *damoi hoi en Lindia polei*,[62] elected thirty of their foremost citizens to represent them, and a decree in honour of their success gives a small sketch of the dispute (*IG* XII.1 761.38–43):

> They showed themselves good men standing together in defence of the Lindians so that elections are held in Lindos of priests, *hierothytai, hieropoioi* and the other officers in charge of public affairs from the Lindians themselves and as written in the laws, and that those who have not taken part before, will not take part in the sacred affairs of Lindos. The *mastroi* and the Lindians decided.

> ἄνδρες ἀγαθοὶ ἐγένοντο συνδιαφυλάξαντες Λινδίοις ὅπως
> ταὶ αἱρέσιες γίνωνται ἐν Λίνδωι τῶν ἱερέων κ[αὶ] ἱεροθυτᾶν κα[ὶ]
> 40 ἱεροποιῶν καὶ τῶν ἄλλων τῶν ἐπὶ τὰ κοινὰ τασσομέν[ω]ν ἐξ
> αὐτῶν Λινδίων καθ' ἃ καὶ ἐν τοῖς νόμοις γέγραπται κα[ὶ μ]ὴ μετέ-
> χωντι τῶν ἐν Λίνδωι ἱερῶν οἳ μὴ καὶ πρότερον μετεῖχον, δεδό-
> χθαι τοῖς μαστροῖς καὶ Λινδίοις·

If the Lindian demesmen of the Peraia and Karpathos were behind the effort to move Lindian elections away from Lindos, they failed; but it appears that the overseas demesmen of the Physkioi were at the same time pursuing a different strategy.

An *epidosis* held in Lindos in those very years (late fourth century BCE) is perhaps indicative of the ambitions of some of the disenfranchised Lindian

---

[60] *RIPR 22* with Bresson's comments; Thomsen 2018.
[61] *Lindos II* 378.
[62] *Lindos II* 347; 349.

demesmen. The *epidosis* was undertaken to collect funds for 'the replacement of the adornment of Athana and for (sacred) vessels' and was joined by the leading citizens of the day, among them no fewer than eleven priests of Athana Lindia, all listed according to their deme.[63] Unsurprisingly, these included all the twelve island demes of Lindos, but a large number of demesmen of the Physkioi, a Lindian deme on the Peraia, also answered the call. Though relegated to what was presumably the end of the list, the Physkioi entered with no fewer than forty-four contributors, outdone only by the sixty-five members of the island (and city) deme of the Lindopolitai who headed the list.

In the light of the legal dispute, it is tempting to see in the massive Physkian entry not only a coordinated effort to demonstrate their loyalty and devotion to the *polis* of Lindos and to its patron deity, but perhaps also an attempt to prepare the ground for a request for admission into the privileged ranks of the island demes, and with it to reach for the important *polis* steps on the *cursus*.[64]

But the Lindians – that is, the members of the twelve Lindian demes on the island of Rhodes – could not be turned on the issue through cajoling or legal threats. Once successfully defended, the demes were again free to compete against each other for the priesthood of Athana Lindia. Elections for the eponymous priesthood were guided by a triennial rule – identified (as mentioned above) by Christian Blinkenberg, who first put the list of priests together – according to which each of the three Lindian tribes (each consisting of four of the twelve island demes) took turns in providing candidates for the priesthood (see Table 4.1).[65]

Not all demes were equally successful. Alain Bresson has pointed to an interesting correlation between the relative number of demesmen from each deme appointed by the Lindians as representatives in the legal dispute of the late fourth century BCE (*IG* XII.1 761) and the number of demesmen

---

[63] *Lindos II* 51.1–2 with Blinkenberg's comments.

[64] Bresson 1988: 145–7; Thomsen 2018: 287; Gabrielsen 1997: 132–3; cf. 2000: 194. Momigliano (1936: 61–3) suspects that the Kamireans or Ialysians were behind the challenge, and while the matter cannot decided (nor are these interpretations necessarily at odds) on the available evidence, it is nevertheless relevant to note that both Kamiros and Ialysos, while excluding each other as well as the Lindians, allowed their fellow citizens from outside the island of Rhodes to stand for elections and presumably therefore also to participate fully in internal affairs (see for instance *Tit. Cam.* 280–1, nos. 19 and 20, two fragments of a third-century list of representatives (theoroi?) sent by each of the three cities to the sanctuary of Zeus Atabyrios, which included demesmen of the Peraia among the Ialysian (of the Kryasseis) and Kamirean (of the Tymnians and Amnistians) contingents.

[65] Blinkenberg 1941 and *Lindos II* 1 (with comments). Fraser (1953) points to the recurring number three in boards of Lindian magistrates as indicating that the triennial rule guided the election for other offices too. In the same article Fraser argues that a similar system also guided the election of *damiourgoi* in Kamiros.

Table 4.1 The Lindian demes of the island.

Tribe A	Tribe B	Tribe C
Old Cycle (406–242 BCE)		
Argeioi	Klasioi	Lindopolitai
Pagioi	Dryitai	–
Nettidai	Ladarmioi	–
Kamyndioi	–	–
New Cycle (242 BCE–)		
Pedieis	Argeioi	Klasioi
Brasioi	Pagioi	Nettidai
Kattabioi	Lindopolitai	Ladarmioi
Dryitai	Boulidai	Kamyndioi

Note: This table follows Badoud (2015: 39–6) but assigns the Argeioi to Tribe A (Old cycle), rather than Tribe B (Finkielstjern and Thomsen forthcoming). In 242 a reallotment of the demes seems to have taken place, apparently to counter demographic shifts (Bresson 1988: 145–55; cf. Badoud 2015: 38–41). *Lindos II* 346 and 378, two dedications including lists of *mastroi* (the first only partially preserved) from 43 and 27 BCE, respectively, suggest that the Lindians kept close track of such developments in order to ensure that representation on the council to some degree reflected citizen numbers. The reapportionment of seats on the council of *mastroi* between 43 and 27 BCE seems not to have had an impact on the distribution of the demes between the *phylai*.

in the contemporary *epidosis* (*Lindos II* 51).[66] Pointing to the high number of Lindopolitai and Klasioi in *IG* XII.1 761 and *Lindos II* 51 compared with the other demes, Bresson identified the demesmen of the Lindopolitai and the Klasioi as the leading public associations in Lindos at the turn of the fourth and third centuries. This is in itself significant, but might be explained by assuming the greater numbers of the Lindopolitai and the Klasioi compared to other demes. But we can add to Bresson's observations that a Klasios managed to win three out of four elections for the priesthood of Athana Lindia in which their *phyla* ('Tribe B') was eligible in the long decade that followed the year 338 (336, 333 and 330). In the same period, the Lindopolitai ('Tribe C'), first among the island demes in representation in *IG* XII.1 761 and *Lindos II* 51, enjoyed virtual electoral dominance, winning four out of four possible terms in 338, 335, 329 and 326.[67]

The late-fourth-century electoral success of the Lindopolitai and the Klasioi is instructive. First of all, it is clear that deme affiliation mattered a great deal and that candidates could to a considerable extent rely on the support of their demesmen. Secondly, since their success was not complete (a member of the Druitai would win the priesthood in 294, a year of 'Tribe B' which included the Klasioi), it stands to reason that neither deme was able to dominate through

---

[66] Bresson 1988: 148 (with table 1).
[67] *Lindos II* 1, fragment B with Blinkenberg's notes (1941: 107–8).

sheer numbers alone.[68] Clearly, we must look for other explanations for the late-fourth-century success of the Lindopolitai and Klasioi, and ask how the members of the Lindopolitai managed to achieve such an exclusive hold on the priesthood of Athana Lindia.

For any contender for *polis* priesthoods and civic office, securing the support of their fellow demesmen was paramount. From mid-second-century Kamiros an *epidosis* is preserved which called for the collection of funds to support the local Panathenaia festival. The demesmen of the Arioi promptly answered the call by announcing a contribution of 50 drachmas (*Tit. Cam.* 159):

> Having chosen to increase the honour of the gods and the Panathe-
> naia festival the following announced that they would give money
> as a contribution to the furnishing of sacrificial victims and reservoirs
> and for the banqueting of the demes:
> The *damos* of the Arioi, 50 (drachmas)
> Kritoboulos son of Aristombrotidas
> and on behalf of his wife Nikaina and his sons
> Aristombrotidas and Nausippos, 100 (drachmas)
> Aristombrotidas son of Aristombrotidas . . .

> τοίδε προαιρούμενοι ἐπαύξειν
> τάς τε τῶν θεῶν τιμὰς καὶ τὰν
> πανάγυριν τῶν Παναθηναίων
> ἐπαγγείλαντο δώσειν χρήματα
> 5   δωρεὰν εἰς τὰν κατασκευὰν τῶν
> χρηστηρίων καὶ τῶν ἐλύτρων καὶ
> εἰς τὰν ἑστίασιν τῶν δάμων
>   Ἀρίων ὁ δᾶμος ν΄
> Κριτόβουλος Ἀριστομβροτίδα
> 10   καὶ ὑπὲρ τᾶς γυναικὸς
> Νικαίνας καὶ ὑπὲρ τῶν υἱῶν
> Ἀριστομβροτίδα καὶ Ναυσίππου ρ΄
> [Ἀριστομβ]ροτίδας Ἀριστομβροτίδα
> [- - - - - - - - - - - - - -]

Immediately after the contribution of the Arioi, a couple of their wealthiest demesmen made their own additional contributions, before the inscription

---

[68] Regarding the relative strength of numbers of the demes, it is interesting to note that the one *phyla* ('Tribe A') for which all four demes are known was responsible for almost precisely one third of the island deme contributors to the *epidosis* in *Lindos II* 51 (60 of 196). The distribution between the demes of 'Tribe A' is Pagioi 17 per cent, Kamyndioi 28 per cent, Argeioi 30 per cent, Nettidai 25 per cent.

breaks off. Among them was Aristombrotidas son of Aristombrotidas, the priest of Athana and *damiourgos* of 171. Family again played a part, and Aristombrotidas' brother Kritoboulos heads the list and gave 100 drachmas. Here the inscription breaks off, but on analogy with the Lindian *epidosis* of the late fourth century through which the demesmen of the Lindopolitai in particular asserted themselves as a significant group within the *polis*, we may guess that other Kamirean demes, in cooperation with their leading members, also joined the subscription.

The competition among demes for prestige is also evident in yet another Kamirean subscription from the second century. It records the contributions of various *koina*, including demes, to an unknown public building project.[69]

[–]

1 ....ν πατ [ριωτᾶν κοινὸν – – – –]
.....στᾶν τῶν ἐγ Κα[μίρωι κοινὸν – –]
...λιδᾶν πατριωτᾶν κοινὸ[ν – – – – –]
[Ε]ὐριαδᾶν δαμετᾶν κοινὸν δισ[χιλίας]
5 Ἑρμαιστᾶν τῶν ἐν τῶι ἄστει κοιν[ὸν – –]
Κυμισαλέων κοινὸν δισχιλίας
Λοξ[ι]δᾶν κοινὸν δισχι[λί]ας ....κοσ[ίας]
Ἀμνιστ[ί]ων [κ]οιν[ὸν δισ]χιλ[ίας]
Βο[υλι]δᾶν κοινὸν πεντακοσίας
10 Φε.....ᾶν [πατρι]ωτᾶν κοινὸν π[ε]ντακοσίας
Ευ........τ[.. κο]ινὸν χιλίας
Σωκλε[.......... κ]οιν[ὸ]ν πεντακοσίας
        vacat(?)
13 Γλαυκε.....ν[ιδ]ᾶ[ν] κ[οιν]ὸν πεντακοσία[ς]
[Κ]τησινε[ί]ων Σ[..... κ]οιγὸν π[ε]ντα[κοσίας]
15 ...θαγ.ογτι..γ κοιγὸγ δισχιλίας
[– – – – – – – – – – – – – – – –]

The Kymisaleis (l. 6) gave 2,000 drachmas as did the Amnistioi of the Kamirean Peraia (l. 8). The Euthenitai, another deme of the Peraia, may be restored in line 11 as giving 1,000 drachmas, while the Loxidai (l. 7), clearly not wishing to be outdone, gave 2,000 and some hundred drachmas.

It is possible, of course, that the money – considerable sums ranging from 500 to over 2,000 drachmas – had come from deme treasuries, but, in the light of the coordinated contributions of the Arioi and Aristombrotidas' family for the Kamirean Panathenaia and the late-fourth-century Lindian *epidosis* (*Lindos II* 51) in which the demes were represented solely by their wealthiest

---

[69] *Tit. Cam.* 159a. Migeotte 1992: 135–7. For the private associations in this *epidosis* see below, Chapter 7.

members, it is perhaps more likely that some of it had come from the wealthy members of the demes.

In response to such and other benefactions the demesmen, just as the Lindians, Kamireans and Ialysians did, would regularly express their gratitude to members of the elite through honorific decrees. At Lindos, for instance, the Argeioi, the Brasioi, the Lindopolitai and the Nettidai all voted honours for their own outstanding members.[70] The Brykountioi on Karpathos, as we have already seen, would petition the federal assembly to have their honorific decree announced also in the *asty*, and other demes followed this practice as well.[71] The same deme honours were almost invariably passed for members and therefore betray a remarkable loyalty towards the local deme elite.[72]

In reaching out across deme boundaries, members of the magisterial elite would occasionally appeal to other civic subdivisions (though, as we will see, private associations had an important part to play here as well). At Kamiros, Aristombrotidas son of Aristombrotidas of the Arioi had secured the gratitude of the *triktoinai hai en Leloi*, an organisation presumably joining three Kamirean *ktoinai* in Lelos, the place that probably lent its name to the Kamirean deme of the Lelioi, and, at Lindos, a certain Eualkidas son of Aristolochos of the deme of the Lindopolitai was the benefactor of the *Dryitan patra*, which shared its name with another Lindian deme.[73] Family connections were possibly a more powerful means through which to secure support across deme boundaries. Through adoption and marriage, contenders for the priesthood of Athana Lindia could establish close connections with influential members in other demes and, more importantly, demes of other tribes whose votes, in years where they were not themselves eligible, were not tied by deme loyalties. Much has been made of adoption as a way of circumventing the triennial rule and allowing candidates to run in two years out of three, but it is at least equally important to recognise that at the same time adoption allowed the contender for office in Lindos to form alliances with influential voices in other demes of other

---

[70] Lindopolitai: *Lindos II* 392; 420; Brasioi: *Lindos II* 384b; Nettidai: 391 (216). Kamirean demes too set up honorific decrees: the Silyrioi: *Tit. Cam.* 98 (undated); the Bybassioi: *RIPR* 44; *NSill* 27 (second century BCE).

[71] *IG* XII.1 1032 (see above). Cf. *IG* XII.1 1032.29 and *Lindos II* 216 (base of a statue set up by the Nettidai for Astymedes son of Theaidetos ‘ἀρετᾶς ἕνεκα καὶ εὐνοίας ἂν ἔχων διατελεῖ εἴς τε τὸν σύμπαντα δᾶμον καὶ εἰς τὸν Νεττιδᾶν’.

[72] *Lindos II* 216 (honours for Astymedes son of Theaidetos by the Nettidai) is the single exception among the twelve Lindian demes of the island. Astymedes held the priesthood of Athana Lindia in 154, a year of ‘Tribe A’, but the Nettidai belonged to ‘Tribe C’.

[73] *Tit. Cam.* 84.17–8. Pugliese-Carratelli 1951: 85 (cf. Gabrielsen 1997: 154). *Lindos II* 146 (statue base from Lindos, late third or early second century) and *IG* XII.1 88 (statue base from the *asty*, late third or early second century).

tribes.[74] In this connection it can hardly be irrelevant that in eleven out of the twelve cases of adopted priests of Athana Lindia for which deme membership is known, the priest had been adopted not only into a new deme, but also into a new tribe.[75] The same kind of support could probably be found from in-laws. In Chapter 3 we came across Kleisithemis son of Eratophanes of the Pedieis (a deme in 'Tribe A'). At the time Kleisithemis ran for the priesthood of Athana Lindia in 136 BCE, he counted several important members of other demes among his family. His wife was the daughter of a certain Aristeidas of the Kamyndioi and his daughter Euagis was married to Timokrates son of Hagemon, a member of the Timokratids who belonged to the deme of the Klasioi.[76] Incidentally, neither the Kamyndioi nor the Klasioi were eligible in 136 (both belonged to 'Tribe C'), when Kleisithemis won the priesthood.

A similar situation would arise at the federal level when citizens of all three old *poleis* gathered in assembly in the *asty* for the election of federal officers. At least in electing *stratagoi* '*ek phylon*' the assembly-goers would have been forced to abandon all local patriotism and cast their ballot for a candidate from each of the other *poleis*.[77] It is perhaps therefore not surprising that the Kamirean subscription mentioned above contained not only entries by Kamirean demes, but also 500 drachmas from the Lindian deme of the Boulidai.[78]

The close relationship between the magisterial elite and their demesmen suggests that electoral success to an extent rested on securing the loyalty of one or more public subdivisions. This raises the possibility of regional politics

---

[74] Blinkenberg 1941: 95–6; Fraser 1953: 53; Gabrielsen 1997: 112–20. Recently, Badoud (2015: 41–2) has called into question the examples provided by Blinkenberg (1941: 96), but those collected by Gabrielsen (1997: 137–40) clearly demonstrate that adopted priests could stand for election in a year of their native deme as well as their adopted deme. Nevertheless, as pointed out by Rice (1988; cf. Badoud 2015: 41), and as argued in greater detail in the previous chapter, the sheer number of attested adoptions (in Kamiros and Ialysos as well as in Lindos) must dispel any notion that circumvention of the triennial rule was the primary motivation for even elite adoption.

[75] In four cases both native and adopted demes are known: (1) Eratophanes son of Kleisithemis (Pedieus) and adopted son of Agorakles (Nettidas), priest in 109 BCE; (2) Aristeidas son of Kleisithemis (Pedieus) and adopted son of Agorakles (Nettidas), priest in 100 BCE; (3) Dionysios son of Dionysios (Karpathopolitas) and adopted son of Euanoros (Pagioi), priest in 72 BCE; (4) Zenodotos son of Diophantos son of Zenodotos (Lindopolitas) and adopted son of Onasandros (Brasios), priest in 64 BCE. For the remaining seven cases (the priests of 112 BCE, 108 BCE, 27 BCE, 24 BCE, 16 BCE, 9 BCE, 26 CE) see Blinkenberg's comments to *Lindos II* 1 and Gabrielsen 1997: 137–40.

[76] *Lindos II* 252.I.9–12. Timokrates himself had been adopted out of the Klasioi by a certain Lysistratos. The deme of Lysistratos (Kattabioi) is suggested by Blinkenberg (*Lindos II* 1 s.v. 112).

[77] Dmitriev 1999.

[78] *Tit. Cam.* 159a.9

in which *poleis*, and below them demes, sought to further their own special interests. We may see such special interests behind the championing of their own politically ambitious members, but in the case of the fourth-century legal dispute there can be no doubt about it. When some outsider sought access to the Lindian privilege of access to Lindian office (be it Kamireans, Ialysians or disenfranchised Lindians) the twelve island demes, which otherwise competed against each other for relative positions and not least the offices and priesthoods of the Lindian *polis*, all came together and closed ranks to form a united front against the outsiders.

CHAPTER 5

Private Associations

From the public subdivisions we move now out of the state sphere and into the social, to private associations. From the late third century BCE to the early first century CE, the period with which we are dealing, Rhodes was home to about 200 private associations that we know of.[1] To judge from their names, the associations were primarily concerned with cult, and therefore commonly known as 'religious associations' among modern historians.[2] In the following chapters the associations' relationship with the Rhodian magisterial elite will come to the centre of the discussion, and we will see how associations became part of an elite strategy and helped shaped politics in the Rhodian state. But before we get to that we must first take a look at the internal organisation of the many private associations of Rhodes.

A comprehensive survey of Rhodian associations, however, is confronted by two problems. First, most private associations in Rhodes are known to us simply as names, most employing a theophoric element, such as the *Asklapiastai*, or compounds, such as the *Meniastai Aphrodisiastai*, while on occasion incorporating ethnic or professional elements.[3] Secondly, those same names combined with other evidence indicate profound differences in membership, activity and intensity.

Traditional scholarship about private associations in the Greek world constructed elaborate typologies of associations: cultic, professional, ethnic and

---

[1] Benincampi 2008: 344–52.
[2] Steinhauer 2014; Arnaoutoglou 2003; Jones 1999: 309.
[3] *Asklapiastai*: IG XII.1 164 (undated); 701 (first century BCE); *Lindos II* 391 (10 CE). *Meniastai Aphrodisiastai*: IG XII.1 162 (undated). For a list, see Benincampi 2008: 244–52. Cf. Morelli 1959.

more, often based solely on the names of associations.[4] More recent scholar-ship, however, has largely abandoned this approach, emphasising instead the various pre-existing networks that coalesced in the associations.[5]

A mid-second-century Rhodian association provides a case in point. To judge from the name, the *Asklapiastai Nikasioneioi Olympiastai* might be under-stood simply as a group of devotees of Asklapios (and of the Olympian gods) and left at that, but the chance survival of a list containing the names of a sub-set of the members – namely those who were also its benefactors – allows us a more detailed look at a subsection of the members: the association had been founded by a certain Nikasion of Kyzikos, and he and his immediate family seem to have formed the nucleus of the group. Both his sons, his daughter and five grandchildren were listed, as was his wife, Olympias, whose name should probably be recognised as the root of the name *Olympiastai*.[6] Certain members of the association also shared a profession. The group included the sculptors Theon of Antioch, who in the first half of the second century had become a favourite of the Rhodian elite (and who may have been married to a sister of Nikasion's wife), and his Rhodian associate Demetrios son of Demetrios.[7] The latter was probably the father of Basilis, who married Nikasion's son (a naturalised Rhodian, also named Nikasion) and whose son followed in his maternal grandfather's footsteps as a sculptor.[8] To this we may add that a large section of the membership also shared the common trait of being foreigners settled in Rhodes, and within this group some shared a common origin in, for instance, Antioch or Soloi.[9] The latter included Agathokles, who is also known to have worked as a sculptor and who may have been a relation of Olympias and Eirene, the wives of Nikasion and Theon.[10] This core group of members, in other words, were related through a complex set of family,

---

[4] Foucart 1873; Ziebarth 1896; Poland 1909.

[5] Harland 2003; Thomsen forthcoming c.

[6] *IG* XII.1 127; *MDAI(A)* 25 (1900) 109 no. 108. Boyxen 2018: 334–6; Maillot 2009; Gabrielsen 1997: 12–9. Badoud (2015: 303) suggests the possibility that the association's *phyla* Olympeis was in fact named for Nikasion's daughter, rather than her mother, but there can be no cer-tainty in the matter. For the date, see Badoud (2015: 303).

[7] Badoud (2015: 281 no. 80 and 81) collects the evidence for the sculptors' professional activities. See also the family's stemma (Badoud 2015: 303; cf. Maillot 2009). Theon appears to have been the husband of Eirene of Soloi (Olympias's sister?) who is listed directly below his name (*IG* XII.1 127.67–9).

[8] Demetrios son of Nikasion (*IG* XII.1 127.64) appears as the sculptor in an unpublished inscription reported by Kontorini 1989: 144.

[9] The seven Antiocheans attested (*IG* XII. 127.17, 28, 42, 46, 51, 54, 67) comprise the largest 'ethnic' contingent of the attested members excepting the Rhodians, some of whom were naturalised (such as the children of Nikasion of Kyzikos and Olympias of Soloi).

[10] For the work of Agathokles of Soloi, see Badoud 2015: 283 no. 150.

professional and 'ethnic' ties, which had been brought together under the umbrella of membership in an association.

The members of the association furthermore proclaimed themselves to be *Asklapiastai* and must have met to perform his rituals.[11] As part of their cultic schedule, Nikasion's association celebrated games at which the members, divided into tribes – all named after members of the founder's family – and the victories of each tribe were dutifully recorded on a stele with the name of the *phyla*, their *phylarchos* and the name of the association *agonothetas* who had served in a particular year (Fig. 5.1).[12]

Few Rhodian associations have left us with evidence that affords us such detailed knowledge about their membership and their activities, but the scanty bits of evidence we do have reveal a world of associations characterised by incredible variation. Some associations announced themselves to the world as individuals sharing a particular place of origin, such as the city of Herakleia or Syria.[13] Others, like Nikasion's association, were composed of a mix of individuals from all over the Greek world and therefore sometimes described as 'foreigners' associations', though many demonstrably included also Rhodian citizens.[14]

A number of associations seem to have premised membership on membership in particular public associations such as specific demes, *ktoina* or *patrai*.[15] One such group had formed around a number of *patriotai*, the members of the otherwise unknown *patra* of the Matioi, but at the same time styled themselves *eranistai*, that is, the members of an *eranos* – a word used in Rhodes and beyond to describe a common fund and by extension an association.[16] But though the association professed a certain citizen exclusivism, it apparently had no reservations about forming strong ties with a certain Philokrates of Ilion, a wealthy, privileged metic who had settled in Rhodes.[17] Finally, an association bearing

---

[11] The members could provide their own wine for their feasts and ceremonies from the vineyard the association owned (*Annuario* n.s. 1–2 [1939/40] 150 no. 5.5. Maillot 2009; Gabrielsen 1997: 129).

[12] *IG* XII. 127.1–57.

[13] *Herakleotan* [---]*soneion koinon, IG* XII.1 158 (first century BCE). *Herakleotai Poseidoniastai Polemoneioi hoi syn Agathameroi, Annuario* 64–5 (1986/7) 277 no. 12. *Heraklotai* (*polis* or Rhodian *koinon*?), *IG* XII.1 963 (Chalke, undated); *Annuario* 1–2 (1939/40) 165 no. 19.22 (third century BCE); *Aphrodisiastai Syroi, IG* XII.3 104 (Nisyros, Imperial period); *Adoniastai* [---] *Asklapiastai Syroi, IG* XII.3 6 (Syme, first century BCE). Maillot 2015: 138 with n. 10.

[14] Maillot 2015; cf. 2005: 68–78.

[15] The distinction between the civic subdivisions and the private associations that took their names from them will be discussed in Chapter 7.

[16] *IG* XII. 155.12, 84, 109; *SEG* 39: 737.b.3; *Lindos II* 420.a.26. For *eranos* and *eranistai* in Classical and early Hellenistic Athens, see Thomsen 2015.

[17] *IG* XII.1 157. There is no need to assume, as Gabrielsen (1997: 153) does, that Philokrates had founded the association or even that he was a member. On the meaning of association names derived from the personal names of benefactors, see below.

Figure 5.1 *IG* XII.1 127. List of victorious tribes of the *Asklapiastai Nikasioneioi Olympiastai* (Ephorate of Antiquities of the Dodecanese – © Hellenic Ministry of Culture and Sports (N.3028/2002)).

one of the familiar theophoric names (the [*Diosatabyri*]*astai*) on one occasion qualified that name with a 'those who are *polis* slaves'.[18]

Viewed together, Rhodian associations spanned the entire legal and – as we will see below – social spectrum, and, as is evident from the case of the *Asklapiastai Nikasioneioi Olympiastai*, names need not have told the whole story.

The prospect of drawing general, but also valid, inferences from a small body of evidence concerning associations is less than encouraging. Accordingly, this chapter will be confined to an analysis of the three aspects of the associations that appear to have been shared universally: the concern with cult, a democratic mode of organisation and the relationship with wealthy benefactors.

COMMUNITY BUILDING

As just mentioned, the concern with cult is among the activities most commonly espoused by private associations through their names. These indicate a wide variety in the religious interests of the associations and their members, including all the deities for whom the Rhodians organised worship, but adding others, such as Men or the Agathos Daimon.[19] Even those citizens' associations whose members regarded themselves as the custodians of ancient kinship lines congregated for the worship of what they at least considered to be ancestral gods. The *Euthalidai* (Nettian branch) congregated in the sanctuary of Zeus Patroios and the *diagonia* of the *Hagetoridai* elected a *hierotamias*, or sacred treasurer.[20]

It is pointless therefore to speak of an association as 'religious' or 'social'. All associations were both. It is important, however, to bear in mind that the ostensible preoccupation with matters of cult, funerals and communal meals does not necessarily signify removal from worldly affairs of political, professional or commercial interests. Much of the current orthodoxy on private associations and their relation to the political and economic sphere (or perhaps rather their lack of such a relation) is formed around this misconception about the role of cult and social functions of the association.[21]

Gods and heroes have schedules; that is to say, they have their own important stories which blend in with the passing of the year and the lives of humans.

---

[18] [---]*astai hoi tas poleos douloi, IG* XII.1 31 (undated).

[19] Meniastai: *IG* XII. 1 917 (Lindos, undated); 162 (Rhodes, undated). *Agathodaimoniastai*: *Lindos II* 252. 251 (Lindos, c. 125 BCE); *Annuario* n.s. 1–2 (1939/40) 151 no. 6.4, 11 (Rhodes, early first century BCE); *IG* XII.1 161 (Roman period); *SER* 17 (undated).

[20] *IG* XII.1 890 (cf. *Lindos II* 652); *Cl. Rhodos* 2 (1932) 175 no. 4.7 (cf. *IG* XII.1 922).

[21] Apolitical associations: Jones 1999: 302–10. Veyne (1990 [1976]: 392) even has the violent clashes between clubs associated with political actors as 'quite non-political in character', but see van Nijf 1997; Verboven 2007; Harland 2003.

A ritual calendar from Mytilene dated to the Roman Imperial period gives an impression of the timing and frequency of cultic activities relating to even a single goddess, possibly Kore (*IG* XII Supp. 29):[22]

> [---] on the fourth of the month of Deios. The ascent of the goddess on the seventh. The *hydropsia* on the new moon of the month of Ioulaisos. The procession from the *prytaneion* on the tenth. The *neomata* [the breaking of fallow land] on the 15th of the month of Apollonios. The descent of the goddess on the fourth of the month of Hephaistios. The banquet on the fifteenth of the month of Posideios. Aristippos son of Aristippos inscribed (this) at the command of the goddess.

> μηνὸς Δείου δ΄ ἡ ἀνάβασις τῆς θεοῦ τῇ ζ΄
> ἡ ὑδροποσία μηνὸς Ἰουλαίου νουμηνίᾳ
> ἡ πομπὴ ἐκ πρυτανείου ι΄
> τὰ νεώματα μηνὸς Ἀπολλωνίου ιε΄
> 5   ἡ δύσις τῆς θεοῦ μηνὸς Ἡφαιστίου δ΄
> ἡ κατάκλησις μηνὸς Ποσιδείου ιε΄
> κατὰ κέλευσιν τῆς θεοῦ Ἀρίστιππος Ἀριστίππου
> ἐπέγραψα.

No Rhodian association has left a comparable timetable of their cultic activities. Nevertheless, a handful of inscriptions give evidence that associational life was guided by sometimes busy cultic calendars. This was certainly the case of the *Haliadai kai Haliastai*, a second-century BCE association which met in the *asty* and from which an extensive decree survives (*IG* XII.1 155). Throughout the year the association met in several *synodoi*, each lasting at least two days, during which burnt sacrifices were performed, presumably followed by a shared meal.[23] The state of the evidence does not allow a clear view of such gatherings, but evidence from elsewhere can provide an impression of association sacrifices. In the early third century, two Athenian associations of *orgeones* met once a year on the 17th and 18th days of the month of Hekatombaion to sacrifice to their hero and heroines. Instructions for the *hestiator* or host, an officer of the association, were laid out in an 'ancient decree' of the association (*Agora* 16: 161):

---

[22] *IG* XII supp. 29 fragment A (found at Dardanos in the Troad). Solokowski 1955: 224. Trans. Lupu 2005: 69. Cf. *IG* II² 1367. Poland 1909: 219–21. Lupu (2005: 88–9) rightly notes the difficulty in establishing the identity of the issuing body of festival calendars.

[23] Honours for the *archeranistas* and benefactor of the *Haliadai kai Haliastai*, Dionysodoros of Alexanderia, were to be proclaimed 'at the *synodoi* on the second day, after the sacrifice' (*IG* XII.1 155.26–8, 57–8).

Resolved by the *orgeones*: the *hestiator* is to offer the sacrifices in the month of Hekatombaion, on the 17th and 18th day. On the first day he is to sacrifice first a young pig to the Heroines and an adult animal to the Hero and to prepare an offering table, and on the last day an adult animal to the Hero. He is to render accounts of what he has spent and he must not spend more than the revenue. Let him distribute the meat to the *orgeones* who are present, and up to half a share to their sons, and to the women of the *orgeones*, giving to free women the same share of up to half a share to their daughters and up to half a share to an attendant. He is to give the woman's share to the man.

ἔδοξεν τοῖς ὀργεῶσιν· τὸν ἑστιάτορα θύειν τὴν [θυσί]-
αν μηνὸς Ἑκατονβαιῶνος ἑβδόμει καὶ ὀγδόει ἐπ[ὶ] δ-
έκα· θύειν δὲ τεῖ πρώτει ταῖς ἡρωίναις χοῖρον, τῶι δὲ [ἥ]-
15 [ρ]ωι ἱερεῖον τέλεον καὶ τράπεζαν παρατιθέναι, τεῖ δ[ὲ]
[ὑστερ]άαι τῶι ἥρωι ἱερεῖον τέλεον· λογίζεσθαι δὲ ὅ τι ἂν
[ἀναλ]ώσει· ἀναλίσκειν δὲ μὴ πλέον τῆς προσόδου· [ν]-
[εμέτω] δὲ τὰ κρέα τοῖς {οις} ὀργεῶσι τοῖς παροῦσι καὶ τοῖ[ς]
[ὑοῖς τὴν] εἰς ἡμίσεαν καὶ ταῖς γυναιξὶ ταῖς τῶν ὀργεώ[ν]-
20 [ων, διδ]οὺς ταῖς ἐλευθέραις τὴν ἰσαίαν καὶ ταῖς θυγα[ς]-
[τράσι τὴν εἰς ἡμί]σεαν καὶ ἀκολούθωι μιᾶι τὴν εἰς ἡμ[ί]-
[σεαν· παραδιδότω δὲ τ]ῶι ἀνδρὶ τῆς γυναικὸς τὴν με-
[ρίδα]

One further item in the association's calendar was the annual congregation (in the month of Hyakinthios) at the association's burial plot in the necropolis of the *asty* for the pouring of libations in commemoration of deceased members.[24] Monthly sacrifices – to which assemblies (*syllogoi*) should be added (see below) – may have made the *Haliastai kai Haliadai* a fairly high-intensity association. We have few means of probing the cultic calendars of other associations, but it stands to reason that associations which proclaimed the worship of several deities, such as the *Asklapiastai Pythiastai Hermaistai* or indeed the *Soteriastai Asklapiastai Poseidaniastai Herakleistai Athaniastai Aphrodisiastai Hermaistai Matros Theon* must have had a rather busy cultic schedule.[25]

Thus the associations may be said to practise for their private communities what Plato had prescribed for his ideal city. In the *Laws* Plato called for regular sacrifices (two a month) by the citizens, not only to ensure continued good relations with the gods, but primarily to foster a sense of unity (*homilia*) among the citizens, who, through frequent interaction, would become most familiar

[24] *IG* XII. 155.66–89. Gabrielsen 1994a: 146–7; Boyxen 2018: 175.
[25] *Tit. Cam.* 78 (first century); *IG* XII.1 162 (undated).

(*oikeios*) and well acquainted (*gnorimos*) with one another.[26] Modern social scientists agree with Plato on this point. Frequent interaction between individuals over long periods of time is an important precondition for the development of trust between members, but the social scientists add that in order for real trust to be felt among individuals, their interaction must be weighted with a 'valued and long-term enterprise'.[27] The timely and regular observance of rituals may qualify as a valued and long-term enterprise in itself, since it presupposed not only exposing the collective relationship with the supernatural to the potential neglect, failure or even malfeasance of other participants, but also, as we shall see in a moment, the efforts and not least the money needed to support cultic activities.

Some associations were probably content to congregate in public sanctuaries, but others acquired meeting places of their own. A third-century inscription records the properties given to an association of *eranistai* by a benefactor (*IG* XII.1 736):

> ... gave to the *koinon* of *eranistai*: a gift of land for graves which is in Rogkyos on the road leading from Aggyleia to Hippoteia, twenty-five fathoms in length and sixteen fathoms wide, as marked by *horoi*, a gift of another plot in the *ktoina*, a gift of the *temenos* of Asklapios and of Apollo and of Aphrodite ...

```
1        [ – ]EY[ – – – – – – – – ]
         [ἐ]ρανιστᾶν τῶι κοινῶι ἔ-
         δωκε δωρεὰν ἐς ταφία
         τᾶς γᾶς τᾶς ἐν Ῥογκύ(?)ω[ι]
5        ὡς ἁ ὁδὸς ἁ φέρουσα ἐξ Ἀ[γ]-
         γυλείας εἰς Ἱπποτείαν
         μᾶκος ὀργυᾶν εἴκοσι πέν-
         τε, πλάτος ὀργυᾶν δεκα-
         έξ, ὡς ὅροι κεῖνται·
10       δωρεὰν καὶ ἄλλον τόπον
         ἐν τᾶι κτοίναι· δωρεὰν
         τὸ τέμενος τοῦ Ἀσκλαπ[ι]-
         οῦ καὶ τοῦ Ἀπόλ[λωνος καὶ]
         τᾶς Ἀφροδίτα[ς – – – – – ]
15       ποιούμενος [ – – – – – – ]
         τοὺ[ς] ὅρο[υς – – – – – ]
```

---

[26] Pl. *Leg.* 771a–d, though Plato would have banned private sacrifice (*Leg.* 909d–e). Millett 1991: 151–3.

[27] Tilly 2005: 12–14; Buskens 2002: 10–26, esp. 10–14 and 24–5.

Another register of association properties (including the association's burial grounds), drawn up by the members of the *Aphrodisiastai Hermogeneioi* towards the end of the second century, attests to the purchase made by the members of a house and its adjacent grounds, including a *temenos* for the muses, which had set the members back a staggering 13,000 drachmas.[28] The reference in both these documents to a plot of land to be used for burials points to another association feature, namely the care for deceased members. Several other inscriptions mention the existence of graves belonging to associations.[29] The site of the ancient necropolis of the city of Rhodes still preserves a number of elaborate burial precincts.[30] One such plot, situated in the central necropolis just outside what is today Rodini park, preserves the traces of a plaster-decorated peristyle court flanked by graves and accessible from the ancient street via a small set of stone stairs. The large open court seems perfectly designed to accommodate ceremonies for the dead such as those held by the *Haliadai kai Haliastai*. Inscriptions on *ostheothekai* found within the precinct name both Rhodians and foreigners among the dead, and in one grave a handful of gold leaves, once part of an honorific crown, has been found.[31]

The widespread ownership of association burial grounds is evidence of the profound meaning attached to membership in some associations. It is important to note, however, that we owe our evidence – both archaeological and epigraphic – for association burials to the prime state of preservation of the Rhodian necropolis, which compared to the city itself has undergone only minimal transformation and development over the millennia. The decision to extend association membership even into death represents perhaps an extreme commitment not practised universally. Still, and as such, it is an opportunity to consider the degree of centrality of membership to those who joined an association, and we may speculate that other significant life events were celebrated within the context of the association. Death, perhaps more than any other event in the life, invited commemoration in a durable material and is therefore pronounced in our evidence (even today, most of us await death for

[28] *Annuario* n.s. 1–2 (1939/40) 156 no. 18 (late second century). The stele carries on one side the decree of the association, proposed by one Zenon of Selge (cf. 27: 472), which ordered the appointment of two men (a similar previous decision had called for the appointment of one man, who died subsequently but before the work could be completed) to have the deeds of property inscribed. The other side preserves the record of the purchase, made through an agent, Nikasion son of Nikasion of the Lindopolitai, who is possibly to be identified with a leading member of the *Asklapiastai Nikasioneioi Olympiastai* (Badoud 2015: 303, 391).
[29] *Annuario* 8–9 (1925/6) 322 no. 5 (first century BCE); *Annuario* n.s. 1–2 (1939/40) 156 no. 18 (late second century BCE).
[30] Fraser 1977: 1–8; Patsiada 2013: 123–230.
[31] Patsiada 2013: 279–84, 293. For other gold crowns discovered in the Rhodian necropolis, see Kaninia 1998.

our epigraphic debuts), but members' marriages or the birth of children were probably also causes for celebration.[32]

Worshippers into members

A handful of association documents allow a glimpse into their internal organisation. The ultimate decision-making body of an association was the members (*plethos*), who met in assembly (sometimes known as *synodoi*) to deliberate and make decisions in the form of laws (*nomoi*) and decrees (*psephismata*). Association decrees often carry a 'ratification clause', which is distinctive of decrees enacted by Rhodian assemblies at the federal, *polis* and deme levels, suggesting an acute awareness among association members of local democratic procedures.[33] Associations elected magistrates (known collectively as *archontes*) charged with various tasks, such as heralds (*karykes*) and auditors (*logistai*), but also appointed members ad hoc to take charge of special tasks.[34] Here too, associations seem to have taken their cue from Rhodian political institutions, naming their magistrates *epistatai* or *hierotamiai*, in close parallel with the leading magistrates of Lindos and Kamiros.[35]

Though the particulars may have varied from association to association, there can be little doubt that all were committed to a democratic form of internal government. The one activity attested for practically all private associations in Rhodes – indeed, for most, the only evidence we have for their existence – was the passing of honorific decrees awarding crowns of gold or foliage to a benefactor and recorded by the benefactor himself in a monument to his own social importance. Each of these references to crowns given by associations – brief though they may be – gives evidence of a procedure intimately connected to democratic institutions: a decision in the form of a formal motion proposed by a member of an association and subsequently debated in an assembly, before it was eventually passed by a majority and effectuated by

---

[32] The Delphic Labyadai (*CID* I 9 and 9bis, Delphi, 525–350 BCE), for instance, took notice of both births and marriages (Sebillotte 1997), as did the association established in Kos by Diomedon (*IG* XII.4 348.114–55, Kos, late fourth or early third century BCE). The *nomoi* of an early-first-century CE association from Tebtunis in Egypt required the members to contribute – in addition to the monthly membership fee – small sums of money on special occasions, which included marriage, the birth of children (2 drachmas per son and 1 per daughter), the purchase of property and livestock (*P. Mich.* V 243.2–5, Tebtunis, 14–37 CE. Venticinque 2010: 274 with n. 4).

[33] Boyxen 2018: 126 (for similar imitation in Athens, see Harris 2017: 114). For the public decrees, see Rhodes with Lewis 1997: 273 with examples 265–72. One of these examples, *IG* XII.1 155, belongs in fact not to the Rhodian state or its subdivisions, but to a private association.

[34] *IG* XII.1 155.30 (*hierokaryx*), 54 (*logistai*); 890.15 (*karyx*?).

[35] Association *epistatai*: *IG* XII.1 155.30, 54–5, 60; 890.14–15; 922.6, 13–14; *SEG* 33: 639.14. Association *hierotamias*: *IG* XII.1 890.26; *Cl. Rhodos* 2 (1932) 175 no. 4.7.

magistrates charged with procuring the crown and proclaiming it to the members of the association and perhaps beyond.

The management of the association's finances seems to have occupied much of the agenda when members met in assembly. The decree of honour voted by the *Haliadai kai Haliastai*, which awarded their long-serving *archeranistas*, Dionysodoros of Alexandria, touches only briefly on Dionysodoros' service to the association, but lays out in full detail the fairly complicated procedure by which the money for his gold crown was to be collected from among the members and how, after its use in the ceremony at the association's graves, the crown was to be sold and the money returned to the association's treasury.[36] The care with which such minutiae were formulated, presented and possibly debated before being ratified by the members suggests a membership deeply engaged in all the practical and financial aspects of running the community.

Through the continued maintenance of cultic activities supported and administered by the members themselves, an association became an important – and for some perhaps even the primary – organisation in life. In the case of the *Asklapiastai Nikasioneioi Olympiastai*, with which we began, it is possible that the personal relationships which resulted in marriages between members (or between members and daughters of other members, to be more precise) or professional collaboration post-dated membership and were, at least in part, the result of the familiarity and trust produced by shared devotion to the gods and the management of their association's affairs. As has already been pointed out, the evidence for many of the activities that associations engaged in comes from a small group of associations whose activities stretched even into the afterlife and which acquired the necessary real estate for associational burial grounds, and from a few of their wealthiest members who, like Dionysodoros of Alexandria, placed enormous value (not to mention time and money) on his membership. Associations were bonded over one or more shared attribute: a shared profession, membership in a public subdivision, origin, lineage and so on. It is therefore highly likely that these groups also had a shared interest in the world beyond the association. If they did, they certainly had the experience and organisational means with which to pursue those interests. Whether they recognised or acted upon them is of course an altogether different matter, and we must proceed on a case-by-case basis.

EQUALITY AND INEQUALITY IN PRIVATE ASSOCIATIONS

Overall, the private associations seem very much committed to an egalitarian ideal. Some explicitly rested on the principle that each member contributed

[36] Gabrielsen 1994a.

to the common funds of the association. A number of associations regarded themselves as *eranoi*, and the term was occasionally used as a catch-all for private associations.[37] Since at least the Classical period, *eranos* designated a shared meal (a potluck supper) or funds collected from contributors known as *eranistai*, or indeed an association.[38] Furthermore, and as we have seen, all associations had chosen a democratic model of organisation, which insisted that every member had the same rights to participate in cultic activities, to speak his mind in the assembly, vote and stand for office. But at the same time, the associations welcomed some members to take a leading role and encouraged benefactions from wealthy members or outsiders. The *Haliadai kai Haliastai* had been served by the same *archeranistas*, or leader of the *eranos*, for a full twenty-three years by the time the association decided to vote him perpetual honour (see below), while another association, the *Paniastai*, had been served for eighteen years by theirs, who happened in fact to be the same man.[39] The associations, in other words, had their own magisterial elite, which at certain points overlapped with that of the Rhodian state: Archokrates son of Archipolis and adopted son of Lysistratos had been elected *hierotamias* of his association, the *Hagetoridan diagonia*, 'many times', but his fellow citzens had placed him first in the priesthoods of Poseidon and of Athana Lindia in Lindos, and eventually in that of Halios.[40]

Wealthy members were encouraged to take the lead in footing the bill for association activities. The *epidosis* for the purchase of a burial plot by the *Eranistai Samothraikiastai Hermaistai Aristobouliastai Panatheniastai hoi syn Ktesiphonti* provides a handy demonstration (*SEG* 39: 737). Though every member contributed something to the *epidosis*, a number of wealthy members took the lead in providing the necessary funding for the plot, contributing more than 70 per cent of the total funds collected, while most contributors (and perhaps most members) gave a modest 5 drachmas, contributing less than 20 per cent of the total sum.[41] One of these top contributors, Ktesiphon of the Chersonesos, had earned himself the title of *euergetas tou koinou*, presumably in response to expenditure on behalf of the association, either on this or on another occasion.[42] The title was a staple of the associational vocabulary and those who earned it carried it like a cognomen

[37] *Lindos II* 420.26 (see Chapter 7).
[38] Thomsen 2015. Cf. Faraguna 2012; Arnaoutoglou 2003; Vondeling 1961.
[39] *IG* XII.1 155. Gabrielsen 1994a.
[40] *Hierotamias* of the *Hagetoridan diagonia*: *Cl. Rhodos* 2 (1932) 175 no. 4. Priest of Athana Lindia (in 202 BCE): *Lindos II* 118 (for the date, see Badoud 2015: 344–6). Priest of Halios (in 185 BCE): *Lindos II* 134. For the dates, see Badoud 2015: 169.
[41] Migeotte 2013: 119–20.
[42] *SEG* 39: 737.a.1–3 (c.1–3).

in every association context; it appears not infrequently on funerary monuments found in the Rhodian necropolis.[43]

With it came certain privileges. In Ktesiphon's case his *euergesia* had been supplemented by the explicit recognition of his leadership of the association, which had appended to its name 'those with Ktesiphon'. Similarly, Dionysodoros' enduring position as *archeranistas* of two associations was based on his willingness over the years to spend from his own means for the common good. Even before the *Haliastai kai Haliadai* voted Dionysodoros a perpetual crown, both associations had recognised him as a *euergetas tou koinou*,[44] and when the *Haliastai kai Haliadai* eventually granted him this chief honour they recalled the 'many and great services he had performed for the association'.[45] The relationship, in other words, was nothing new, but one that had developed over time as Dionysodoros had made his private means available to his fellow members, who had responded not only with the stock symbols of recognition of his generosity and superior moral character, but also by yielding to him the leadership of the association. Similarly, the generous member of an unknown association of the late third century who offered to pay out of his own means for the repair of damages to association property caused by an earthquake was also the *archeranistas* of the association; and when a certain Zenon of Selge in the late second century introduced a motion before the assembly of his association, he did so as Zenon of Selge *euergetas*.[46]

A plaque discovered in what was once the Kamirean deme of the Thyssanountioi lists the honours voted by several associations for an unknown benefactor. Apart from gold crowns and announcements of the honours, at least two of the associations had decided to designate a special day every year to re-enact the announcement of their honorific crowns.[47] The details of the ceremony, however, are obscure; but what little is known recalls an arrangement made by the association of the *Haliadai kai Haliastai* by which

---

[43] Foreigner *euergetai tou koinou: IG* XII.1 158; 940; 939; *Annuario* n.s. 1–2 (1939/40) 147 no. 1; 150 no. 5; 151 no. 6; 151 no. 7; 153 no. 11; *Annuario* 2 (1916) 127 no. 4; *Cl. Rhodos* 2 (1932) 214 no. 53; *NSill* 40; 192; *MDAI(A)* 21 (1896) 43 no. 12; *Lindos* II 683. Citizen *euergetai tou koinou: Annuario* 2 (1916) 175 no. 163; *PdP* 5 (1950) 76 no. 2; *Lindos* II 251; 264(?); 285; *NSER* 173 no. 25.

[44] *IG* XII.1 155.3–4, 16–17. Dionysodoros was also a *euergetas* to the Dionysiastai (*IG* XII.1 155.41–2). The fundamentally pecuniary meaning of the phrase 'having enlarged the *eranos*' (ἐπαυξήσαςτὸν ἔρανον) is clearly demonstrated by its inclusion in the call for funds issued by the *Eranistai Samothraikiastai Hermaistai Aristobouliastai Panatheniastai hoi syn Ktesiphonti* (*SEG* 37: 737.B.1–5). For the dual meaning of *eranos* as 'common fund' and 'association', see Thomsen 2015.

[45] καὶ πο[λ] | λὰς καὶ μεγάλας χρείας παρείσχηται τῶι κ[οι] | νῶι, *IG* XII.1 155.d.I.6–8.

[46] *Annuario* n.s. 1–2 (1939/40) 156 no. 18.1, 3, 20.

[47] *RIPR* 126 (identified as a 'decree'). Boyxen 2018: 111 with nn. 70 and 71.

they awarded their long-serving *archeranistas*, Dionysodoros of Alexandria, eternal associational commemoration – even after his death. The *Haliadai kai Haliastai* decreed that they should praise and crown Dionysodoros with a gold crown – the greatest allowed by the law of the association.[48] This crown, it would seem, was to be given only after Dionysodoros had passed away, and the decree of the *Haliadai kai Haliastai* proceeded to lay out the instructions for Dionysodoros' eternal commemoration: to raise the money for the crown, the officers of the association would collect three obols from each member at every meeting of the association, and on the second day of the meetings (after the sacrifices) reannounce the crown to the members.[49] The latter provision closely resembles that recorded on the fragmentary inscription from Thyssanous. After Dionysodoros' death the members of his association would each year congregate, in the month of Hyakinthios (June/July), in the association's burial precinct outside the walls and pour libations for deceased members.[50] During the ceremony, the officers of the association would announce once again to the members the honours which they had bestowed on Dionysodoros and place a gold crown on his memorial (*mnameion*).[51]

Here again, the honouring of a benefactor was made to last long beyond the initial ceremony. The memory of the benefactor and his *areta*, *eunoia* and *philodoxia* was kept alive constantly through announcement at every meeting of the association, his social importance and the gratitude owed to him by the membership being thus continuously reaffirmed.

The relationship between these associations and the individuals after whom they were named was not a distant one. The *Timapoleion koinon* which entered an *epidosis* in Lindos around 125 BCE did so together with a certain Timapolis,[52] the *Aphrodisiastan Hermogeneion koinon* counted the metic Hermogenes of Phasalis among its most prominent members,[53] and the *Asklapiastai Nikasioneioi Olympiastai*

---

[48] Gabrielsen 1994a: 147; cf. Ziebarth 1896: 46; Pugliese Carratelli 1942: 191

[49] *IG* XII.1 155.20–30. Gabrielsen 1994a: 144–5.

[50] *IG* XII.1 155.e.IV.116–22. Gabrielsen 1994a. Cf. Ziebarth 1896: 46; Pugliese Carratelli 1942: 191 with n. 1.

[51] In fact a small altar for Dionysodoros and his brother Iachos has been found in the Rhodian necropolis, possibly a *mnameion* (but not necessarily *the mnameion*) like the one mentioned in the decree of the *Haliastai kai Haliadai*. *NSill* 46. For a discussion of this *mnameion* and its relation to the associations mentioned in *IG* XII.1 155 (Dionysodoros' dossier), see Guarducci 1942 and Gabrielsen 1994a.

[52] *Timapoleion koinon*: *Lindos II* 252.250 (for the date, see Badoud 2015: 232). The Timapolis in question was probably the same person who contributed to the same *epidosis* together with a number of other *koina* (*Lindos II* 252.251–8) and may perhaps be identified with Timapolis son of Euphragoras and adopted son of Timapolis, whose full name is plausibly restored in *Lindos II* 252.86–7, and who had served as priest of Pythian Apollo in Lindos in 138 BCE (*Lindos II* 228.4–6) and as *hierothytas*, *archierothytas* and *epistatas* in Lindos (*IG* XII.1 836; *Lindos II* 223.10–1).

[53] *Annuario* 1–2 (1939/40) 156 no. 18.

took part of their name from their *euergetas*, Nikasion of Kyzikos.[54] This Nikasion, furthermore, was also the founder of the association (*ktistas tou koinou*) and it has been suggested that the *-eioi* form signalled the founder of the association.[55] This, however, can hardly have been a general rule, since we are able in one case to identify the change in name as a result of the exchange between an association and its benefactor. The second-century association of the *Hermaistai* is known to have been the recipient of some benefaction from one Alkimedon son of Alkistratos, a Rhodian *stratagos*, and responded with a gold crown and the title of *euergetas tou koinou*, and is undoubtedly to be identified with the *Hermaistai Alkimedonteioi* which dedicated on the Lindian acropolis a life-size bronze statue of another *euergetas*, Mikythos son of Mikythos and adopted son of Euboulos, who happened to be a priest of Athana Lindia with a long priestly résumé.[56] Whether founder or highly regarded benefactor, it is clear that these individuals and the associations to which they gave their names shared a connection even stronger than those they shared with other benefactors.

The concept of *euergesia*, whether given as a title or not, instituted a basic dichotomy between ordinary members of the association and those whose private expenditure merited special recognition. Honorific decrees testify to the gratitude of associations towards their benefactors and the imperative of rendering due thanks for benefactions, and not least to be seen rendering due thanks. It is rarely possible to establish with any certainty whether a benefactor was in fact a practising member of the associations he or she had supported. In one case the monument of an unknown member of the Rhodian elite compiled the honours voted by no fewer than twenty-three different private associations.[57] The sheer number of associations would suggest that he did not take part in every sacrifice and every funeral. In practice, however, it did not matter a great deal. Once a benefaction was accepted, the gratitude of the members was equally due to any *euergetas* regardless of membership, and the patronage of a private association, as we shall see, became a convenient way of tapping into the social and human resources of an association. But here we

---

[54] *IG* XII.1 127.b.58–9; *Annuario* n.s. 1–2 (1939/40) 150 no. 5. The name of the association, the *Askalapiastai Nikasioneioi Olympiastai*, is found in *MDAI(A)* 25 (1900) 109 n. 108.4 and is generally identified as the (unnamed) association of *IG* XII.1 127 (Boyxen 2018: 110; Maillot 2009; Gabrielsen 1997: 128; Poland 1909: 273; Hiller von Gaertringen and Saridakis 1900: 109).

[55] Poland 1909: 73–6; Gabrielsen 1997: 126–7. Maiuri (1916: 141) notes the gentilical ring to association names ending in *-eioi* and contrasts them with what he believed were the commoners' version (*hoi syn tōi deini*). We can agree to the first part, but not the second. Andrewes (1957: 32–3) notes that names of *patrai* take two different forms, some ending in *-dai* and some in *-eioi*. He surmised that the different forms suggested origins in different periods, before their earliest attestations, but for obvious reasons the hypothesis cannot be tested.

[56] *JÖAI* 9 (1906) 85–8; *IG* XII.1 50.13; *Lindos II* 251 with Blinkenberg's comments. Boyxen 2018: 131.

[57] *Annuario* n.s. 1–2 (1939/40) 165 no. 19. See Maiuri 1916: 139–42; Maillot 2005: II 18–23.

must be careful that our conclusions are not forced upon us by the nature of the evidence. Our only evidence for this exchange is the benefactions that were accepted and, so to speak, made it into stone in an inscribed decree. These often include all-embracing hortatory clauses exhorting anyone to imitate the behaviour of their benefactor, but in reality associations may have been pickier. The associations were only too aware that benefactions came with strings attached and there is no reason to assume that they would have accepted everything from every would-be benefactor.

CHAPTER 6

Private Associations and Human Resources

Towards the end of the preceding chapter, we came upon the monument of an unknown member of the Rhodian elite. It catalogued twenty-three different private associations which had all been attached to him through the exchange of benefactions and honours. The monument, unique for its sheer number of associations, nevertheless represents a clear trend. Together, the monuments of the elite give evidence of an associational arms race in which the members of the magisterial elite constantly sought to establish relations with more and more private associations. This requires explanation; and falling back on the idea of a disinterestedly sociable Rhodian elite clearly will not do.

The preceding chapter traced an outline of private associations in Rhodes and analysed how continued interaction of members and the placing of trust in others for the maintenance of important activities, such as proper observance of rituals, the maintenance of burial plots and association finances, resulted in the development of strong ties of loyalty and reciprocity. I have argued that such associations were formed around pre-existing networks whose members shared one or more trait, such as a common occupation or membership in public subdivisions. As a result we posed the question: how and under which conditions were the human resources of the associations exploited?

THE RICH AND THE TALENTED

The arts

The Rhodian state on various levels invited its citizens in their various public associations to compete against each other in putting on the most splendid choruses. At the federal level each of the three old *poleis* competed as tribes (*phylai*) in several festivals held in the *asty*. The Alexandria and Dionysia festivals featured choric competitions in several disciplines. At the *polis* level the Lindian Sminthia in honour of Apollo enjoyed worldwide fame and was the subject of a treatise by Philomnestos.[1] The festival involved a competition of six choruses, paid for by wealthy citizens on behalf of the three Lindian tribes.[2] Sometime in the first half of the second century the Lindian tribe of Argeia was triumphant with a comic chorus under the *choragos* Onasandros son of Euphanes, priest of Lindos in 165 BCE and at some stage also *grammateus* of the Rhodian *boula* and the *prytaneis*.[3]

Chapter 4 treated the enthusiasm with which the Rhodian elite embraced the opportunity to display and employ their wealth to the benefit of their fellow demesmen and citizens as well as the state as a whole. And there was much prestige to be had. Although they were acting on behalf of their *polis* or tribe, victory belonged in no small part to the *choragoi* personally. At the Rhodian festival of Alexander and Dionysos the successful *choragos* was honoured with a crown.[4] To this each of the three *poleis* might add its own token of recognition, as the Lindians did in 129 BCE when they voted to honour the *choragos* who had sponsored the presumably victorious Lindian bid at a federal festival.[5] Ubiquitous reference to triumphs as *choragoi* in elite monuments reflects the prestige associated with the performance of this liturgy and especially with producing a winning chorus. Consequently, in the private monuments of the elite, the reference to such sponsorship, χοραγήσαντα – 'having been *choragos*' (in itself an achievement worthy of recognition) – was often followed by the proud assertion καὶ νικάσαντα, 'and having won'.[6]

The precise costs involved cannot be uncovered, and while the few existing references to several terms as *choragos* (never more than four) are evidence that multiple terms were allowed, their rarity suggests that competition was fierce and for most members of the elite a once-in-a-lifetime opportunity.[7]

Being *choragos* not only meant financing the performance. With the office, and the expenditure it entailed, came also the responsibility for selecting and hiring poets and instructors, and generally ensuring the quality of the chorus.

---

[1] Athen. 10.445a.

[2] *IG* XII.1 762 (discussed in detail below), a Lindian decree of 23 CE, lays out the rules for the election of *choragoi* for the Sminthia, which henceforth would include both citizen and foreign *choragoi*. Thomsen 2018: 283–5.

[3] *Lindos II* 199; *Cl. Rhodos* 2 (1932) 198 no. 31.I.11–13.

[4] *Cl. Rhodos* 2 (1932) 201 no. 33.5–6; *Lindos II* 197f.

[5] *Lindos II* 233.

[6] E.g. *Lindos II* 131d (early first century BCE); 199 (165 BCE); *IG* XII.1 71 (undated); *Annuario* n.s. 1–2 (1939/40) 155 no. 16 (first century BCE); *Tit. Cam.* 63 (undated).

[7] Multiple terms as *choragos*: e.g. *Lindos II* 236 (two terms, c. 129 BCE); *Cl. Rhodos* 2 (1932) 193 no. 21 (four terms, first half of second century BCE).

As cultured men, some members of the Rhodian elite dabbled in writing for the stage themselves,[8] but those whose civic ambitions exceeded their artistic gifts turned to professionals. A marble base from the Lindian acropolis once supported a dedication in commemoration of two victories of the Lindians, that is, the tribe of *Lindia*, in an unknown federal festival in the late fourth century (*SER* 7):

> When Nikomnastos was priest (of Halios) and Anaxipolis son of Timaratos was *agonothetas*,
>   Arideikes son of Timaratos was *choragos*, Lindia won for the boys' (choruses). Arideikes son of Timaratos was *choragus*. Dexilaos of Thallos was flute player
>   Aristonidas son of Mnasitimos made (it)

> When Dama[---] was priest (of Halios) and [---] was *agonothetas*, Lindia won for the boys' (choruses). Phileratos son of [---] was *choragos*. Dexilaos of Thallos was flute player

a.1   ἐπ' ἱερέως Νικομν[άστου]
       καὶ ἀγωνοθέτα Ἀν[αξιπ]όλι[ος] τοῦ Τιμ[αράτου]
       Ἀριδείκης Τιμαράτ[ου ἐ]χοράγησ[ε],
       Λινδία παίδω[ν ἐ]νίκη·
5   Ἀριδείκης Τ[ιμα]ράτου ἐχοράγε[ι]·
       Δεξίλαος Θ[άλλ]ιος αὔλει.
                    vacat
7   Ἀριστωνίδας Μν[ασιτί]μου Ῥόδ[ιος
       ἐποίησε].

b.1   ἐπ' ἱερέως Δαμα[– – – – – – –]
       καὶ ἀγωνοθέτα [– – – – – – –]
       Λινδία π[αίδων ἐνίκη]·
       Φιλήρατ[ος – – – – ἐχοράγει]·
5   Δεξίλα[ος Θάλλιος αὔλει].

Each victory is dated by the Halios priest and the *agonothetas*, and gives the name of the Lindian *choragos*.[9] For each win, the inscription also records the name of

---

[8] According to Philomnestos in a passage from his treatise *On the Sminthian Festival at Rhodes*, paraphrased by Athenaeus (10.445a–b), a certain Antheas of Lindos wrote several comedies, but these were apparently meant for and performed by his *symbakchoi* (perhaps an association?).

[9] Several members of the family of Arideikos son of Timaratos are named in a Lindian *epidosis* of the late fourth century (*Lindos II* 51.III.18–21). Phileratos, the other *choragos*, is otherwise unknown (Blinkenberg commentary to *Lindos II* 696).

a flute player, the same man for both years, a certain Dexilaos of Thallos. The inclusion of Dexilaos, the flute player, in the monument along with the *choragos* suggests that his contribution to the victory had been instrumental in a double sense and that he perhaps had been the leading creative force behind the Lindian bid (according to Theophrastos, the omission of the flute player in a choregic monument was a tell-tale sign of the Illiberal Man).[10] Evidently, Phileratos, the *choragos* of the following year, kept him on the payroll for his production too – a decision which seems to have paid off.

Though Dexilaos may have been the kingpin in these two choral victories, the successful production depended on a much larger cast whose skill was every bit as important for the quality of the chorus and the outcome of the judgement. Evidence for Classical Athens, though this practice does not necessarily match the Rhodian in every detail, at least gives an impression of the personnel needed for putting on a decent chorus: first of all a poet and instructor (in Classical Athens the poet was in the pay of the state), an assistant instructor (*hypodidaskalos*), actors, dancers, chorus members, whose numbers varied according to the type of performance, and the all-important flute player. Behind this on-stage ensemble worked teams of costume makers, set painters and other craftsmen – also highly sought-after artists.[11] To assist him in the management of these human resources, but also in the financial matters involved in keeping such a troop running for the year over which recruitment and rehearsals could easily stretch, one Athenian *choregos* found it necessary to take on no fewer than four administrative assistants.[12] But recruitment of the necessary talent posed a challenge to the *choragos*: first of all he had to seek out key professionals, judge their skills and whether they suited the production, and negotiate terms of employment – before they were snatched away by other *choragoi* who competed not only for the same honours, but also for the same professionals. Then he had to fill up his chorus and find suitable rehearsal facilities, while in most cases having no practical experience with any of these matters. In the late third century, a certain Hagetor gave his name to the *Hagetoreioi Polystrateioi hoi peri Dionyson kai tas Mousas technitai*, along with a certain Polystratos, and was also a benefactor of two further artists' associations, the *hoi peri ton Dionyson ton Mousagetan technitai Eudameioi* (to whom a certain Eudamos was also a benefactor) and the *technitai hoi peri tas Dionysou Mousas*.[13]

---

[10] Theophr. *Char.* 22.2; Wilson 2000: 215.

[11] Le Guen 2001: 73.

[12] Wilson 2000: 61–93 (Antiph. 6.12).

[13] *Annuario* n.s. 1–2 (1939/40) 165 no. 19. All three associations of *technitai* are listed as having honoured an individual whose name is not preserved. However, the fact that no fewer than four of these associations carry the name of *Hagetoreioi* suggests that a Hagetor may be presumed to be the person honoured (cf. Polykles and the associations of *Polykleioi* in *NSill* 18).

As evident from Le Guen's prosopography of members in the five 'world-wide' associations of Dionysiac *technitai*, such groups had skilled experts in virtually every field of choral performances, processions and even festival management, and were capable of offering in-house solutions to practically all problems faced by a *choragos*.[14] Two similar associations, *hoi technitai hoi peri ton Kathegem[ona Dionyson hoi en] toi hieroi tou Dionysou* and *[hoi peri] ton Dionyson technitai I[---]*, are found in Lindos towards the end of the second century. Both were among those associations that honoured an unknown member of the Lindian elite who had held several priesthoods including those of Athana Lindia, Artemis Kekoia, Pythian Apollo and at least one more (we may guess Dionysos). Like Hagetor, he had kept up good relations with a pair of associations whose members possessed the very artistic skills needed for successful choral competition. It is therefore hardly surprising that the same man could boast of 'having been *choragos* and having won'.[15] One of these associations, the *technitai hoi peri ton Kathegem[ona Dionyson hoi en] toi hieroi tou Dionysou*, had apparently made the Lindian sanctuary of Dionysos their home, suggesting that the state too had benefitted from the association's cultic and artistic expertise, and probably also from their administrative abilities. If our nameless Lindian priest and *choragos* were in fact also a priest of Dionysos, we can further speculate that he had been instrumental in tying this group directly to the sanctuary – an affiliation which was probably to the mutual advantage of the members of the association, who found steady employment, and the Lindians, who could draw on the *technitai*'s expertise.

The fleet

Though the word 'trierarch' was derived from the command of a special type of warship, the three-banked warship or trireme, the title was used irrespective of the class of ship with which it was associated. Several Rhodians were commemorated as trierarch of an aphract warship[16] or even of the larger quinqueremes,[17] a fact which suggests that the trierarchy was considered a liturgy first and a military position only second. This is further underlined by the existence in Rhodes of a formal substitute for the trierarch as captain of the ship,

---

[14] Le Guen 2001: I 41–74; cf. Aneziri 2003.
[15] *Lindos II* 264.
[16] *IG* XII.1 44.3–4; *Lindos II* 707.6 (c. 40–30).
[17] *NSill* 21.4 (second/first century BCE); *Cl. Rhodos* 2 (1932) 188 no. 18.22 (first century BCE?); *Lindos II* 303 (c. 90–70 BCE) mentions two trierarchs subordinate to *hagemones* of quinqueremes. Trierarch of a *dikrotos*: *Lindos II* 707.2–3. For the nature of this ship see Gabrielsen 1997: 103. Trierarch of a trireme: *NSill* 18.15 and 17.

the *epiplous*.[18] Though the monuments of the Rhodian elite often draw attention to trierarchy and to personal fighting experience, only two inscriptions refer to both,[19] and the trierarchy is often listed among other liturgies such as the sponsorship of choric and agonistic events.[20] Though this, of course, does not mean that these trierarchs never took to the sea themselves (they certainly did),[21] their monuments appear to be first and foremost concerned with the liturgical aspects of the trierarchy as part of a demonstration of individual wealth and euergitism. As in Classical Athens, the Rhodian trierarch was responsible for getting a state-owned vessel in fighting condition. In order to inspire great care and greater expenditure on the part of the trierarchs a review of ships (*apodeixis tas naos*) was held before the fleet set out, and the trierarch with the most impressive ship was awarded a prize.[22]

It was not uncommon for a company of soldiers to set up a monument in honour of their fallen comrades or of successful officers and gods who had seen them through the trials of war.[23] An example of such a monument is the honorific monument dedicated by the crew of a warship (probably a quadrireme) under the trierarch Theupropos to one Alexidamos son of Alexion sometime in the first half of the first century BCE. The list of dedicators is set under the heading *hoi systrateusamenoi* or 'those who served together', and proceeds to name forty-eight individual crew members under their particular ratings. Apart from the officers, deckhands, craftsmen and a doctor, the ship's crew included two catapult operators, nineteen marines and six archers, but the largest part of the crew, the rowers, were left out.[24] An interesting feature of the crew list is that it is possible to identify several family relations within it. When putting together his crew, Theupropos was apparently drawing on a pre-existing network in which family ties played an important part, and it is not at all improbable that most of the remaining crew members were in some way connected by family or friendship.[25] This made good sense, since it facilitated recruitment and lowered the risk of bad choices in manning the ship. Whether the crew of Theupropos' ship would continue to gather after

---

[18] Segre 1936: 231–3; Gabrielsen 1997: 101 with n. 96.
[19] *Lindos II* 707; *NSill* 18.
[20] *Hermes* 36 (1901) 440 no. 1; *SER* 19 .
[21] *IG* XII.5 913 (second century BCE); *IG* XII Supp. 317 (second century BCE).
[22] *NSill* 18.15–16.
[23] Poland 1909: 127–9; Launey 1949–50: 1002–8; Chaniotis 2005: 237–40.
[24] *Cl. Rhodos* 8 (1936) 227; Gabrielsen 1997: 104–5.
[25] Fifteen family ties were identified by the editor Mario Segre (see commentary for *Cl. Rhodos* 8 [1936] 227 and Gabrielsen 1997: 104 with n. 112). Other Rhodian crew lists are: *SER* 62; *IIR I* 6; *NSill* 4; *Cl. Rhodos* 2 (1932) 176 no. 5; *NSill* 5; *Annuario* n.s. 48–9 (1986–7) 280 no. 16; *Lindos II* 88 (which also includes at least eight pairs of brothers and fathers/sons [*Lindos II* 88, comments; Gabrielsen 1997: 104 with n. 115]).

the end of their service is impossible to know. But a number of crews formed themselves into permanent associations. These associations took names, which often consisted of the participle *systrateuomenoi* (or *systrateusamenoi*) in combination with a theophoric element, for instance [*stra*]*teuomenoi Athanaistai*.[26] The proper name, as opposed to a generic reference to *hoi sysstrateuomenoi* (with reference to a particular commander), suggests a permanent corporate identity and an organisation which endured beyond any single campaign. One military association (*koinon*), the *Aristomachioi syskanoi Hermaizontes*, added the specification *hoi en toi astei* to their name, associating themselves with a particular place (the Rhodian *asty*) in a further indication that the association was of some permanency.[27] Such groups could continue to exist even beyond the life span of any individual member. The Lindian *Panathenaistai sysstrateuomenoi* was maintained through a period of more than a century, from the late second or early first century BCE to the early first century CE – a remarkable feat, and evidence of a strong organisation that must have managed several organisational changes of the guard (see below).

Some associations reveal through their names an increased specialisation and segmentation of the military staff of Rhodian warships. Lindos was home to an association of *Panathenaistai Herakleistai dekas*, an association formed around the worship of Athana and Herakles, but whose members also formed a military unit (*dekas*) of ten marine soldiers under the command of a *dekatarchos*.[28] Another association is found organising specialist crews who worked below deck. The *Samothraikiastai mesoneoi* are found among the military associations which honoured an unknown naval commander (but also *prytanis*) around the time of the First Mithridatic War (88–85 BCE).[29] Though several explanations for the nature of this group, particularly the name *mesoneoi*, have been put forth, the military nature of the association has long been clear from their connections with the unknown naval commander, who also kept an association of *Samothrakiastai kai Lemniastai synstrateusamenoi* as part of his entourage.[30] A passage in Aristotle's *Mechanical Problems*, however, suggests that *mesoneos* was in fact not

[26] *Lindos II*, 264 (c. 125–100 BCE).

[27] *AD* 24 B2 (1969) 461 (undated).

[28] *Cl. Rhodos* 2 (1932) 210 no. 48.15; *SEG* 15: 497. A *dekatarchos* is mentioned in a dedication by the crew and officers of a Rhodian warship on the island of Paros (*IG* XII Supp. 210.3–4). Gabrielsen 1997: 124 with n. 56.

[29] *IG* XII.1 43.9, 12–13.

[30] *Mesoneoi* as (military) sailors: Gabrielsen 1997: 124; Launey 1949–50: 1021 with n. 1. Several other explanations have been offered based on various interpretations of *mesoneioi*: a *patra* (phratry) (Ziebarth 1896: 120; van Gelder 1900: 364), based on similarity with names in *Tit. Cam.* 1 (see Chapter 2), an age group (Ziebarth 1896: 120), based on etymology and parallels with groups of *halikiotai* (*IG* XII.1 43.4; *NSill* 18.23–4; *Lindos II* 703.6) and the crew of special carriers for the initiated of the Samothracian mysteries.

a general term for 'rower', but a technical term for a particular section of the rowers of warships, the 'mid-ship-men'.[31] The Aristotelian treatise illustrates the mechanical principle of the lever by pointing to the *mesoneoi*, the rowers positioned at the broadest sections of the hull. Due to their greater distance from the thole-pin they could exert greater leverage on their oars, thereby producing a greater thrust than their colleagues in the aft and stern sections of the ship. This suggests that the *Samothraikiastai mesoneoi* organised a vital resource for the Rhodian navy's most famous and feared quality, its speed and manoeuvrability. Polybios, not a man easily impressed, relates with some admiration how a small Rhodian fleet of warships managed to wreak havoc on the forces of Philip V at the battle of Chios (201 BCE) due to their superior seamanship.[32]

The organisation of specialised and experienced military manpower into formal associations eased recruitment and probably acted as a guarantee of the quality of the crew. These benefits would also have been obvious to the trierarch looking to hire a competent fighting crew or well-trained rowers. It is hardly surprising that several members of the Rhodian political and naval elite acted as benefactors to such associations: Hagetor, the late-third-century *stratagos* and *hagemon*, was a benefactor of the *stratiotai Hagetoreioi* and the *Astymedeioi sysstrateusemenoi*.[33] A certain Hesteios, perhaps father of a Lindian *hierothytas* of the year 74 BCE,[34] commanded a squadron of quadriremes around the time of the First Mithridatic War.[35] He also sponsored an association, the *Haliastai Haliadai*, which added his name to theirs, making them the *Haliastai Haliadai Hesteioi*. The association appears among those who honoured Timarchidas son of Hagesitimos, another Lindian with naval exploits on his résumé, around the time when Hesteios himself saw active duty.[36] Similarly, one Antiochos, who also served as a naval squadron commander (*archon*), sponsored an association of *Apolloniastai Antiocheioi sysstrateusamenoi*, and Theaidetos son of Astykrates, the priest of Athana Lindia in 62, who had fought in the same war in a cataphract warship and was honoured along with its crew by the Rhodian people, sponsored the *Theaideteioi synst[rateusamenoi]*.[37]

---

[31] Aristotl. *Mech.* 4 (850b10–29).
[32] Pol. 16.4.4–5.9; cf. App. *Mith.* 25.
[33] *Annuario* n.s. 1–2 (1939/40) 165 no. 19.13, 37. The *akolo[uth]esantoi st[ratiotai]* (l. 11) should perhaps be added and it is possible that the *Pausistra[teio]i* (l. 4) were sponsored by Pausistratos, the Rhodian nauarch of Polybian fame (Pol. 21.7.5; Livy 33.18; 37.11.13; so Gabrielsen 1997: 126 with n. 77; Maillot 2005: II 20–1), but it must be borne in mind that Pausistratos is a relatively common name and that the dating of the inscription (Maiuri 1916: 139) rests only on epigraphic criteria.
[34] The name is exceptionally rare and found only in Lindos. For the *hierothytes* Timokrates, son of Hesteios, see *Lindos II* 299 c.35. *LGPN* s.v. Ἕστειος (1) and (2).
[35] *Lindos II* 303.13.
[36] *Lindos II* 292.6 (see below).
[37] *IG* XII.1 43 and *NSill* 18.26–7; *IG* XII.1 75.

The steady supply of naval manpower was, according to Strabo, a prime concern for the political leadership of Rhodes even at the end of the first century BCE. 'The people (*demos*)', he wrote,

> is supplied with provisions and the wealthy support those in need according to an old custom. They have liturgies through which the poor are provided with food, with the result that the poor receive support and the city has no lack of available manpower, particularly as regards the fleet.[38]

To this public support system the Rhodian elite added its own private system for the maintenance of well-integrated fighting units who could be called up at moment's notice and who would have owed some loyalty to their benefactors and commanding officers.[39]

No military association was more sought after than the Lindian *Panathenaistai strateuomenoi*. The association is first heard of around 121 BCE and was still in existence in the early first century CE, when our epigraphic material becomes less plentiful. The *Panathenaistai strateuomenoi* seem to have had their finest moments during the war with Mithridates. This they shared with a great many members of the Lindian elite who in the years following took great pride in their personal military experience.[40] One of these was Timachidas son of Hagesitimos, whom we have already come across as the compiler of the Lindian *anagraphe* in 99 BCE. Timachidas had fought on both aphract and cataphract warships in the war against Mithridates in the early first century BCE. The inscription on the base of his statue mentions that Timachidas had shown himself a 'good man in the fighting' (*Lindos II* 292.3–4), which could suggest that Timachidas was killed in the course of action:[41]

---

[38] Strab. 14.2.5: σιταρχεῖται δὴ ὁ δῆμος καὶ οἱ εὔποροι τοὺς ἐνδεεῖς ὑπολαμβάνουσιν ἔθει τινὶ πατρίῳ, λειτουργίαι τέ τινές εἰσιν ὀψωνιζόμεναι, ὥσθ᾽ ἅμα τόν τε πένητα ἔχειν τὴν διατροφὴν καὶ τὴν πόλιν τῶν χρειῶν μὴ καθυστερεῖν καὶ μάλιστα πρὸς τὰς ναυστολίας. Gabrielsen 1997: 25; Migeotte 1989; 1992: 109.

[39] Gabrielsen 1997: 124–8.

[40] Whereas earlier monuments stress military command (e.g. *IG* XII.1 1036), private (Lindian) monuments of this period place emphasis on personal fighting experience and invariably begin with *strateusamenos*, 'having fought (onboard)', and then name the type of vessel and occasionally the commander: *IG* XII.1 41; 43; *Lindos II* 292 (see below); *Cl. Rhodos* 2 (1932) 190 no. 19; *Cl. Rhodos* 8 (1936) 227; *NSill* 18; *SEG* 43: 527. Eventually references to personal fighting experience drop through the lists of achievements, but are still included after the first century CE (*Lindos II* 707; *IG* XII.1 58).

[41] For the trope of the 'good man' in Rhodian inscriptions, see Kontorini 2014: 345–6 and throughout.

Timachidas son of Hagesitimos who served on the aphract vessels and on the cataphract vessels and in battle showed himself to be a good man. He was crowned by the *koinon* of the *Haliastai Haliadai Hesteioi* with a gold crown and by the *koinon* of the *Panathenaistai systrateusamenoi syskanoi* ('tent-mates') with a gold crown. The messmates: Dionysos son of Hierokles, Aristokrates son of Hagesandros, Dionysios son of Leon, Hagesandros son of Hagesandros son of Athanodoros, Aristeidas son of Pythodoros and adopted son of Aristeidas, Alexidamos son of Aristophilos because of his *eunoia* towards them. To the gods. Agathokles of Antioch made (it).

> Τιμαχίδαν Ἀγησι[τίμου]
> στρατευσάμενον ἔν τε τοῖς ἀ[φράκτοις]
> καὶ ἐν ταῖς καταφράκτοις ναυσὶ [καὶ ἐν τοῖς]
> κινδύνοις ἄνδρα ἀγαθὸν γενόμε[νον]
> 5   [σ]τεφανωθέντα ὑπὸ Ἀλιαστᾶν Ἀλ[ιαδᾶν]
> Ἑστείων κοινοῦ χρυσέωι στεφά[νωι καὶ]
> ὑπὸ Παναθηναϊστᾶν συστρατευσαμένων
> συσκάνων κοινοῦ χρυσέωι στεφάνωι.
>   οἱ σύσσιτοι·
> 10   [Δ]ιονύσιος Ἱεροκλεῦς
> [Ἀρ]ιστοκράτης Ἀγησάνδρου
> Δ[ι]ονύσιος   Λέοντος
> Ἀ[γή]σανδρος Ἀγησάνδρου
>   τοῦ Ἀθανοδώρου
> 15   Ἀρ[ισ]τείδας Πυθοδώρου
> κ[αθ]᾽ ὑοθεσίαν δ[ὲ] Ἀρ[ιστεί]δα
> Αἰσ[χί]νας   Αἰσχ[ί]να
> Ἀλε[ξί]δα[μ]ος Ἀρ[ι]στ[ο]φίλου
> εὐνο[ία]ς ἕνεκα τᾶς εἰς αὐτούς.
> 20   θεοῖς.
> [Ἀγαθοκλῆς] Ἀντ[ιοχ]εὺς ἐποί[η]σε.

The inscription goes on to list two associations which had honoured Timachidas. One was the *Haliastai Haliadai Hesteion*, an association sponsored by the naval archon, or squadron commander, Hesteios; the other was the *Panathenaistai strateuomenoi*, or more precisely a subsection of the association, the *syskanoi*, or 'those who encamp together'. His statue was dedicated by seven surviving *syssitoi* or 'messmates' – which presumably was a further subsection within the *syskanoi*.[42]

---

[42] Other *syskanoi* subsections of military associations: the *Athanaistai strateuomenoi syskanoi* (*Lindos II* 392.b.16–17, 9 BCE), a subdivision of the *strateuomenoi Athanaistai* (*Lindos II* 264, c. 125–100 BCE)?, and the *Aristomachioi syskanoi Hermaizontes en toi asti*, no doubt a subdivision of the *Aristomachioi* (*AD* 24 B2 (1969) 461). Gabrielsen 1997: 124.

The names of these *syssitoi* were recorded on the base of the statue and allow for a glimpse into the social composition of the group. (1) Timachidas himself has already been mentioned. He was the son of Hagesitimos, the Lindian *hierothytas* of 148 BCE, who suggested compiling the Lindian *anagraphe* and putting his son in charge. (2) Dionysios son of Hierokleus is found as a contributor to a statue of a gymnasiarch around 68 BCE.[43] So is (3) Hagesandros son of Hagesandros son of Athanodoros, who also fathered the priests of Athana Lindia in 22 and 21 BCE respectively.[44] (4) Aischinas son of Aischinas was the son of the priest of Athana Lindia in 108 BCE and grandson of the priest of 157 BCE. (5) Alexidamos son of Aristophilos probably also appears in the list of contributors to a gymnasiarch monument and was probably the brother of a former priest of Dionysos mentioned in a Lindian monument dated to 43 BCE.[45]

Apart from their membership in the top strata of the Lindian elite, the group may have shared another trait, namely age. Timachidas' statue must have been dedicated at the time of the First Mithridatic War, since the inscription mentions the association sponsored by Hesteios, and since the sculptor Agathokles of Antioch is known to have made a statue of Damokrates, the priest of Athana Lindia in 104 BCE.[46] If the sons of Hagesandros held the priesthood of Athana Lindia in the late 20s BCE, they can hardly have been born long before c. 90 BCE and Hagesandros therefore, like Timachidas, must himself have been a young man at the time of the dedication. The appearance of these young aristocrats within a subdivision of the *Panathenaistai strateuomenoi* suggests that the association provided the organisational framework for the rearing of one of the most treasured resources of Rhodes, namely the highly skilled naval officer.

The association was apparently a large one. Sometime before the First Mithridatic War, an unnamed Lindian was honoured by the *Panathenaistai strateuomenoi* on two occasions and by several subdivisions of the association, each associated with a particular warship on which they served (*Lindos II* 303):

[– – – – – – – – – – – – – – – – – –
– – –]
[καὶ] στεφανωθέν[τα πλεονάκις θαλλίνοις καὶ χρυσέοις?]
[στ]εφάνοις ὑπὸ Πα[ναθηναϊστᾶν στρατευσαμένων]

---

[43] *IG* XII.1 46.

[44] *Lindos II* 292.12–14 and *IG* XII.1 46.18–19. The sons of Hagesandros: *Lindos II* 1 s.v. 22 and 21; *Lindos II* 347 (statue base signed by Athanodoros son of Hagesandros); *IG* XII.1 847 (base of honorific statue for Athanodoros son of Hagesandros adopted son of Dionysios). For the career of the sculptor Athanodoros son of Hagesandros and possible identification with the Lindian priest of 22 see Rice 1986: 233–50.

[45] *IG* XII.1 46.63; *Lindos II* 346.II.76.

[46] *Lindos II* 260. The command of Hesteion is mentioned in *Lindos II* 303, in which Damagoras (son of Euphranor), the later nauarch in the war against Mithridates, is mentioned as a trierarch.

5   [κοιν]οῦ τῶν τε ὑπὸ ἄρχ[οντα τετρηρέων ..]εα[− −]
    καὶ τριήραρχον Δαμαγόρα[ν καὶ τῶν ὑπ]ὸ ἄρχοντα
    Ἀριστώνυμον καὶ τριηράρχ[ους ..5..α]νδρον καὶ
    Σῶσον καὶ ὑπὸ ἄρχοντα Πασι[..5..] καὶ τριήραρχον
    ..ιστ...αν ἀρετᾶς ἕν<ε>κα καὶ εὐνοί[α]ς καὶ φιλοδοξίας τᾶς
10   [ε]ἰς αὐτούς, καὶ στεφανωθέντα χρ[υ]σέοις στεφάνοις
    [ὑπὸ Πα]ναθηναϊστᾶν στρατευσαμ[έ]νων κοινοῦ τῶν τε
    [ὑπὸ ἄρχοντα] τετρηρέων Τιμόθεο[ν] καὶ ἐπίπλουν
    [− − − καὶ τ]ῶν ὑπὸ ἄρχοντα τ[ετρηρ]έων Ἐστει{ει}ον
    {Ἐστειον} καὶ
    [ἐπίπλουν − − − −] ἀρετᾶς ἕνε[κα καὶ] εὐνοίας καὶ φιλοδοξίας
15   [τᾶς εἰς αὐτούς].

... and who was honoured [many times with foliage and gold] crowns
by the *koinon* of the Pa[*nathenaistai strateusamenoi*], those who served under
the archon [of the quadriremes(?) ---] and the trierarch Damagoras, [and
by those under] the archon Aristonymos and the trierarchs [---]andros and
Sosos and under the archon Pasi[---] and the trierarch [---], because of his
areta and *eunoia* and *philodoxia* towards them, and who was honoured with
gold crowns by the *koinon* of the *Panathenaistai strateusamenoi*, those who
served [under the archon] of the quadriremes Timotheos and the *epiplous*
[---], and those who served under the archon of the quadriremes Hestios
and ---, because of his *areta* and his *eunoia* and *philodoxia* [towards them].

On one occasion (ll. 3–10) the nameless honorand was honoured by groups:
(1) those of the *Panathenaistai strateuomenoi* who served with the trierarch
Damagoras under an unnamed squadron commander (*archon*); (2) those
who served with the trierarchs [---]andros and Sosos, under the archon
Aristonymos; and (3) one more subgroup associated with a trierarch and
archon whose names are all but missing from the inscription.[47] We do not
know the type of ship on which the members of the association served
(Blinkenberg restored *tetrereon* on analogy with line 12, but there can be
no certainty), but on a second occasion the same man was again honoured
by (1) the *Panathenaistai strateuomenoi* who served with an unknown *epiplous* under the archon Timotheos, as well as (2) those who served with
an unknown trierarch or *epiplous* under the archon Hesteios. The two
archons Timotheos and Hesteios are specified as commanders of quardri-
remes (*archontes tetrereon*). The dedication to Alexidamos, by the crew of a
quadrireme, which we mentioned earlier, numbered some forty-eight crew
members (without the rowers). If the *Panathenaistai strateuomenoi* likewise

---

[47] *Lindos II* 303.

did not include rowers, the number of those who honoured the unnamed Lindian of *Lindos II* 303 might still be close to 100 members. The same inscription also shows that the *Panathenaistai strateuomenoi* was connected to practically every Lindian known to have taken part in the war against Mithridates. These included the highest echelons of the Rhodian naval command. Damagoras, who in *Lindos II* 303 is named a trierarch, would be appointed nauarch and held supreme command of Rhodian forces for the campaign against Mithridates. His military advisor (*symboulos nauarchoi*), Polykles, who was probably a relative of Sosos the trierarch, was voted gold crowns by the association, as was Lysimachos, one of the *hagemones*.[48]

The adoption of the name *Panathenaistai* also represented a clear commitment to the Lindian *polis*. On analogy with other military associations whose members were associated with overseas mysteries, particularly the *Samothraikiastai mesoneoi* and the *Samothraikiastai Lemniastai*, Christian Blinkenberg suggested that the *Panathenaistai strateuomenoi* were theoric groups who participated in the Athenian Panathenaia. The possibility cannot be excluded, but other options need to be considered. Across the island from Lindos, the Kamireans celebrated a Panathenaia – apparently a public festival (*panagyris*) of some importance in the city in which the demes participated, and which included athletic games (*agones*) and was the preferred venue for various public announcements.[49] This is hardly surprising given the fact that Athana Polias was the patron deity of Kamiros. The question is whether the Lindians also celebrated a Panathenaia (the *Panathenaistai strateuomenoi* are completely unattested in Kamiros). The question is complicated by the fact that our knowledge of Lindian public festivals is extremely poor. While a handful of Kamirean honorific decrees specify the proclamation of honours at particular festivals and games, including the Panathenaia; their Lindian counterparts refer simply to the *panegyreis* or the *agones*.[50] But it is possible that generic references to 'festivals' and 'games' conceal a Lindian Panathenaia, since after all Athana Lindia was the patron deity of the city and the inhabitant of the largest temple on the Lindian acropolis.[51] Panathenaia or not, the *Panathenaistai strateuomenoi* through their adoption of their native

---

[48] Damagoras as nauarch: *IG* XII.1 41.4–5; *NSill* 18.14; App. *Mith.* 25; Diod. 37.28.1 (Berthold 1984: 224–6; van Gelder 1900: 162–4). Polykles: *NSill* 18 (see also below). Lysimachos son of Aristeidas: *Cl. Rhodos* 2 (1932) 190 no. 19.

[49] *Tit. Cam.* 110; 106 and 159 (an *epidosis* of the Kamirean deme of the Arioi for repair of buildings and the celebration of the Panathenaia).

[50] E.g. *Lindos II* 281a.9 (c. 100 BCE); 379b.5 (c. 25 BCE); *SEG* 39: 758.12–13 (after 78 BCE).

[51] For comparison, the Lindian Sminthia festival, which was the subject of a treatise by Philomnestos (Athen. 10.445a), is only mentioned once in a very rare decree of the Lindians from 23 CE (*IG* XII.1 762; see below).

city's patron deity displayed a profound commitment to the city and to those of their patrons who served the goddess as priests.

In the years that surround the First Mithridatic War, the *Panathenaistai strateuomenoi* enjoyed connections with, or indeed the sponsorship of, several Lindian military (especially naval) officers, including the supreme commander of Rhodian naval forces and his personal advisor. In the years following the war, the achievements of the war heroes were commemorated in private monuments in Rhodes, but especially on the Lindian acropolis. Any visitor would time and again find the name of the *Panathenaistai strateuomenoi* associated with the city's most celebrated sons. Though large-scale naval engagements became a thing of the past with the turn of the first century, the *Panathenaistai strateuomenoi* retained their presence in Lindos as crews of several *triemoiliai* stationed there.[52] Their public standing had not diminished and their endorsements were continually sought by the leading men and women of Lindos. The association or its subsections can be found among the private associations that honoured the priests of Athana Lindia of the years 10 and 23 CE and their wives.[53]

POLITICAL ASSOCIATIONS

A number of associations drew their members exclusively from the subdivisions of the Rhodian state. Among them we find associations of *patriotai* whose members were also members of *patra*, for instance the *Grennadai patriotai* who were active in first-century CE Lindos, but whose *patra* may have been as old as the fourth century BCE.[54] Similarly, some members of particular *ktoina* set up private associations as *ktoinetai*, like the first-century BCE *Matioi ktoinetai eranistai Philokrateioi*.[55] That these were in fact private associations and not the public subdivisions from which they drew their members is suggested by two things. First of all, the terminology of the public subdivisions is different. The associations in question refer to themselves as *koina* plus the personal plural derived from the type of public subdivision to which they also belonged – *koinon patriotan* or *koinetan*, from *patra* and *ktoina*.[56] When at some point in the second or first century BCE a Lindian citizen was honoured by the Lindian *patra* of the Druitai with a statue, in the inscription which accompanied it, the *patra* appears simply as *ha patra ha Druitan* without the use of *patriotai*.[57] Also, the

---

[52] *Lindos II* 420a.10–15 (23 CE).
[53] *Lindos II* 391.32–3; 392a.13–14, b.6–7; 394.6–7; 420a.13–15.
[54] *Lindos II* 391; 392; 394; 615 (fourth century BCE). Gabrielsen 1997: 141.
[55] *IG* XII.1 157.9–10.
[56] *Tit. Cam.* 159a (*koinon patriotan, damatan*); *IG* XII.1 157 (*ktoinetai*).
[57] *IG* XII.1 88.6. cf. *Lindos II* 206; *IG* XII.1 832. Gabrielsen 1997: 141–2.

Lindian *Euthalidai patriotai* had two distinct branches, one in Netteia close to the western shores of the Lindian territory, and another in an unknown location called Oiai.[58] How precisely these two groups are related to each other is difficult to tell, but the split into two is evidence of a sort of organisational freedom which is not found in public subdivisions. Furthermore, the *Haliatadai patriotai Aristokleioi* (which seem to have merged with another association)[59] had adopted the name of their benefactor, one Aristokles, a phenomenon which is unattested for public subdivisions, but common among private associations. A similar pattern of terminology is evident for the *ktoina* which appears as such (*ha ktoina ha Epibomous*) as opposed to the private association of the *Matioi ktoinetai eranistai Philokrateioi*.[60] This last association is especially interesting since it explicitly identifies it members as *eranistai*, that is, members of an *eranos*, a form of association that belongs squarely to the non-public sphere. Another element of the association's name was again derived from the name of their benefactor, a certain Philokrates from Ilion. Furthermore, as mentioned earlier, the fact that this association was sponsored by someone from Ilion need not indicate that the *ktoina* of the Matioi was accessible to foreigners; rather, it demonstrates the flexibility in membership that was inherent in private associations. Lastly and on analogy with the associations of *patriotai* and the *ktoinetai*, the *Euriadan dametan koinon* which appears in a Kamirean *epidosis* (*Tit. Cam.* 159a.4, above), may well have been a private association formed by members of the Kamirean deme of the Euriadai. Demes appear as *damos* plus proper personal plurals or even as *koinon Loxidan, Physkion* and so on.[61]

The *diagonia* of the *Hagetoridai* most likely also drew their members from the same *patra*, but as their name suggests the members were also kinsmen.[62] Sometime during the first half of the second century BCE, one of their number, Alkidas son of Kleustratos, appeared before the Lindian assembly to make a special announcement. Alkidas was probably familiar with the assembly; after all, it had at some point elected him priest of Artemis Andromeda.[63] Chances

[58] *Lindos II* 652 (*ek Netteias*); *NSill* 18.22–3 (*en Oiais*). The editor, Maiuri, considers Oiai to be a Lindian deme. The place is otherwise unattested and if it was a deme it was certainly not among the twelve island demes, all of which are well known (Papachristodoulou 1989: 56–81; Blinkenberg 1941: 19–23).

[59] Gabrielsen 1997: 142.

[60] *IG* XII. 157.9–10.

[61] As *damos*: *IG* XII.1 978; 994; 995; *Lindos II* 216; *Tit. Cam.* 159; *NSill* 27; *RIPR* 6; 10; 124. As *koinon*: *Tit. Cam.* 159a; *Lindos II* 51.II.36.

[62] *IG* XII.1 922. Andrewes (1957: 33–5) assumes that the *diagoniai* were public associations subdividing the *patrai*. His attempt at constructing a hierarchy of Archaic public subdivisions has been convincingly refuted by Gabrielsen (1997: 141–51).

[63] *Lindos II* 220.16.

are that what he had to say to his fellow citizens was something of a surprise, for he announced before them that his brother Alexandros had been honoured with a gold crown 'because of the *areta* and *eunoia* he held towards the Lindian *plethos*'. This in itself was not unusual; several prominent Lindians who, like Alexandros, had served in a priestly or civic office had received similar awards for their *areta* and *eunoia* for the Lindians.[64] It may nevertheless have come as a surprise, for the honour had been enacted not by the Lindians themselves, but by the members of the *diagonia* of the *Hagetoridai*. This association had further-more petitioned the Rhodian *boula* and *damos*, presumably for the permission to set up the decree in a public sanctuary.[65] But in the light of the close con-nection between Alexandros and the *Hagetoridai* expressed through an hon-orific decree, the question naturally arises: when Alexandros announced his candidacy for office or priesthood in Lindos, whom did the members of the *Hagetoridai* vote for?

The answer is provided by a quick review of the individuals who formed ties with such citizens' associations. (1) Apart from Alexandros and his brother, the *Hagetoridai* had voted honours half a century earlier for their long-time treasurer Archokrates son of Archipolis and adopted son of Lysistratos who won the priesthood of Poseidon in 221 BCE and that of Athana Lindia around 202 BCE, before he became priest of Halios in 185 BCE. (2) An unnamed *strata-gos* and *hagemon* received the endorsement of the *Pankiadai patriotai* in the late third or early second century BCE.[66] The *Euthalidai patriotai* in Netteia counted among their trusted members (3) Euphranor son of Dardanos, the priest of Sarapis of 148,[67] while their colleagues in Oiai backed (4) Polykles, the *stratagos* and *prytanis* and part of the Rhodian high naval command in the war against Mithridates (88–85 BCE). We will have more to say about Polykles shortly, but first we must add the two Kamireans, (5) Aristombrotidas son of Aristomb-rotidas and (6) Eukleitos son of Eukles, whose rise to prominence in Kamiros and their connections with private association need special attention.

Private associations in local politics

In the first half of the second century, two members of the Kamirean civic elite joined in making a donation to the city together with the *Sarapiastai hoi en Kamiroi* (*Tit. Cam. Supp.* 220, 157b):

---

[64] *IG* XII.1 922. Alexandros son of Kleustratos: *Lindos II* 208.5; 220.4.
[65] Gabrielsen 1994b.
[66] *Annuario* n.s. 1–2 (1939/40) 165 no. 19.21.
[67] *IG* XII.1 890; *Lindos II* 224.7.

This association may have been among the contributors to a Kamirean *epidosis* in which only demes and private associations contributed.[79] Another group, the *Hermaistai en toi astei*, certainly contributed. The two associations bear strikingly similar names: both were *Hermaistai*, but one was based in Kamiros and the other in the *asty*. Clearly, the two were contemporary and their names suggest that they were well aware of each other's existence. Furthermore, the two share a geographical connection, as the *Hermaistai hoi en toi astei* participated in a Kamirean *epidosis*. The fact that the Lindian *Euthalidai*, as we have seen, had two branches in different locales (the *Euthalidai ek Netteias* and the *Euthalidai patriotai en Oiais*) raises the possibility of a Kamirean asociation (the *Hermaistai hoi en Kamiroi*) with a branch office in the Rhodian *asty* (*Hermaistai hoi en toi astei*). If the former was an asset to an individual with local political ambitions, then the latter might also be so to one with federal ambitions, and Aristombrotidas son of Aristombrotidas was just that.

The federal level

That patronage of several associations might provide the infrastructure for an elite network is evident from the case of a certain Polykles, a Lindian who came to occupy a central place in Rhodian and international politics in the early years of the first century. Polykles' impressive career is known to history through an inscription which accompanied a private monument dedicated by four grandchildren. The stone on which the inscription can be read provides almost no clues as to the appearance of the monument, but does suggest that it was rather large.[80] As a military commander, Polykles had paid to equip a trireme and commanded squadrons of both light vessels and the heavy quinqeremes. Clearly a man of extraordinary ability in military affairs, he had been elected *hagemon* of the *hagemones* and *stratagos* of the Peraia, and was eventually made *symboulos* or advisor of the famous nauarch Damagoras, who held supreme command of those Rhodian naval forces who fought against the Pontic king in Rome's First Mithridatic War. Polykles' military career was complemented by an equally splendid civic career, which included the presidency of the jury courts and a term as secretary of the *boula* before he won election as *prytanis* 'in wartime' – presumably during the same war with Mithridates. It would be fair to say that Polykles managed to put himself in positions of great influence in these crucial years as part of both the political and military leadership. No doubt he was gifted both in the field of military strategy and in oratory; we may nevertheless add another and probably crucial skill: networking.

[79] See Chapter 4.
[80] *NSill* 18 with Maiuri's comments.

In addition to its elaborate account of Polykles' civic and military career, the inscription also records the names of no fewer than ten private associations that had all voted honours for Polykles, presumably in return for some benefaction:

The *Panathenaistai strateuomenoi*
The *Haliatadai patriotai*
The *Aristokleion kai Kydagoreion diagonia*
The *Epektoridai patriotai*
The *Euthalidai patriotai hoi en Oiais*
The *Aphrodisiastai halikiotai Polykleioi*
The *Hierombroteioi Klysimeioi Polycharmeioi*
The *Apolloniastai Antiocheioi sysstrateusamenoi*
The *Polykleioi Boarsai*
The *Boarsai [---]sagoreioi*

Several of these associations carried the name of a benefactor. Apart from the *Aphrodisiastai halikiotai Polykleioi* and the *Polykleioi Boarsai*, which were apparently sponsored by Polykles himself, two more benefactors may be identified:

1. The *Apolloniastai Antiocheioi sysstrateusamenoi* were closely associated with a certain Antiochos who served as a naval squadron commander in the First Mithridatic War.[81]
2. The *Aristokleion kai Kydagoreion diagonia* were formed around Aristokles and Kydagoras, and the rarity of the latter name makes it highly likely that the association was sponsored by the father of Kydagoras son of Kydagoras, a Lindian of the deme of the Lindopolitai whose son (Kydagoras) was *hierothytas* in 47 BCE and *mastros* in Lindos four years later.[82]

Though Aristokles, Polycharmos, Klysimos, Hierombrotos and [---]sagoras cannot be identified it seems reasonable to suppose, given their support of associations, that they too belonged to the Rhodian elite. All, however, were influential members of their associations and were probably instrumental in securing the support of these for Polykles. Therefore, it is possible to see in Polykles' inscribed list of associations the petrified remains of a powerful political network of the early first century (Fig. 6.1): a small group of political leaders centred on Polykles, a dominant political figure of his day, and each with a group of followers organised into private associations; a *hoi peri ton Polyklen* to match the *hoi peri ton Philophrona kai Theaideton*, the pro-Roman

---

[81] *IG* XII.1 43.
[82] *Lindos II* 344.I.14; 346.II.96; cf. *SER* 4.b.10–12.

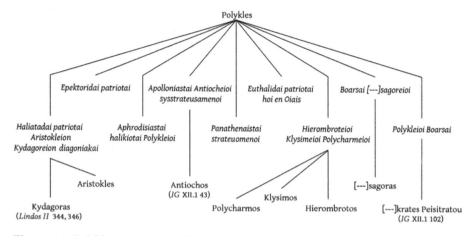

Figure 6.1 Polykles' network (*NSill* 18).

faction of Philophron and Theaidetos, or the *hoi peri ton Deinona kai Polyaraton*, the pro-Macedonian faction of Deinon and Polyaratos, which, according to Polybios, were the dominating 'parties' of Rhodian politics in the period of political unrest leading up to Rome's Third Macedonian War.[83]

Polykles' network of elite friends and associations comes extremely close to the political factions of fourth-century Athens as identified by Demosthenes in yet another lambasting of the Athenian assembly:

> Men of Athens, you used to pay your taxes by symmories, now you conduct your politics by symmories. There is a *rhetor* in charge of each, and a *strategos* as his henchman, and 300 to do the shouting and the rest of you are divided in one group or another.[84]

> ὦ ἄνδρες Ἀθηναῖοι, κατὰ συμμορίας εἰσεφέρετε, νυνὶ δὲ πολιτεύεσθε κατὰ συμμορίας. ῥήτωρ ἡγεμὼν ἑκατέρων, καὶ στρατηγὸς ὑπὸ τούτῳ καὶ οἱ βοησόμενοι, οἱ τριακόσιοι· οἱ δ᾽ ἄλλοι προσνενέμησθε οἱ μὲν ὡς τούτους, οἱ δ᾽ ὡς ἐκείνους.

Apparently, the Athenian assembly was split into distinct and rival factions similar to the *hoi peri ton Polyklen*. The 300 'shouters' were directly attached to the *rhetor* or speaker and his *strategos*, but Demosthenes provides no hint as to how they were organised. Polykles' monument may at least suggest an answer.

---

[83] Pol. 28.2.3 and 28.16.3.
[84] Dem. 2.29. Trans. Hansen 1991: 285.

The potential of private associations as a power base for politicians of Polykles' league is perhaps further underlined by the conspicuous absence from his inscription of any mention of public subdivisions or indeed office in one of the old *poleis* (Polykles was almost certainly Lindian). This may of course be due to mere chance. The stone which preserves the inscription is only one out of several which would have gone to make up his monument. He might also have set up another inscription back in Lindos commemorating his local civic career. But it is at least certain that Polykles never held the priesthood of Athana Lindia and it therefore becomes tempting to ask: may we be justified in seeing in Polykles a new species of Rhodian political animal who had found political support in private associations, a support that rendered the traditional approach through local office and courtship of public subdivisions obsolete?

CHAPTER 7

The Civic Aspirations of Private Associations

No ancient author as far as we know ever undertook a comprehensive description of the association phenomenon. When ancient authors did comment on private associations it was usually with scepticism and occasionally with outright criticism. For Polybios, private associations were directly responsible for the downfall of the formerly proud people of Boeotia:

> For childless men, when they died, did not leave their property to their nearest heirs, as had formerly been the custom there, but disposed of it for purposes of junketing and banqueting and made it the common property of their friends. Even many who had families distributed the greater part of their fortune among their clubs, so that there were many Boeotians who had each month more dinners than there were days in the calendar.[1]

> οἱ μὲν γὰρ ἄτεκνοι τὰς οὐσίας οὐ τοῖς κατὰ γένος ἐπιγενομένοις τελευτῶντες ἀπέλειπον, ὅπερ ἦν ἔθος παρ᾽ αὐτοῖς πρότερον, ἀλλ᾽ εἰς εὐωχίας καὶ μέθας διετίθεντο καὶ κοινὰς τοῖς φίλοις ἐποίουν: πολλοὶ δὲ καὶ τῶν ἐχόντων γενεὰς ἀπεμέριζον τοῖς συσσιτίοις τὸ πλεῖον μέρος τῆς οὐσίας, ὥστε πολλοὺς εἶναι Βοιωτῶν οἷς ὑπῆρχε δεῖπνα τοῦ μηνὸς πλείω τῶν εἰς τὸν μῆνα διατεταγμένων ἡμερῶν.

Though Polybios does not condemn the activities of associations as such, he is nevertheless clear about the detrimental effects the association habit had on

---

[1] Pol. 20.6.5–7. Trans. Paton 2012.

the state.[2] Associations turned the attention of the citizens away from political society and had a damaging effect on the family too.

Livy was less restrained in his criticism of associations, both of internal matters and of their effects on the state. Associations enter his history of Republican Rome through the vehicle of a Greek sorcerer, who preached a gospel of drunkenness and sexual depravity in Etruria. From there it soon spread to Rome, according to Livy, who has Hispala, a freedwoman with some knowledge of the group, divulge their secrets to the consul:

> At first that shrine had been limited to women, she said, with no male admitted there. They had three days a year set aside for initiation in the Bacchic rites in a daylight ceremony, and married women were usually appointed to the priesthood in turns. It was Paculla Annia, a priestess from Campania, who had made the radical changes, supposedly at the prompting of the gods. She was the first to have initiated males (her own sons, Minius and Herennius Cerrinius) and she had made it a nighttime as opposed to a daylight ceremony, with five days of rites per month instead of three in a year. Ever since the rites were integrated, with men mixed with women, and with darkness giving participants freedom of action, there was no crime and no shameful act omitted from them. There were more sexual assaults inflicted on the men by other men than on the women, continued Hispala, and any who showed reluctance to submit to abuse or hesitated to engage in crime became sacrificial victims. To consider nothing sinful – that, among them, was the essence of religion, she said. Men who appeared deranged would utter prophesies with a furious shaking of their bodies. Married women wearing the dress of Bacchants and with hair streaming would run down to the Tiber carrying blazing torches; they would plunge them in the water and draw them out again still aflame because of a mixture of pure sulfur and calcium contained in them. Some whom they tied to a crane and whisked out of sight into hidden caverns were said to have been 'taken by the gods,' and they were those individuals who refused to join the conspiracy, be involved in crimes, or submit to sexual abuse. The number of participants was enormous, by now virtually amounting to a second city-population, and included certain men and women from the nobility. In the past two years, Hispala said, it had become established that no one above the age of twenty be initiated; the targeted age groups were those susceptible to corruption and sexual abuse.[3]

---

[2] The communal meals of private associations received some attention in Classical Athens: Arist. *Eth. Nic.* 4.2.20 (1123a20–2); Aesch. 3.251.

[3] Livy 39.13.8–14. Trans. Yardley 2018.

If the admittedly rather thick layer of scandal may for a moment be set aside, the associations described by Livy exhibit many similarities to the associations we have come across so far: a clearly defined membership which included individuals of different statuses and standing, a formalised leadership and cult celebrations.

According to Livy 'these nocturnal gatherings were a danger to the state'; at least the members of the senate thought so, but if Livy can be believed on this point, the threat of these associations was not obvious to most Romans.[4] Livy's account, written centuries after the events, is obviously to be taken with a (large) pinch of salt. What can be said is that the Roman senate issued a state-wide ban on associations (*collegia*), suggesting that associations as such, rather than 'impure and obscene' nocturnal rites, were at the time considered the root of the problem.[5] None of this refers to associations in Rhodes and, as we shall see, it seems unlikely that such views were generally shared by Rhodians or even the Rhodian elite.[6] Yet they do illustrate the sort of criticism to which private associations might be subjected.

It is possible, therefore, to see in the associations' epigraphic output and in their behaviour towards the state, its institutions and its personnel, an attempt to counter potential accusations of anti-social behaviour. Their inscribed monuments display a profoundly different image of orderly conduct and a strong commitment on behalf of the association to conduct itself in the manner befitting a state.

THE PUBLIC RELATIONS OF PRIVATE ASSOCIATIONS

Members of private associations were keenly aware that their behaviour shaped outsiders' perception and attitudes towards them. The motivation for the *koinon ton en Symai katoikounton* to honour a benefactor who had taken it upon himself to repair a public sanctuary was expressly 'that the *koinon*

---

[4] Livy 39.14.1–10. Apparently, it was a case that needed some pleading, and Livy in his account has the consul concede before the people, 'some of you fancy that it is a particular form of worship; others think that it is some permissible kind of sport and dalliance; its real nature is understood by few' (Livy 39.15.6).

[5] *CIL* I.2 581. The decree bans congregations of more than five people and forbids key features of private associations such as the election of magistrates (*magistri*), priests (*sacerdotes*), the ownership of sanctuaries and the collection of common funds (*neve pecuniam quisquam eorum comoinem habuise*) unless with the expressed permission of the senate. Roman authorities would continue this scepticism well into the era of the Roman Empire (Cotter 1996).

[6] Though Athenaeus preserves a story about the Rhodian Antheas who often led out his *symbachoi* in procession, to the amusement of all (10.445a–b). Cf. Dem. 18.259–60, for Demosthenes' malicious ridicule of the rites which Aeschines and particularly his mother performed. Parker 1996: 151–98.

may appear to be thankful and reverent towards the good among men'.[7] In a similar case the imagined audience for an honorific decree was 'everyone' (*pantes*).[8] The *Euthalidai* too wished to broadcast their decision to honour one of their members 'so that what has been decided may be visible after this time'.[9] In the case of the *Euthalidai* this intention was directly related to the decision to inscribe their decree and to have it set up in public, in the sanctuary of Zeus Patroos in Lindian Netteia.

Though such formulae are stock phrases of honorific decrees, both private and public, they should not be brushed aside as mindless platitudes. After all, in both cases the associations took the trouble of electing members to go before the Rhodian *boula* and petition for the permission to set up these decrees in public sanctuaries.

Associations on display

The acropolis was the civic and religious heart of the Rhodian *asty* as well as in the three old *poleis*. Within these the main sanctuaries stood, and crowded around them were the monuments that combined to make up the civic memory of each *polis*. Members of the Rhodian elite competed with each other for monumental presence and prominence within these civic-epigraphic 'hotspots'.[10]

The well-excavated acropolis of Lindos (Fig. 7.1) provides us with the best view of the use of public sanctuaries as display spaces. From the late fourth century BCE it had been customary for the priests of Athana Lindia to set up life-size statues of themselves commemorating their tenure of the prestigious priesthood. That tradition persisted into the first century CE, but over the centuries the priestly portrait statues were added to with statues for other priests and magistrates, and those others to whom the Lindians, the demes or prominent families saw fit to grant a statue, eventually creating a veritable forest of statues.[11]

Few association dedications seem to have made it into these 'hotspots'.[12] The *Diosoteriastai Philokrateioi* managed to dedicate a statue of their benefactor

---

[7] IG XII.3 1270.A.18–20: ὅπως οὖν καὶ τὸ κοινὸν φαίνη | ται εὐχάριστόν <τ>ε ἐὸν καὶ τιμοῦν τοὺς ἀγαθοὺς τῶν | [ἀν]δρῶν. Cf. SEG 33: 639.3–5; IG XII.1 155.d.I.8–13; 890.17–8; AEMÖ 18 (1895) 121 no. 1; Cl. Rhodos 2 (1932) 175 no. 4; Lindos II 652; Annuario 33–4 (1955/6) 174 no. 27.1–2 (NSill 27).

[8] Annuario 33–4 (1955/6) 174 no. 27.1–2 (NSill 27).

[9] IG XII.1 890.17–8: εἰς τὸν μετὰ ταῦτα | χρόνον φανερ[ὰ ἦι τὰ δ]όξαντα.

[10] See for instance the exedra of Timodikos son of Moiragenes, Lindos II 131a–e.

[11] See Chapter 4, above. Thomsen forthcoming b; cf. Sosin 2005.

[12] For the acropolis of Rhodes there can be no certainty, since its monuments and dedications have been heavily quarried in subsequent centuries. Though many inscribed association monuments have been found in the city there is no telling whether they were originally placed there or brought there later from either the acropolis or the necropolis.

Figure 7.1 Model of the Lindian acropolis (© National Museum of Denmark).

on the Lindian acropolis – one of only two private associations, as far as we know, to ever do so.[13] Given the number of preserved inscriptions from the Lindian acropolis and the number of association dedications preserved from the Rhodian necropolis, this is a strikingly low figure. It is immediately clear from the dedication of the *Diosoteriastai Philokrateioi* that there was no ban on dedications on the Lindian acropolis by outside groups, and we will have to look for other reasons.[14] One explanation may be found in the conditions of the 'hotspots' of civic epigraphy. A stroll around the excavated areas of the Lindian acropolis or the agora of the fountain house in Kamiros is all that is needed to realise the problem: too many dedications and not enough space. In the case of the public sanctuary of Asklepios in the Rhodian *asty*, the accumulation of dedicated monuments, which may have included some from private associations, had reached a point where they made it difficult to move around the *temenos*. In the attempt to put a stop to the crowding of the sanctuary the wardens managed to cram in one more stele, bearing a decree of the *boula* and *damos* banning any further petitions for permission to dedicate anything in the sanctuary, and instructed the *astynomoi* to remove any dedicated objects placed there in disregard of the decree.[15] Evidence from both Rhodes and elsewhere in the Greek world suggests that the associations to some extent preferred their own sanctuaries and burial precincts.[16] Somewhere in the necropolis of Rhodes in the association's *topos* the *Aphrodisiastai Hermogeneioi*, presumably with considerable pride in their own success, set up an inscribed list of all their real estate possessions. The decree carved on the back of the same stele called for its placement in 'the most visible and safe place' and it seems likely that the association believed it would make an impression on anyone who saw it.[17]

Though association sanctuaries, *oikoi* and burial precincts were less public than the civic-epigraphic 'hotspots' of *acropoleis* and other public sanctuaries, they were not necessarily clandestine or inaccessible to outsiders. The major roads leading from the *chora* and the old cities to the new city passed right by the burial precincts, and the *asty*'s Hippodamian street plan extended into the necropolis.[18] The city of the dead was closely connected with that of the living, and came alive (sometimes too much alive)[19] with, among other

---

[13] *Lindos II* 285 (93 BCE); 251 (115 BCE). Boyxen 2018: 131.

[14] Gabrielsen 1994b.

[15] *SER* 1; see Gabrielsen 1994b.

[16] For the use of sanctuaries as display spaces by associations in Hellenistic Athens, see Thomsen forthcoming a.

[17] *Annuario* n.s. 1–2 (1939/40) 156 no. 18.12–3. See also Chapter 5.

[18] Fraser 1977: 1–5; Gabrielsen 1997.

[19] Occasionally a burial precinct may have been put to good if less than respectful use: βόεα μηδὲ | βοτέα | μὴ ποτάγειν ('grazing cattle and sheep may not enter', *NSill* 17).

things, the activities of the numerous associations which set up their head-
quarters there.[20] What these sites offered was complete control over space
and the objects displayed within them. This is illustrated by placing-formulae,
well-attested in Attic associations from whose hands an impressive number of
honorific decrees have been preserved. Allowing the honorand a say in the
display of monuments was in itself a prize, though not one to be bestowed
lightly: 'place the stele where he wishes', instructed one decree of a generous
Attic association; 'wherever he wishes, excepting the *naos* and the *pronaos*',
instructed a decree of a less generous Delian association,[21] and 'let the dedication be set up in the sanctuary wherever he wishes – after he has asked the
thiasotai', instructed a decree of an association whose members were only too
aware that display space was prime real estate, and attempted to have their cake
and eat it.[22]

As argued above, some association activities and facilities were open to
outsiders, and even a seemingly unapproachable *oikos* might be opened for
the right people. This is illustrated by the well-known association of Berytian
Poseidoniastai in Delos. From the outside, their *oikos* was impressive for its
size, but the beautiful column hall and its in-house sanctuary of Poseidon
and Roma would remain unseen by all who did not have business with the
'shippers, merchants and warehousemen' whose association it housed. The
oikos nevertheless functioned as the association's display window to the world,
through a carefully orchestrated show.

Every year, on the day following the festival of Apollo, the *Poseidoniastai*
gathered at their *oikos* for a feast in honour of Marcus Minatius, a wealthy
Roman banker and benefactor of the association. The banquet was no small
matter, and the association set aside no less than 150 drachmas every year for
its celebration – the same amount allocated for the purchase of the ox that was
to be displayed in the procession for Poseidon. The feast was a private event,
but Marcus was allowed to bring two guests of his own choice to it. Since the
event was hosted by the *Poseidoniastai*, the guests can only have been outsiders. Though the choice is left entirely up to Marcus, we may speculate that
the members of Marcus' circle of friends would have shared some of his basic
characteristics, most notably wealth and influence. At the feast these two guests
would have an opportunity to visit the beautiful peristyle courtyard where a
statue of Marcus Minatius had been erected by the *Poseidoniastai*, among other
dedicated objects, which eventually included the association's dedications in
honour of the state (the Athenian *demos* and the goddess Roma) as well as its

---

[20] Van Nijf (1997: 34–9), highlighting the Rhodian necropolis. Boyxen 2018: 171–5.

[21] *ID* 1520.23–5

[22] τὸ δὲ ἀνάθημα ἀναθεῖναι ἐν τῶι ἱερῶι οὗ ἂν βούληται αἰτήσας τοὺς θιασώτας, *IG* II²
1263.25–7. Cf. Thomsen forthcoming a.

agents.[23] Over time these were augmented by several other dedications, which likewise testified to the generous behaviour of the associations towards its benefactors and the state. Finally, the guests would have been able to inspect the decree voted by the association in honour of Marcus Minatius, which also stood somewhere in the peristyle courtyard. Secondly, while it is true that only a few association dedications have been found in civic-epigraphic hotspots like the Lindian acropolis, the associations nevertheless had a strong presence. Their names were recorded in the monuments of those members of the elite who acted as their benefactors. This gave them a conspicuous presence in the civic hearts of the old city-states as well as in the *asty* and, equally important, in the good company of the most respectable members of the Rhodian elite.

This outsourcing of public relations, and the keen interest which members of the elite approached the task, will be the subject of the following section. Before we get there, however, we must examine the image that private associations displayed to the world around them.

Imitation of the *polis*

Imitation is important. It is, as the saying goes, the most sincere form of flattery. The image displayed through inscribed decrees is one of an orderly association guided by the same fundamental principles as the state: decisions were made collectively by the members and executed by elected officers who were accountable to the membership.

Honorific decrees, furthermore, were explicitly concerned about the appropriate, *kataxias* (literally 'quite worthy'), response to benefactors, and the appropriate response was the *polis*' response.[24] The prizes given – a crown, a statue, front-row seats at festivals – were carefully copied from the state, and the moral qualities identified as the benefactor's motivation were drawn from not just a state vocabulary, but a distinctively Rhodian set of *polis* virtues (see below). Furthermore, reference to inscribed laws or *nomoi* of associations gave an impression of orderliness and manners. Though no such *nomoi* survive from Rhodes, they are occasionally referred to in published decrees. For the members of the *Haliadai kai Haliastai*, failure to meet the financial obligations of membership meant being 'guilty under the enduring *nomos* concerning injustice towards the *koinon* and it will be permissable for any of the *eranistai* who want to denounce him with a view to obtaining the fine'.[25] In a single honorific decree the *Haliadai kai*

---

[23] Honorific decree for Marcus Minatius son of Sextus: *ID* 1520. Dedications found at the *oikos*: *ID* 1778 and 1779 (Roma); 1782 (Roman general). For the *oikos*, see Hudson McLean 1996 and Trümper 2006.

[24] *IG* XII.1 155.d.I.8–12; *SEG* 33: 639. Verboven 2007.

[25] *IG* XII.1 155.d.III.93–5.

Haliastai make no fewer than four references to their laws, which seem to have regulated every aspect of official conduct.

Associations as benefactors of the state

By the middle of the second century a sanctuary of Athana on the island of Syme was in a bad state of repair. The displacement of two walls had left the *naos* barely standing. A decree of a private association in honour of the man (probably a member of the association) who eventually took it upon himself to foot the bill of repair mentions that the *ktoinetai,* to whom the sanctuary belonged, opened up a subscription for the collection of funds and that 'promises of money for the repair were made by both *koina* and private individuals'.[26]

We do not know which *koina*, if any, answered the call, for the *epidosis* of the Symian *ktoina* does not survive, if it ever made it into stone (according to the decree of the private association, the promised funds failed to materialise).[27] But other *epidoseis* from both demes and *poleis* preserve the contributions made towards various public building projects by private associations.

From Kamiros there also survives a fragment of an *epidosis* entered only by *koina*, which has already been mentioned (Chapter 5). Among those *koina* which answered the call of the Kamireans were five demes from both Kamiros and Lindos, island and Peraia. The fragment, however, contains another nine entries which can be partly restored. Each of these names a private association and its contribution (*Tit. Cam.* 159a):

```
I       . . . . . . . . ν πατ[ριωτᾶν κοινὸν – – – – ]
        . . . . . στᾶν τῶν ἐγ Κα[μίρωι κοινὸν – – ]
        . . . λιδᾶν πατριωτᾶν κοινὸ[ν – – – – – ]
        [Ε]ὐριαδᾶν δαμετᾶν κοινὸν δισ[χιλίας]
5       Ἑρμαιστᾶν τῶν ἐν τῶι ἄστει κοιν[ὸν – – ]
        Κυμισαλέων κοινὸν δισχιλίας
        Λαρξ[ι]δᾶν κοινὸν δισχι[λί]ας . . . . κοσ[ίας]
        Ἀμνιστ[ί]ων [κ]οιν[ὸν δισ]χ ιλ[ίας]
        Βο[υλι]δᾶν κοινὸν πεντακοσίας
```

[26] *IG* XII.3 1270.10–11 (face A is quoted below). The decree is dated by the Halios priest Sosikles, assigned by Finkielsztejn (2001) to the year c. 155/4 (cf. Badoud 2015: 258). Recently, Constantakopoulou (2015: 223–31) has argued that the association in question functioned as joint political body of all the inhabitants of Syme, both citizens and foreigners. There is, however, nothing to suggest that the association included foreigners as members or that every citizen inhabitant was a member.

[27] *IG* XII.3 1270.10–11 (see the decree with a translation below, pp. 139–41).

10   Φε.....ᾶν [πατρι]ωτᾶν κοινὸν π[ε]ντακοσίας
      Eυ........τ[.. κο]ινὸν χιλίας
      Σωκλε[.......... κ]ρ[ιν]ὸν πεντακοσίας
            vacat(?)
13   Γλαυκε.....ν[ιδ]ᾶ[ν] κ[οιν]ὸν πεντακοσία[ς]
      [Κ]τησινε[ί]ων Σ[..... κ]ριγὸν π[ε]ντα[κοσίας]
15   ...θαγ.ρντι..γ κοιγὸγ δισχιλίας

Several of these were associations of *patriotai*, that is, whose members were also
members of a particular *patra* (lines 1, 3 and 10), presumably of Kamiros, but
whose full name cannot be restored. Another association was the *Hermaistai hoi
en toi astei*.[28] The specification that this was the association *hoi en toi astei* served
to distinguish the group from their contemporary namesakes from Kamiros,
the *Hermaistai hoi en Kamiroi*,[29] whose name, incidentally, may be restored in
line 2. Two other contemporary Kamirean associations, the *Asklapiastai hoi en
Kamiroi* and the *Sarapiastai hoi en Kamiroi*, however, also fit the preserved text.[30]
The latter certainly took part in another Kamirean *epidosis* into which they
entered, with two distinguished members of Kamiros' citizen elite, Eukleitos
son of Eukles (*damiourgos* of c. 144 BCE) and Aristombrotidas son of Aristombrotidas (*damiourgos* of c. 171 and on whom the association also bestowed a gold
crown), giving 30 drachmas, as we have already seen.[31]

No effort was made to separate the private associations from the demes.
Indeed they mingle freely in the list, and private associations and demes are
both entered as *koina*, as an echo of the unnamed Symian *ktoina*'s call for contributions from both individuals and *koina*. Later in that same century (around
125 BCE) in Lindos, the Lindians called upon the city's wealthy inhabitants to
contribute to an *epidosis* for the purchase of gold crowns to adorn the statues
of Athana, Zeus and Nike (*Lindos II* 252), including several members of the
Timokratid family. The contributors were the leading citizens of Lindos,
who contributed on behalf of their families, but a number of private associations also contributed either alone or with a citizen. The association of the
Athanaistai Timapoleioi participated in a joint contribution with two individuals and the Lindian priests, the *hierothytai* and the *archierothytas*.[32] Timapolis
son of Euphragoras and adopted son of Timapolis, who probably gave his
name to the association of *Athaniastai Timopoleioi*, had entered the subscription for himself and his family, but reappears later in the list at the head of no

[28] *Tit. Cam.* 84.12.
[29] *Tit. Cam.* 84.12.
[30] *Tit. Cam. Supp.* 157b; *Tit. Cam.* 84; 78.
[31] See pp. 120–4.
[32] *Lindos II* 252.221–7.

fewer than six different associations, the *Timapoleioi*, the *Agathadaimoniastai*, the *Soteriastai*, the [---] *kai Apolloniastai*, the *Hagestrateioi kai Leukareioi* and the *Arsi[noeioi kai] Aphrodisiatai*, the last two of which bore the names of other individuals too.[33]

The *epidoseis* offered to elite members of Rhodian society an opportunity to express and, no doubt even more important, display their generosity and care for the city they inhabited.[34] Of course, members of the citizen elite may have felt obliged to contribute, but they were far from alone in contributing. The case of the unnamed Symian *ktoina* which explicitly looked to *koina* as well as individuals, combined with the evidence of actual *epidoseis*, suggests that associations regularly took part. Their motives for doing so were undoubtedly the same as those of the wealthy, namely to display their concern for the civic and religious institutions and the general wellbeing of their fellow citizens in the most conspicuous way possible. The call for a public *epidosis* took the form of a formal decree before the assembly and was followed (if the decree was accepted by the assembly) by public declaration of promises (*epangeliai*) of contributions before the assembly, and here the associations or their representatives must too have risen to pledge their contributions for all to see.[35]

Connections with notables

Back on the island of Syme[36] the sanctuary of Athana had finally been restored by Aristophanes son of Aristophanes, a wealthy citizen of the Ialysian deme of the Politai and resident of Syme, who had taken matters into his own hands and completed the repair of the sanctuary from his private means. In response to this conspicuous display of civic-mindedness, the association of the *katoikountes hoi en Symai* voted to set up a decree in Aristophanes' honour.

[33] *Lindos II* 252.250–8. For Timapolis son of Euphragoras and adopted son of Timapolis, see Chapter 3.
[34] Migeotte 1992: 356.
[35] E.g. *Lindos II* 419.44–61. For a thorough treatment of the subject, see Migeotte 1992.
[36] The precise status of Syme vis-à-vis the Rhodian state is not entirely clear. Fraser and Bean (1954: 139–41) take it to be fully incorporated as part of the deme of the Kasareis (assigned by Fraser and Bean to Lindos, but to Kamiros, and in my oppinion rightly so, by Papachristodoulou 1989: 72 with n. 310). But some objections to Syme's status may be raised. (1) The demoticon Κασαρεύς is remarkably rare in Syme, attested only in one grave marker (*IG* XII.3 1272) and for a member of the association of the *katoikeuntes hoi en Symai* (*IG* XII.3 1269, cf. 1270), a private association whose members included Rhodians of other demes (the Ialysian Politai and Lindian Amioi). (2) The reference in *IG* XII.3 1270.17 to the παρεπιδαμοῦντας τῶν Πολιτᾶν (that is, the resident demesmen of the Ialysian Politai) could also be read as τῶν πολιτᾶν (the resident citizens), which in the context of a private association of Rhodian citizens (with members from all three old *poleis*) would suggest that the Symians were not considered citizens of Rhodes.

When Sosikles was priest (of Halios) and Ktesias was *damiourgos*, on the *ides* of Panaimos, it was decided by the *koinon*, the motion of the *hierothytai*: Since Aristophanes son of Aristophanes of the deme of the Politai continues to be a good man towards the *koinon ton en Symai katoikounton* giving everything with great care and *philotimia*, and has always a hand in the good things that befall the *koinon*. When the temple of Athana on the acropolis was crumbling and a collapse was imminent due to the displacement of two walls, the ones facing towards the east and the south, and as pledges for money for the repair were being made by *koina* and private individuals but the collection of funds was dragging out, besought by the *ktoinetai* in the assembly to complete the work from his personal means, he pledged (the money) and it was done. He also pledged to procure wood for the roofs of the adjacent (buildings) and roof tiles at his own expense. And when it was done he led up (to the temple) the resident citizens and showed them the beautiful work. In order that all may know that the *koinon* is grateful and honours those who are good among men, good fortune, it was decided by the *koinon*, when this decree is ratified, to praise and crown Aristophanes son of Aristophanes of the Politai with a gold crown because of the *areta* and *philodoxia* he continues to show the *koinon ton en Symai katoikounton* and his piety towards the gods . . .

A.1   ἐπ' ἱερέως Σωσικλεῦς καὶ δαμιουργοῦ Κτησία, Πα-
       ναίμου [δ]ιχομηνίαι, ἔδοξε τῶι κοινῶι, ἱεροθυτᾶν γνώ-
       μα· ἐπειδὴ Ἀριστοφάνης Ἀριστοφάνευς Πολίτας
       ἀνὴρ ἀγαθὸς ὢν διατελεῖ περὶ τὸ κοινὸν τῶν ἐν Σύμαι
   5   κατοικούντων, τὰν πᾶσαν σπου[δ]ὰν καὶ φιλοτιμίαν πα-
       ρεχόμενος καὶ ἀεί τινος ἀγαθοῦ παραίτιος γινόμενος
       τῶι κοινῶι, πονέσαντός τε τοῦ ναοῦ τοῦ ἐν τᾶι ἄκραι τοῦ
       τᾶς Ἀθάνας καὶ ἐγγί[ζ]οντος συνπετεῖν διὰ τὸ ἐξῶσθαι
       τοίχους [δ]ύο, τόν τε κείμενον ποτ' ἀνατολὰς καὶ τὸν πο-
  10   τὶ μεσαμβρίαν, καὶ εἰς τὰν ἐπισκευὰν αὐτοῦ γενομενᾶν
       ἐπαγγελιᾶν ὑπό τε κοινῶν καὶ ἰδιωτᾶν, τᾶς δὲ ἐπισυναγω-
       γᾶς τοῦ διαφόρου γινομένας πολυχρονίου, παρακληθεὶς
       ἐν τᾶι ἐκλησίαι ὑπὸ τῶν κτοινετᾶν συντελέσαι ἰ[δ]ίαι τὰ
       ἔργα ἐπαγγείλατο καὶ συνετέλεσε, ποτεπαγγείλατο
  15   δὲ καὶ ξυ[λ]ωσεῖν τὰς στέγας τὰ ποτι[δ]εόμενα καὶ κερα-
       μωσεῖν τελέσμασι τοῖς αὐτοῦ· καὶ συνετέλεσε ἀναγαγών
       τε τοὺς παρεπιδαμοῦντας τῶν πολιτᾶν³⁷ ἐπέδειξε τὰ
       ἔργα κα[λ]ῶς γεγονότα· ὅπως οὖν καὶ τὸ κοινὸν φαίνη-
       ται εὐχάριστόν <τ>ε ἐὸν καὶ τιμοῦν τοὺς ἀγαθοὺς τῶν

---

³⁷ The editor of *IG* XII.3 prefers τῶν Πολιτᾶν, that is demesmen of the Politai, Aristophanes' deme.

20   [ἀν]δρῶν, τύχαι ἀγαθᾶι, δε[δ]όχθαι [τ]ῷ κοινῶι, κυρω-
     [θέντο]ς τοῦδε τοῦ ψαφίσματος, ἐπαινέσαι καὶ στεφα-
     [νῶσαι Ἀρι]στοφάνη Ἀριστοφά[ν]ευς Πολίταν
     [χρυσέωι σ]τεφ[ά]νωι ἀρετᾶς ἕνεκα καὶ
     [φιλοδοξίας ἃν ἔχων] διατ[ελεῖ ε]ἰς [τ]ὸ κοινὸν τῶν
25   [ἐν Σύμαι κατοικούντων καὶ τᾶς ποτ]ὶ τοὺς θεοὺς
     [εὐσεβείας· –]

Interestingly, Aristophanes' service to the association is only vaguely hinted
at ('he always had a hand in the good things that befall the *koinon*') and the
uninitiated reader, ancient as well as modern, is left to guess whether Aristophanes was also a benefactor of the association. His services to the community,
the local *ktoina* (the name of which does not survive), on the other hand, are
described in great detail. On the reverse (not given above) the stele bears
a fragmentary additional decree which called for the election of a member
to be charged with petitioning the Rhodian *boula* and *damos* – presumably
for permission to set up the decree in a public sanctuary.[38] The request was
obviously granted, and given the subject matter of the decree it seems likely
that the sanctuary in which it was set up was that of Athana in the unknown
Symian *ktoina*, which may or may not have been the centre of the association's
cultic activities. Here the decree stood to remind any visitor to the sanctuary
not only of Aristophanes' generosity and care for his fellows, but also of the
admiration felt by this upright member of the community for the *en Symai
katoikountes*.[39]

Other associations too took pride in their connections and made an effort
to demonstrate their relationships with notable figures in the public sphere.
When the *Dioskouriastai Philokrateioi* honoured their benefactor, Nikagoras son
of Nikagoras and adopted son of Peisios, with a statue on the Lindian acropolis,
they made sure to mention the priesthoods of Athana Lindia and Artemis Kekoia
which Nikagoras had held.[40] Similarly, when the *Aphrodisiastai Soteriastai* voted
to dedicate a statue of their benefactor, Ploutarchos son of Heliodoros, they took
great care to demonstrate that the man who, so they claimed, had made them
the object of his *areta*, *philotimia*, *eunoia* and *dikaiosyne* was an important man in

---

[38] For similar petitions see *IG* XII.1 890 and Gabrielsen 1994b.
[39] There is no mention in the decree of any contribution by the association to the repair of the
sanctuary. The decree does, however, say that funds were promised by *koina* and private individuals, but that these promises were never honoured. Perhaps we are justified in detecting a
touch of embarrassment on behalf of this association behind all the accolades?
[40] *Lindos II* 285 (after 93 BCE), found on the Lindian acropolis below the stoa.

Rhodes.[41] Sacrificing eloquence for comprehensiveness, they listed every public office Ploutarchos had held. These included virtually every important office in the federal state: *agonothetas, tamias, stratagos, klarotas ton dikastan, epimeletas ton xenon* and *prytanis*. As with the *en Symai katoikountoi*, the benefactions towards the association are never explicated, but only glossed by the abstract moral qualities that supposedly motivated Ploutarchos. The fact that Ploutarchos was a well-known and revered artist, whose works could be seen in the *acropoleis* of Lindos, Kamiros and in the *asty*, is not even mentioned.[42]

Futhermore, the inscription included references to honours voted for Ploutarchos by three groups (*koina*) of Rhodian *synarchontes*: the *prytaneion synarchonton kai boulas grammateos koinon*, the *stratagon synarchonton koinon* and the *tamian synarchonton koinon*.[43] This further endorsement of Ploutarchos by the state's most esteemed officers reflected well on the association which enjoyed Ploutarchos' favour.

That the opinions of others, expressed through honours, counted for something and furthered the prestige of the association is underlined by a *koinon* of *Samothraikiastai Aphrodisiastai Borboritai*, also from the island of Syme, which included as their benefactor's credentials not only the honours bestowed upon him by another association, the *Adoniastai [---] Asklapiastai Syroi*, but also those voted for him by two of the island's *ktoinai*:[44]

> The *koinon* of the *Samothraikiastai Aphrodisiastai Borboritai* (set this up) over Euphrosynos of Idyma,[45] the metic and benefactor of the *koinon*. He is to be praised and crowned with a gold crown for the *areta* and *eunoia* he continues to hold towards us for all time, and he was crowned with gold crowns by us (for a third time?) and he was crowned by the *Adoniastai [---] Asklapiastai Syroi* with a gold crown and by the *ktoina* of [− − −] with a gold crown and by the *ktoina* of Epibomes with a gold crown for the *kalokagathia* he continues to hold towards the *koinon*. To the gods.

---

[41] *Annuario* n.s. 1–2 (1939/40) 151 no. 7.

[42] See Chapter 8, below.

[43] The same boards of magistrates also honoured a Kamirean citizen and, among other things, priest of Halios (*SEG* 33: 644). The occasion for these honours was his discharge of the prytany. Unlike Ploutarchos he was apparently never *stratagos* or *tamias*, and the honours for Ploutarchos were probably also voted in connection with his term as *prytanis* (mentioned immediately before; *Annuario* n.s. 1–2 [1939/40] 151 no. 7.10–13).

[44] *IG* XII.3 6.

[45] Or perhaps Sidyma.

[τ]ὸ κοινὸν Σαμοθρᾳκι[α]στᾶν Ἀ[φ]ρο[δισιασ]-
[τ]ᾶν Βορβοριτᾶν ὑπὲρ Ε[ὐ]φροσύνο[υ]
Ἰδυμέως μετοίκου [εὐ]εργέτα
[τ]οῦ κοινοῦ· ἐπαιν[εῖ] καὶ στεφανοῖ χρ[υ]-
5   [σέ]ῳ στεφάνῳ [ἀρε]τᾶς ἕνεκα καὶ
[εὐ]νοίας ἂν ἔχων διετέλ[ε]ι 'ς ἀμὲ τὸ[ν]
[ἅπ]αν<τα> χρόνον· καὶ ἐστεφανωμένο[ν]
[χ]ρυσέοις [στ]εφάνοις ὑπ' ἀμῶν τὸ τ[ρίτον]
[καὶ] ἐστεφανωμένον ὑπο Ἀ[δ]ωνιασ[τᾶν Ἀφροδισιασ]-
10   [τᾶν(?)] Ἀσκλαπιαστᾶν Σύρων [χρ]υσ[έῳ στεφάνῳ]
[καὶ] ὑπὸ τᾶς κτοίνας τᾶς ΗΛ – – –
χρυσέῳ στεφάνῳ καὶ ὑπο τᾶς κτο[ί]-
[ν]ας τᾶς Ἐπι[β]ωμοῦς(?) χρυσέῳ στε-
[φ]άνῳ καλοκἀγαθίας ἕνεκα ἄν ἔ-
15   [χ]ων [δ]ι[ε]τέ[λει] 'ς [τὸ κ]οινὸ[ν]
θεοῖς.

Similarly, the *koinon* of the *Samothraikiastai*, on the base that supported the funerary stele of a certain Moschion of Phaselis, recorded not only the gold crown they had voted for him, but that two other associations, the *Aphrodisiastai* and the *Panathenaistai*, had also found their benefactor worthy of praise.[46]

When it came to association benefactors, quantity was apparently a quality in itself. A plaque of Lartian marble from the eastern necropolis of Rhodes preserves the lower part of a list containing the names of eight benefactors, citizens and foreigners, followed by the abbreviations ΧΡΥ or ΘΑΛ for a gold or foliage crown respectively (Fig. 7.2). Clearly this plaque was meant to showcase the association's attractiveness to well-off and respectable members of the community.[47]

---

[46] *NSill* 43.

[47] *NSill* 47. The list does bear some resemblance to an inventory (*NSill* 7, second century) from the *asty* in which a number of citizens (men and women) are recorded for dedicating crowns. In this case, however, names are in the nominative and followed by either the verb *anethekan* (for a crown of foliage) or the preposition *apo* (for a gold crown). In *NSill* 47 the names are all in the dative case, which I take to signify that they were the recipients rather than the givers of crowns. A similar list of awards for benefactors is known from late-fourth-century Attica. Under the heading τούσδε ἐστεφάνωσεν τὸ κοινὸν τῶν | θιασωτῶν ἀρετῆς ἕνεκα | καὶ δικαιοσύνης τῆς εἰς τὸ κοινὸν τῶν θιασωτῶν, twenty-seven names appear, though without specification of the type of crown awarded (*IG* II² 2347).

Figure 7.2 *NSill* 47. List of crowns awarded (Ephorate of Antiquities of the Dodecanese – © Hellenic Ministry of Culture and Sports (N.3028/2002)).

PUBLIC RECOGNITION

No Rhodian association seems to have managed better to cultivate its relationship with the state than the *katoikeuntes hoi en Lindia polei kai georgeuntes hoi en tai Lindiai*. The association, which seems to have been formed by foreign merchants living in Lindos, had consistently found favour with the priests of Athana Lindia in a period stretching well over a century. A plethora of monuments on the Lindian acropolis bears evidence of their remarkably good connections with the Lindian establishment over a period of some century and half. Lindian priests, such as Aristodamos son of Onasandros, and *epistatai*, such as Kallianax son of Kleisimbrotos and Peisistratos son of Aglon, regularly and presumably with some pride added the name of this association to their personal monuments on the Lindian acropolis with reference to the honours which they had received from the association.[48] In these monuments the *katoikeuntes en Lindiai*

---

[48] *Lindos II* 300 (Aristodamos son of Onasandros, priest of Apollo and priest of Athana Lindia in 121 BCE and Artemis Kekoia); 249 (*epistatai* of 117/16 BCE); 264 (priest of Athana Lindia and perhaps *epistatas* c. 125–100 BCE); 391 (Lapheides son of Lapheides, priest of Athana Lindia in 10 CE). *Cl. Rhodos* 2 (1932) 210 no. 48 (priest of Apollo, c. 100–50 BCE). See Thomsen 2018 for a full review of the evidence.

polei kai georgeuntes en tai Lindiai are often mentioned directly after, but clearly separated from, the boards of civic-religious magistrates, the priests, the *archiero-thytas* and the *hierothytai*.

By 121 BCE, if not before, the *katoikeuntes hoi en Lindiai polei kai georgeuntes hoi en tai Lindiai* (appearing here simply as *katoikeuntes hoi en Lindiai polei*) are found interacting with Lindian civic-religious magistrates when they voted a crown to the priest of Athana Lindia.[49] In 117 or 116 they apparently joined with the college of Lindian *synhiereis* and the *archierothytas* in crowning the two *epistatai* elected by the Rhodian *damos* to take charge of the naval detatchment stationed at Lindos.[50] Their ambition to move closer to those members of the Lindian elite who regularly sought and obtained the major priesthoods is further stressed by the fact that the association for a while added *Athanaistai* to their name.[51] The close coordination among boards of public magistrates and a private association becomes even more curious since the private association seems to have replaced the *hierothytai*, who were otherwise always included with the priests and the *archierothytas*:

When Sosiphilos son of Aristes and Kallianax son of Kleisimbrotos were priests of Athana and Zeus Polieus, Peisistratos son of Aglon was elected *epistatas* by the (Rhodian) *damos* and crowned by the priests and the *archierothytas* and the *katoikeuntes en Lindiai polei*. To Athana Lindia and Zeus Polieus.

ἐπ᾽ ἱερέων τᾶς Ἀθάνας κ[α]ὶ
τοῦ Διὸς τοῦ Πολιέως
Σωσιφίλου τοῦ Ἀρ[ισ]τῆ
[Κ]αλλ[ι]άνακτος [Κ]λεισιμ[βρ]ότ[ου]
5   [Π]εισίστρατο[ς] Ἀγλῶνος
χειροτονηθεὶς ἐπ[ι]στάτα[ς] ὑπὸ [τοῦ]
δάμου καὶ στεφανωθεὶς ὑπό τε τ[ῶν]
ἱερέων καὶ τοῦ ἀρ[χιε]ροθ[ύ]τα
καὶ τῶν κατοικού[ν]τω[ν ἐ]ν Λινδίαι πόλ[ει]
10   Ἀθάναι Λινδία[ι κα]ὶ Διὶ Πολιεῖ.

In 38 BCE the name of the association appears in a joint dedication by the Lindian priests of that year for the priest of Athana Lindia. The twelve island

[49] *Lindos II* 264.3–6. If Blinkenberg's restoration of the second half of the inscription may be trusted, it would seem that the relationship between the priest and the *katoikeuntes hoi en Lindia polei kai georgeuntes hoi en tai Lindiai* stretched back to the former's term as priest of Pythian Apollo.
[50] *Lindos II* 249.7–10.
[51] *Lindos II* 300 with Gabrielsen 1997: 129 n. 94. Cf. Thomsen 2018.

demes of Lindos also joined in the dedication, but the private association blends in almost as a 'thirteenth deme' – a remarkable position not even afforded the demes of the Peraia or the islands, much less any other private association, and a good indication that the *katoikeuntes en Lindia polei kai georgeuntes en tai Lindiai* in terms of status had reached parity with the most privileged subdivisions of the Lindian state.[52]

As the year 23 CE was coming to an end, the *epistatai* in Lindos proposed to the *mastroi* and the Lindians that they change the way *choragoi* or chorus sponsors were elected for the Sminthia festival, or perhaps more precisely to expand eligibility. Hitherto the Lindians had elected their *choragoi* from among wealthy citizens only. This had also been practised in the *asty*, but at some point in the early first century BCE the Rhodians had opened up the liturgy to wealthy foreigners too. An unknown foreigner from Herakleia could boast of his *choragia* in a private monument found in the *asty*.[53]

The decree, proposed by the *epistatai*, contains the decision by the Lindian *mastroi* and assembly to select *choragoi* from both citizens and foreigners in accordance with the procedure employed by the federal state. In the event that no foreigner volunteered for one of the six spots reserved for foreigners, the *epistatai* are instructed to appoint foreign *choragoi* from among the members of the *katoikeuntes hoi en Lindia polei kai georgeuntes hoi en tai Lindiai* (IG XII.1 762):

> Concerning *choragoi*. Under the priest of Athana Kallikrates and the priest of Halios Rhodopeithes on the eleventh day of the month of Diosthyos it was decided by the *mastroi* and the Lindians. Motion of the *epistatai*. Since the Rhodian *damos* out of the greatest foresight act to preserve the honour of Dionysos in a good way and to pay for games and processions and sacrifices in every Sminthia, they hold elections of *choragoi* both from citizens and from foreigners and so also the Lindians may strive to be reverent to the god, it is to be decided by the Lindians when this decree is ratified: All the rest concerning the Sminthia is to be according to the old custom of the Lindians. The *epistatai* who are at any time in office shall further select in addition to the citizens (number?) elected *choragoi* and the rest of the *choragoi* from the *katoikeuntes kai georgeuntes in Lindiai polei* six foreigners if none volunteer, and those elected must each prepare the

---

[52] Thomsen 2018.

[53] *Annuario* n.s. 1–2 (1939/40) 151 no. 6; the ethnicon is all that remains of the name. Non-citizen *choragoi* appear in undated inscriptions: *IG* XII.1 157 (Philokrates of Ilion who was given *epidamia* and was *choragos* three times); 383 (Epigonos, a metic and former slave who was 'freed by the *polis*' and who had been *choragos* twice); 385 (Aristoboulos of Termessos, who was *choragos* three times); *NSill* 21 (Apollonios of Antioch, who was *choragos* twice); *AD* 25 B2 (1970) 524 no. 1 (Dorion, who was given *epidamia* and *enktesis* and was *choragos* twice [late Hellenistic]).

procession for the Sminthia just as the others . . . and they must do the
burning of incense . . .

frg. A.1 [ἐκκλησίας γενομένας συλλόγου γενομένου]
[ἐν Σμινθίῳ; θεάτρῳ;] περὶ χορα<γῶ>ν [ἐπ᾽ ἱερέως]
[τᾶς Ἀθάνας Καλλι]στράτου, τοῦ δὲ Ἁλίου Ῥοδο-
πε[ί]θευς, <Δ>ιοσ[θύ]ου ἑνδεκάτᾳ, ἔδοξε μαστροῖς
5   καὶ Λινδίοις· ἐπιστατᾶν γν<ώ>μα· ἐπειδὴ πλείσ-
ταν πρόνοιαν ὁ σύμπας δᾶμος <π>[οιεῖται(?)] εἰς τὸ
τὰς τοῦ Διονύσου τειμὰς συν[τηρεῖν καλῶς καὶ]
ἀγῶνας τελεῖν καὶ πονπὰς καὶ θυσίας [εἰς ἁ-]
εἰ Σμ<ιν>θ[ίοις;] χοραγῶν ποιούμενοι αἵρ[εσιν]
10   καὶ πολειτᾶν καὶ ξένων, ὁμοίως δὲ κα[ὶ Λίνδι-]
οι εἰς τὰν ποτὶ τὸν θεὸν εὐσέβειαν [φιλοτειμοῦν-]
ται, δεδόχθαι Λινδίοις, κυρωθέντος τοῦ-
δε τοῦ ψαφίσματος· τὰ μὲν ἄλλα πάντα γεί-
νεσθαι περὶ τ<ῶ>ν Σμινθί<ω>ν κατὰ τἀρ[χαῖον]
15   ἔ<θ>ισμα Λινδί<ω>[ν, ποτ]αιρείσθων [δὲ τοὶ ἐπιστάται]
τοὶ ἀεὶ ἐν ἀρχᾷ ἐόντες ποτ[ὶ τοῖς ἐκ πολειτᾶν]
αἱρουμένοις χοραγοῖς καὶ ἄλλο<υ>ς χοραγο<ὺ>ς
ἐκ τῶν κατοικεύντων καὶ γεωργεύντων ἐν
Λινδίᾳ πόλει ξένους ἕξ, εἴ κα μ<ή> τινες ἐπαν-
20   γέ<λλ>ωνται· τοὶ δὲ αἱρεθέντες στελλόντω [τὰν]
πο<νπ>ὰν ἐν τοῖς Σμινθίοις ἕκαστος καθά-
περ καὶ τοὺς ἄλλους <γ>έ<γ>ρα<π>τα<ι κ>αὶ ποι-
είσθων ἐ<π>ιθυσίαν ΑΝΕ[.]ΕΙΟΝΤΩΞΕΝΟΥQΙΝ
ΤΩΙ[- - - - - - - - - - - - - - - - -]

The decree has traditionally been read in the light of another decree of the
same year in which several measures were taken by the Lindians to remedy the
serious financial difficulties of the sanctuary of Athana Lindia (*Lindos* II 419).[54]
Though the sanctuary of Athana Lindia seems to have fallen on hard times, it
does not follow that the number of Lindian citizens who could afford to pay
for choruses had similar financial problems. At any rate it cannot account for
the decision of the federal assembly to allow foreigners to sponsor choruses.
The pride with which foreign residents of the *asty* advertised their choric liturgies is perhaps indicative that pressure to open up the choragy came from an
ever-growing class of wealthy foreigners whose civic ambition was matched
only by their wealth.[55] The details of this process are of course irretrievably

---

[54] Blinkenberg 1941: 581–2. *Contra* Thomsen 2018: 303–4.
[55] Thomsen 2018: 284 n. 2. Cf. Boyxen 2018: 240–9.

lost to us, but we may venture a guess: the fact that the Lindians made the *katoikeuntes hoi en Lindia polei kai georgeuntes hoi en tai Lindiai* stand as guarantors of the new system may perhaps be taken as an indication that the association had favoured a change in the system. They certainly had the connections within the top circles of the Lindian elite, as well as a clearly detectable civic ambition.

That ambition was seemingly fulfilled in 23 CE. With the passing of *IG* XII.1 762, the members of the *katoikeuntes en Lindia polei kai georgeuntes en tai Lindiai* gained special access to the prestigious liturgy – a probably coveted tool for the status enhancement of the individual member.[56] If what set 'public associations' apart from 'private associations' was the former's formal function vis-à-vis the *polis*, then the *katoikeuntes hoi en Lindia polei kai georgeuntes hoi en tai Lindiai* may be said to have almost made the transition from private association to public when it became a *polis*-recognised tax group.[57]

Theirs is a truly remarkable case, but as we shall see in the following section, its uniqueness consists in the degree to which they were integrated into the public organisation, and their popularity with the Lindian elite. Other associations remained wholly private, but displayed their admiration for the *polis* in imitation of its institutions and its values, as well as in benefactions made to the state.

One clear indication that members of associations were held in high esteem by their contemporaries is the overwhelming interest and attention with which the latter cultivated relationships with associations and the pride with which they displayed these connections before their *polis* and their peers. This status, as we shall see next, was at one and the same time both the result and the prerequisite for what was arguably the associations' most precious resource and most sought-after commodity: their endorsements.

CIVIC VIRTUES AND ASSOCIATION VIRTUES

Sometime in the early first century BCE, the *koinon* of the *Polykleioi Boarsai*, one of the associations sponsored by the Rhodian statesman Polykles, dedicated a statue to another benefactor of the association (*IG* XII.1 102):

> The *koinon* of the *Polykleioi Boarsai* honoured Peisikrates son of Peisistratos and adopted son of Nikasios with a gold crown and a

---

[56] The choragy is linked most clearly to social advancement in the case of Epigonos, a former slave from Lycian Rhodiapolis, who was manumitted by the *polis* and given status as a metic, and who sponsored two choruses (*IG* XII.1 383). Wilson 2000: 291.

[57] Thomsen 2018.

bronze statue because of the *areta* and *eunoia* and *philodoxia* which he continues to hold for the *koinon* of the *Polykleioi Boarsai*

[τὸ κ]οινὸν τὸ Πολυκλείων Β[οαρσᾶν]
ἐτίμασε
[Πεισι?]κράτη Πεισιστρά[του]
[κα]θ᾽ υοθεσίαν δὲ Νικάσιος
[χρυσ]έωι στεφάνωι καὶ εἰκόνι χα[λκέαι]
[ἀρετ]ᾶς ἕνεκα καὶ εὐνοίας κ[αὶ]
[φιλ]οδοξίας ἂν ἔχων διατελε[ῖ]
[εἰς] τὸ Πολυκλείων Βοαρσᾶν κοιν[όν].

We do not know how or in what capacity the son of Peisistratos had served the association. Such mundane matters are often left out of honorific inscriptions, both public and private, and the observer, ancient and modern, is instead provided with a list of virtues identified as the benefactor's motivation, in this case the honorand's *areta*, *eunoia* and *philodoxia*.

The inscription bears a rather striking resemblance to another honorific statue set up around that same time by the Rhodian *damos* (*IG* XII.1 90):

The people of Rhodes honours Gaios Ioulios Theuponpos son of Artemidoros because of the *areta* and *eunoia* which he continues to hold for the people of Rhodes

ὁ δᾶμος ὁ Ῥοδίων
ἐτίμασε
Γάϊον Ἰούλιον
Θεύπονπον Ἀρτεμιδώρου
ἀρετᾶς ἕνεκα καὶ εὐνοίας
ἂν ἔχων διατελεῖ
εἰς τὸ πλῆθος τὸ Ῥοδί[ω]ων.

Apparently, it was the same virtues that motivated both men: *areta* and *eunoia*, and in the case of the son of Peisistratos also *philodoxia*, another civic virtue common in public honorific monuments.[58]

The virtues identified by the associations as the source of their benefactors' behaviour towards them were all drawn from the *polis* vocabulary of civic virtues: *areta* (virtue), *eunoia* (goodwill), *philodoxia* (love of honour) and *dikaiosyne* (justice) are staples of the civic vocabulary not just in Rhodes but throughout

---

[58] E.g. *IG* XII.1 851 (Lindos); *Tit. Cam.* 110.46 (Kamiros); *IG* XII.1 1033.7 (*ktoina* of the Potidaioi, Karpathos).

the Greek world.[59] Each political community, however, had its preferences (which may have changed over time): the *andragathia* or *sophrosyne*, for instance, so important elsewhere were not used by any public body in Rhodes.[60] Nor are they found among the justifications for association honours and private associations. Overall, the dedicatory inscriptions of private associations show remarkable similarities with those of the state and its subdivisions – not only in form, but also in content. There was, in other words, no such thing as an 'association virtue', or rather, the virtues praised by Rhodian associations were the very same as those recognised by the state, with no additions of their own. When, for instance, *philotimia* begins to appear in public honorific decrees around the turn of the second and first centuries (it would only replace *philodoxia* completely after the first century CE), the associations reacted promptly by voting honours for their benefactors in response to their *philotimia*.[61] Since only few Rhodian decrees survive and even fewer preserve any motivational clause, we lack the sufficient context for an analysis of the precise contents of the virtues, and we must make do with their general meaning. Though each probably had a nuance that set them apart from one another, they all referred to the same basic condition, namely a contribution in person or from purse to the community, whether state, public subdivision or association, beyond what was expected of every citizen or member.

As we saw above, the associations took care that every benefaction received the proper response in the form of recognition of the benefactor and his virtues, and this to a degree which suggests that failure to respond appropriately was a violation of an unwritten but universally accepted norm of exchange between benefactor and beneficiary. As van Nijf has suggested, the demands of this norm of reciprocity may have worked the other way too, and the voting of honours and their announcement to the world may have caused the

---

[59] Veligianni-Terzi 1997: 216–27; Thomsen forthcoming a.

[60] *Andragathia*: Samos 54; 372. Athens: e.g. *IG* II² 103 and 500. *Sophrosyne* occurs a couple of times in Rhodes, but seems to have gone out of use by the late fourth century: *Lindos* II 40 (c. 350); *Cl. Rhodos* 9 (1938) 83 (c. 350); *AE* (1967) 128 (fourth century).

[61] Public recognition of *philotimia*/*philoteimia*: *IG* XII.1 1032 (second century or later); *Annuario* 8–9 (1925/6) 321 no. 4 (Roman) Associations: *Lindos* II 652 (undated, but association attested in 129); *IG* XII.1 156 (undated, but association attested in second century BCE) 937 (first century CE?). The personal name Philotimos makes its appearance in the second century. A certain Philotimos son of Philotimos was priest of Apollo Erethmios in Ialysos in 38/7 BCE (*SER* 5b), and a Pythagenes son of Philotimos appears in a list of names dated by prosopography to 100–68 BCE (*SEG* 39: 732; Kontorini 1989: 32). Since two associations are attested in the second century (one in 129) it would in fact be possible to argue that private associations were first movers of the 'philotimatic turn'. This, if true, would reverse the chain of causality and be evidence for a remarkable importance of associations in shaping civic discourse. Though certainly possible, the nature of the evidence, both the state of preservation and the lack of precise and secure dates, however, condemns this interpretation to the footnotes.

'benefactor' to reciprocate.[62] A variation of this scheme is possibly found in the decree by the *hoi en Symai katoikeuntes* for Aristophanes son of Aristophanes, who was explicitly honoured for a benefaction made not to the association but to a *ktoina*. Is it possible that the association was in fact angling for a new benefactor? The cost of having a decree inscribed on stone and the trouble of travelling to Rhodes for permission may be thought to be too extravagant, but it must be remembered that the decree had value to the association in itself. Even if the trap failed to snap shut, the association would still have made an important contribution to their own public image by putting themselves in line with the state and its subdivisions or even other private associations.

CORPORATE ENDORSEMENTS AND THE RHODIAN MONUMENTAL ORDER

One way for the state to show appreciation of the behaviour of an individual towards it was through the erection of a statue of him or her. In the late first century CE Dio Chrysostom accused the Rhodians of handing out statues 'like parents who buy those cheap dolls for their children'.[63] This seems to have been an old custom among the Rhodians. The practice was not just restricted to the Rhodian assembly. The three old *poleis* and their demes also dedicated statues in honour of outstanding citizens.[64] On the Lindian acropolis alone, close to thirty bases of honorific statues have been found, all issued by the Lindians. Across time and space, from the mid-third century into the Roman period and in the Peraia or on the island, and from all levels of the Rhodian state, the inscriptions display a remarkable similarity bordering on uniformity. One such honorific statue with its inscription (*Lindos II* 415) from early-first-century CE Lindos may serve as an example.

Nothing of the statue survives, but from cuttings on the rectangular marble base it may be presumed that it once supported a bronze statue of a man in a walking posture.[65] An inscription on the base informs the spectator of the situation which resulted in the erection of the statue and the relationship between the honouring body and the honorand.

In fairly large letters (0.025–0.027 m), as if in a heading, the first line of the accompanying inscription reads: 'The Lindians honoured'. Only in the second

---

[62] Van Nijf 1997: 113–20.
[63] Dio Chrys. *Or.* 31.153.
[64] Honorific statues dedicated by the Rhodians: *IG* XII.1 61; 85; *AIV* 57 (1898) 259, no. 2; by the Lindians: e.g. *Lindos II* 169; 307; *IG* XII.1 846; by the Kamireans: *Tit. Cam.* 86; 92; by the demes: *NSill.* 27 (Bybassioi); *RIPR* 6 (Kedreatai); *Lindos II*, 216 (Nettidai).
[65] *Lindos II*, 415 with Blinkenberg's comments.

and third line, inscribed in smaller letters (0.015–0.018), do we encounter the
name of the object of the honouring, Melanthios son of Zenon and adopted
son of Iason, who was presumably also the subject of the bronze statue above.
The inscription then continues to flesh out the meaning of 'honoured' through
a list of the prizes conferred upon Melanthios by the Lindians: a gold crown,
a bronze statue, front seat at the games, dining in the *hierothyteion*, the privilege of wearing the crown in those festivals that the Lindians hold, and the
proclamation of these honours. Only at the very end of the inscription are
we informed that the Lindians will do this in recognition of Melanthios' piety
towards the gods and his *eunoia* and *philotimia* towards the Lindians and the
people of Rhodes. What benefaction or public service lay behind 'goodwill'
and 'generosity' is never explicated. This is all the more curious since we know
that Melanthios served as priest of Athana Lindia in 20 CE. This might indicate that he was honoured sometime prior to his term as priest, but none of
the surviving inscriptions which accompanied honorific statues gives additional
information on the honorand, and in at least one case a priest of Athana Lindia
was honoured after his term.[66]

In the second century the famous Rhodian (but also Lindian) politician Astymedes son of Theaidetos was honoured with a similar statue on
the Lindian acropolis.[67] Not far from it stood another statue of Astymedes
given by the demesmen of the Nettidai.[68] The wording of the accompanying
inscription echoes that of the Lindians. Whether Astymedes was dissatisfied
with the number or quality of the statues is impossible to say, but he commissioned the famous sculptor Demetrios son of Diomedon, who was at the
height of his career and popularity, to execute yet another statue which he
set up on the Lindian acropolis.[69] To judge from their bases, all three were of

---

[66] This seems to be Blinkenberg's assumption in dating *Lindos II* 415 to 'before 20 CE'. Though
several priests of Athana Lindia were honoured by the Lindians alone or by the *mastroi* and
the Lindians, none had their priesthood (or any other priesthood or office) mentioned in
the inscriptions that accompanied their statues. Zenodotos son of Diophantos and grandson
of Zenodotos can be found in *Lindos II* 1 as priest of Athana Lindian of the year 64. He was
honoured by the Lindians on two separate occasions, the first time in *Lindos II* 281b under the
same name. Whether that was before or after his priesthood we cannot tell, but by the time of
the second occasion (*Lindos II* 309) he had been adopted, presumably at a very advanced age,
by a certain Onasandros (perhaps the son of Aristodamos?). Priests honoured by (the *mastroi*
and) the Lindians: *IG* XII.1 846 (118); 847 (22); 852/856 (154); *Lindos II* 243 (124); 297 (74); 307
(65); 379 (25).

[67] *IG* XII.1 852/856.

[68] *Lindos II* 216.

[69] *Lindos II* 217. Among other statues, Demetrios had made that of Eudamos son of Dexicharis
(*Cl. Rhodos* 2 [1932] 192 no. 20); see Chapter 3 above.

bronze and of similar size. What was different was the situation from which they resulted. While the first two were dedications of the Lindians and the Nettidai respectively and kept Astymedes in an honorific (but also passive) place, the third offered Astymedes an opportunity to assert himself independently. The inscription simply reads: 'Astymedes son of Theaidetos who was priest of Athana Lindia and Zeus Polieus', the first and only indication that Astymedes had in fact won and held the prestigious priesthood.

Astymedes was not alone in taking the opportunity to dedicate a monument for himself. On the acropolis of Lindos, in the agora of the Fountain House in Kamiros and in the Rhodian *asty* several such personal monuments have been found, dedicated by prominent members of the Rhodian elite or by members of their families. In form and content the accompanying inscriptions display enough similarity for us to speak of a distinct genre.

One such monument of self-aggrandisement (*Tit. Cam.* 84, Fig. 7.3) was put up for Aristombrotidas son of Aristombrotidas, the Kamirean priest of Athana and *damiourgos* of c. 171 and later *epimeletas ton xenon* of Rhodes (whom we have come across several times already), by members of his immediate family:

Aristombrotidas son of Aristombrotidas
Kritoboulos son of Aristombrotidas for his brother, Aristombrotidas and Nausippos sons of Kritoboulos for their uncle, Damaineta daughter of Kritoboulos for her husband, who was priest of Athana Polias and Zeus Polieus and who was *damiourgos* and who was honoured and crowned by the Kamireans with a gold crown and who was crowned by the *Asklapiastai hoi en Kamiroi* with a gold crown and who was crowned by the *Hermaistai hoi en Kamiroi* with a gold crown, and who was crowned by the *Sarapiastai hoi en Kamiroi* with a gold crown, and who was crowned by the *Kouriastai hoi en Kyteloi* with a gold crown, and who was crowned by the *hoi Triktoinoi en Leloi* with a gold crown. To the Gods. Pythokritos and Asklapiodoros son(s) of Zenon Rhodians made (it).

    Ἀριστομβροτίδας Ἀριστομβροτ[ίδα].
    Κριτόβουλος Ἀριστομβροτίδα ὑπὲρ τοῦ ἀδ[ελφοῦ]
    Ἀριστομβροτίδας καὶ Ναύσιππος Κριτοβούλου ὑπὲρ τοῦ [θία]
    Δαμαινέτα Κριτοβούλου ὑπὲρ τοῦ ἀνδρὸς
5   ἱερατεύσαντος Ἀθάνας Πολιάδος καὶ Διὸς Πολιέως
        καὶ δαμιουργήσαντος
      καὶ τιμαθέντος καὶ στεφανωθέντος
        ὑπὸ Καμιρέων χρυσέωι στεφάνωι
      καὶ στεφανωθέντος χρυσέοις στεφάνοις

Figure 7.3 *Tit. Cam.* 84. Inscribed statue base of Aristombrotidas son of Aristombrotidas set up by his family in Kamiros (Ephorate of Antiquities of the Dodecanese – © Hellenic Ministry of Culture and Sports (N.3028/2002)).

10 ὑπὸ Ἀσκλαπιαστᾶν τῶν ἐν Καμίρωι
   καὶ στεφανωθέντος χρυσέωι στεφάνωι
   ὑπὸ Ἑρμαιστᾶν τῶν ἐν Καμίρωι
   καὶ στεφανωθέντος χρυσέωι στεφάνωι
   ὑπὸ Σαραπιαστᾶν τῶν ἐν Καμίρωι
15 καὶ στεφανωθέντος χρυσέωι στεφάνωι
   ὑπὸ Κουραιστᾶν τῶν ἐν Κυτήλωι
   καὶ στεφανωθέντος χρυσέωι στεφάνωι
   ὑπὸ Τρικτοίνων τῶν ἐν Λέλωι
   θεοῖς.
20 Πυθόκριτος καὶ Ἀσ<κ>ληπιόδωρος Ζήνωνος Ῥόδιοι ἐποίησαν.

The inscription may be broken down into four sections or themes. (A, l. 1)
First comes the name of the honorand, in this case Aristombrotidas son of
Aristombrotidas. (B, ll. 2–4) This is followed by the *oikos*, consisting of his
wealthy brother Kritoboulos, who often spent his money on public building
projects, and his politically ambitious nephews Nausippos and Aristombrotidas,
who in their turn would become prominent members of the magisterial elite,
and last his wife and cousin (or perhaps niece), Damaineta. (C, ll. 5–8) Next
are the civic subdivisions. The civic-religious offices are mentioned before the
section is rounded off with a reference to the fact that the citizens of Kamiros
had endorsed Aristombrotidas' civic virtues by voting him honorific crowns.
(D, ll. 9–18) The honours from the Kamireans are immediately followed by
those from five private associations. First were the *Asklapiastai en Kamiroi*, the
Hermaistai en Kamiroi and the *Sarapiastai en Kamiroi* with which Aristombrotidas
had joined an *epidosis*. Finally come the *Kouriastai en Kyteloi* and an association
of *ktoinetai* based in Lelos.

To the ancient observer this must have been a familiar code. When a crown
was awarded it was inevitably in response to the civic virtues of *areta*, *eunoia*
and *philodoxia*, which were so intimately connected with the procedure that
they hardly needed mentioning. Every so often, however, and just in case, the
more meticulous among the elite added the motivation: 'because of his *areta*
and *eunoia*', or the like, so as to leave no one in doubt.[70] And here too quantity
was a quality. Polykles, the Lindian statesman, recorded the honours voted by
eight different associations, but was outdone by another (but unnamed) Rhodian with naval exploits to his name. His monument stood somewhere in the
asty, but only a single fragment survives. He had cast his social net wide, for the
fragment records the names of no fewer than twenty-three associations that at

[70] *Tit. Cam.* 96a; *IG* XII.1 43; 827; *Lindos II* 303; 400.

some point had honoured him.[71] The range not only attests to the diversity of the associations in Rhodes, but also shows that members of the Rhodian elite sought to establish relationships with a wide variety of groups. The associations include groups of soldiers, fellow magistrates, kinsmen, teachers, *technitai*, citizens, foreigners and devotees of both domestic and 'foreign' gods.[72] Though to us most of them are hardly more than a name or yet another association, to the inhabitants of the Rhodian *asty* they might very well have been familiar, even household names.

The importance of such corporate endorsements is further underlined by the tendency for members of the elite to found their own associations or to enter into steady relationships with existing ones. Astymedes son of Theaidetos, along with his father, sponsored an association, as did another Theaidetos, the son of Autokrates, a priest of Athana Lindia with naval exploits in his résumé[73] and several other Rhodian naval commanders.[74] Polykles, who seems to have endeavoured to surpass everyone in everything, sponsored two different associations, the *Polykleioi* and the *Polykleioi Boarsai*, but even he was outdone by Timapolis son of Euphragoras and adopted son of Timapolis, who cultivated no fewer than six associations.[75]

ASSOCIATIONS AS CIVIL SOCIETY

Hieroboula daughter of Gorgosthenes has the honour of being one of the few women, as far as we know, to have been honoured with a statue on the

---

[71] *Annuario* 1–2 (1939/40) 165 no. 19. Maiuri assigned the inscription to the third century on epigraphic criteria (*Annuario* 2 [1916] 139 no. 10). Maillot (2005: II 20–1), however (following Berthold 1984: 44), suggests that the Pausistratos who gave name to the *Pausistra[teio]i* (l. 4) may be identified as the nauarch of 190 BCE, the first to use Greek fire (Pol. 21.7.5), and that the Astymedes who gave name to the *Astymedeioi sysstrateusan[toi]* was the son of Theaidetos, also of Polybian fame (see above). Berthold, however, misread lines 4–5 as saying that Pausistratos' association was one of *technitai*, whom he suggests may have been behind the invention of Greek fire. The *technitai*, however, were the τεχνιτᾶν τῶν π[ερὶ τ]ὰς Διονύ[σου] Μούσας and though undoubtedly crafty people probably did not invent Greek fire. Maillot further points to the existence of a Λητοδωρείων Πα[υσιστρατείων κοινον] (*Lindos II* 264), but there is no reason to think the two connected. Pausistratos is not an uncommon name and for the Lindian association the restoration is far from secure. As for Astymedes, he very probably did sponsor an association, but whether this association also belonged to him is less certain.

[72] *Annuario* n.s. 1–2 (1939/40) 165 no. 19.

[73] *Lindos II* 1; 293.bII.21 (*hierothytas*, 86 BCE); benefactor of the *Theaideteioi synst[rateuomenoi]* (*IG* XII.1 75).

[74] Antiochos, the naval archon mentioned in *IG* XII.1 43, probably gave his name to the *Apolloniastai Antiocheioi sysstrateusamenoi* (*NSill* 18.26–7); *Haliastai Haliadai Hesteioi* (*Lindos II* 292). Gabrielsen 1997: 127–8.

[75] *Lindos II* 252 (see above, p. 138).

Lindian acropolis. Her statue and accompanying inscription formed part of a larger monument, which included a statue of her husband Kallistratos son of Kallistratos, a prominent member of the Lindian elite who had been priest of Athana Lindia in 23 CE.[76]

Both husband and wife had at some point been honoured by the Rhodian *boula* and by the Lindian *mastroi* in 22 CE, the year before her husband served as priest of Athana Lindia, and again by the *mastroi* a year later. But here Hieroboula's and Kallistratos' lists of honours diverge. Kallistratos was honoured by a number of boards of civic officers: the Lindian *epistatai* under the leadership of one Hippias and perhaps also by representatives of the Lindian *phyla* and the Rhodian *stratagoi* of which he had himself been part. To these were added a parade of civic-religious officers who had served in the year in which Kallistratos had been priest: the *hierotamiai* of Dionysos and the priests of Pythian Apollo, Serapis, Dionysos, Artemis Kekoia, Apollo Olios, Poseidon Hippios, Apollo Kamyndos, Apollo Karnios, the *archierothytas* and the twelve *hierothytai*. Finally the list included the *epistatai* under Hippias (again), the *molpos* and the *architekton*.[77]

Hieroboula, on the other hand, was honoured by a number of private associations. (1) First were two sections of the *Panathenaistai strateuomenoi*, one that served on the *triemiolia* Euandria under the archon Lysimachos and an unknown *epiplous*, and another that served on the *triemiolia* Eirena under an unknown archon and the *epiplous* Diodotos.[78] Both groups awarded her a gold crown. (2) These were followed by the *patriotai ton Grenadai*, who bestowed honours on Hieroboula which included gold crowns as well as the dedication of a statue in painted armour on her behalf. This was done in cooperation with (3) the *katoikeuntes en Lindiai polei kai georgeuntes en tai Lindiai*. Finally (4) the association of *Athaniastai Lindiastai Damageteioi* are noted for a gold crown before the list is rounded off with the rather sweeping statement that she had been 'crowned by all the *eranoi* in the year of Kallistratos because of the *areta* and piety she showed the gods and the *eunoia* and generosity she showed them [i.e. the *eranoi*]'.[79]

This clear division of labour (if receiving praise may in itself be considered laborious) can hardly be incidental. It reflects a conscious division of labour between the priest and his wife: while Kallistratos had sought recognition from the state and its agents, Hieroboula had courted the private associations.

Most surprising is that the organisations which we have throughout identified as 'private associations' seem to have been recognised as a distinct section of Lindian society, separate from the state and its institutions. No comprehensive

---

[76] *Lindos II* 420.
[77] *Lindos II* 420b.
[78] See Chapter 6.
[79] *Lindos II* 420a (quotation at 420a.26–30).

label for this section of society is provided; it does, though, come close to what modern social scientists call 'civil society'.

Civil society, however, is a troubled and troubling concept caught half-way between ideal and heuristic concept. As an analytical concept it is under constant pressure from its idealistic counterpart, hailed both inside and outside academia as an unqualified social good, which must be defended where it is found and exported to where it does not exist.[80]

Civil society, according to most definitions, is a polite society. Associations working in violence, such as the mafia, or for-profit associations, such as business corporations, are usually excluded for being 'uncivil'.[81] What constitutes 'civility' is usually the commitment to a set of values or ideals about social interaction that constitute the Good Society. In fact, it is the percieved abillity of private associations (or voluntary associations, as they are often called) to school the individual in these values through repeated face-to-face interaction that has led some social scientists to see in private associations the remedy to just about every evil in society.[82]

The values that combine to constitute civility are usually what may be called democratic values: (1) voluntarism, the freedom to engage with society uncoerced, especially by the state; (2) equality; (3) non-violence; and (4) non-sectarianism.[83] This concept of civility is of course shaped by a particular historical process in Europe and North America from the seventeenth century onwards, and as such is not immediately applicable to the ancient world. However, it is perhaps not completely applicable to the modern world either, since all the components of civil society are ideals (which one may both aspire to and fail to achieve), which again leaves the concept of civil society lost somewhere between what is and what ought to be.

This might be thought to render civil society altogether useless for analytical purposes, but alternatively we might embrace the concept and find that its heuristic value lies precisely in the tension between ideal and reality.[84] But if we are to do so, we must first modify our definition of 'civility' to fit the context of Hellenistic Rhodes; and no institution was more civil than the *polis*. Man was after all, as Aristotle wrote, by nature a *polis* animal. In fact, membership in a *polis* was what separated man from other creatures: 'a man who is incapable of entering into partnership, or who is so self-sufficing that he has no need to do so, is no part of a *polis*, so that he must be either a lower animal or a god'.[85]

[80] Hann 1996: 2–3; Seligman 1992: 201–6.
[81] Edwards 2004: 40–9.
[82] Edwards 2004: 37–53.
[83] Edwards 2004: 40–9; Putnam 2000: 21–4; Doyle 1977: 333–4.
[84] For a criticism of the concept of 'uncivil society' and the value judgement it entails, see Bob 2011.
[85] Arist. *Pol.* 1253a27–9, 'ὁ δὲ μὴ δυνάμενος κοινωνεῖν ἢ μηδὲν δεόμενος δι' αὐτάρκειαν οὐθὲν μέρος πόλεως, ὥστε ἢ θηρίον ἢ θεός'.

The commitment to the democratic *polis* mode of organisation is a defining feature of private associations. It drives a wedge through society, separating the private and civil associations we have come across so far from uncivil society, a section of Rhodian society which we have not mentioned until now. This is due to the nature of our evidence for Rhodian society, which is almost entirely epigraphic and therefore dependent on adherence to the democratic *polis* mode of organisation, with the epigraphic habit it entailed. But we have come across their Roman counterparts in the passage from Livy quoted at the beginning of this chapter. Livy's associations were secret societies bent on outrageous promiscuity before they turned to murderous intrigue against the state and against polite society. To these we could add the secret sworn societies of late-fifth-century Athens, which, according to Thucydides, lurked and plotted behind closed doors until the democracy, shaken by defeats in the Peloponnesian War, was ripe for toppling.[86] Another example would be the so-called 'hellfire clubs', also of Classical Athens, which even took names such as *Kakodaimoniastai*, a malicious inversion of *Agathodaimoniastai*, presumably in mockery of what they thought was the most pretentious behaviour on the part of the *hoi polloi*;[87] plainly they did not care about civility.

But others did. To distance themselves from such uncivil society (be it real or imagined), private associations adopted the guise of the *polis*, the quintessential civil society, and conducted themselves in the same manner. They constantly interacted with the *polis* by behaving like public subdivisions, rallying with the demes, for instance, to join public subscriptions, and by seeking the patronage of the state's agents, the magisterial elite.

When Hieroboula claimed that she had been 'crowned by all the *eranoi*', she of course did not mean to say that she had been honoured by every more-or-less formal group of individuals in Lindos. What she did mean to say was that she had received golden crowns from everyone of a particular kind of group: namely those groups which had assumed the democratic *polis* mode of organisation, each of which had made its collective decision to bestow a gold crown (itself a *polis* prize) by voting in assemblies organised by magistrates, and most likely recording the decision on a stele.

In the centuries that preceded Hieroboula and Kallistratos, members of the Rhodian magisterial elite had cultivated this civil society alongside their patronage of the state and its subdivisions. One reason was surely its flexibility. New associations could be formed and membership regulated in ways not possible with their public counterparts.

---

[86] Thuc. 8.54.4. Calhoun 1913.

[87] Lys. frg. 53. (Cf. Dem. 54.14–20, 39. Calhoun 1913: 32; Parker 1996: 335–6.)

CHAPTER 8

The Corporate *Polis*

We began this study by noting the existence of two different *poleis* within the ancient Greek city-state. One was the state, an exclusive community of the citizens; the other was the city, or the social sphere, a 'corporate *polis*' made up of various corporate groups, recalling Aristotle's association of associations. At the centre of both *poleis* stood a small group of wealthy families who became benefactors and, through benefactions, also the leading members of those associations, both public and private, to which they belonged. The central contention of this study has been that the relationships formed within and between individuals, families and associations greatly influenced – in fact, shaped – the course of politics in Hellenistic Rhodes, and our findings may be briefly summarised.

The first concern the families themselves. Family ties meant access to two important resources: wealth and experience. Despite the scanty nature of the sources, we nevertheless have ample evidence of father–son cooperation in politics, with that of Theaidetos and Astymedes being the most famous. Through marriage and adoption, members of the elite formed alliances between families which could offer either experience or wealth, or both. Wealth and experience were key resources without which entry into the ranks of the magisterial elite was seriously hampered. Those who were without distinguished pedigree and therefore without the patronage of experienced members of the magisterial elite resorted to marriage and adoption in order to secure access to the family networks through which these resources flowed.

The same individuals who occupied high office on the federal level also took a keen interest in the public subdivisions to which they belonged. The three old *poleis* still retained a measure of independence and competed against each other at the federal level. In both Lindos and Kamiros, demesmen sought

to expand and maintain the reputation and status of their demes through benefactions to the state. In this effort they were aided by the elite, who often gave
their money on behalf of their demes. In return they won the loyalty of their
demesmen, who also seem to have taken no small pride in the success of those
of their numbers who achieved high office. On the available evidence it is difficult to see what local interests were behind the local patriotism of the demes.
Furthering their own standing was certainly one, but in one case, in the early
fourth century BCE, the demesmen of the twelve Lindian demes displayed a
keen awareness that their interests were being threatened, and reacted promptly
in denying outsiders access to Lindian office. In this effort they found support
in their own members of the magisterial elite, for whom Lindian office was an
important stepping stone to federal office, and for whom the threat of outside
intrusion into Lindian civic institutions provided an excellent opportunity to
act as protectors and strengthen ties with both their demesmen and the Lindian
community as a whole. For those who wanted in, the deme was also a platform.
As the Lindian island demes drew closer together to fight off the attempt to
widen access to Lindian magistracies and priesthoods, leading members of the
Physkioi organised an effort to display their 'Lindian-ness' through a strong
contribution to the adornment of Athana Lindia's sanctuary.

Patronage of the public subdivisions was augmented by the formation of
relationships with a number of private associations. The associations which
cultivated strong ties between members in some cases provided neat reservoirs
for key human resources, especially concerning the successful performance
of liturgies. More importantly, however, a large number of Rhodian citizens
organised themselves into associations and established ties with leading members of the Rhodian magisterial elite. Through these associations, members
of the elite had access to the one of the most precious political resource the
associations had to offer, namely their political support.

But political support went beyond votes. Equally important, the connections between members of the elite and private associations were broadcast,
both by the associations and by the elite, through monumental epigraphy, and
both took considerable pride in their connections. From the point of view of
the associations, cooperation with the elite formed a vital step in the process
of claiming a respectable position in Rhodian society. This process was begun
by assuming the guise of the *polis* and mimicking the behaviour of the demes
in contributing to state *epidoseis*, and completed through the establishing of ties
with the foremost agents of the Rhodian state. Their collective efforts resulted
in the creation of a separate section of the corporate *polis*; one marked by the
adherence to *polis* values, or, as we suggested in the preceding chapter, a civil
society.

Members of the elite were not slow to realise the political potential of the
associations. Through benefactions, the elite secured access to vital human

resources, above all votes. But these alliances were not made in the proverbial smoke-filled rooms out of public view. On the contrary, members of the elite publicised them widely and added the names of several associations to the monuments they set up in commemoration of their civic careers. The civility of the associations rubbed off on their benefactors, and the honours were presented as testimonials to their benevolence and civic-mindedness; their *areta*, *eunoia* and *philodoxia*.

The efforts on behalf of members of the elite to tie associations ever more closely to themselves, as reflected through the adoption of a benefactor's name, is in itself good evidence that some associations reserved a good measure of independence for themselves. In turn this suggests that behind the polite salutations of a benefactor's civic virtues lay special interests, which members thought to further through contact with a member of the political establishment. If this is so, then politics not only extended into society as a means by which political leaders consolidated their power; it also emanated from it.

The relationship between the individual and the state (or perhaps rather the state's agents) was mediated and informed by the associations, both public and private. For any Rhodian citizen, politics was guided by membership of one of the old *poleis* and then of a deme with its own special interests. To these were added the private associations, which formed strong ties with particular members of the magisterial elite and which acted in support of their benefactor. All these introduced a measure of representativeness into the otherwise direct democracy of Hellenistic Rhodes. In other words, the *polis* as a political community was never simply a union of the citizens. The citizens themselves were split between their membership in various associations, both public and private. Whether in the sense 'state' or 'city', the *polis* of Hellenistic Rhodes was a corporate *polis*.

Bibliography

Anderson, G. 2009. 'The Personality of the Greek State'. *JHS* 129. 1–22.

Andrewes, A. 1957. 'The Patrai of Camiros'. *BSA* 52. 30–7.

Aneziri, S. 2003. *Die Vereine der dionysischen Techniten im Kontext der hellenistischen Gesellschaft*. Stuttgart.

Arnaoutoglou, I. 2003. *Thusias heneka kai sunousias: Private Religious Associations in Hellenistic Athens*. Athens.

Arnold, I. R. 1936. 'Festivals of Rhodes'. *AJA* 40.4. 432–6.

Badoud, N. 2010. 'Une famille de bronziers originaire de Tyr'. *Zeitschrift für Papyrologie und Epigraphik* 172. 125–43.

— 2011. 'L'intégration de la Pérée au territoire de Rhodes' in Badoud, N. (ed.), *Philologos Dionysios: Mélanges offerts au professeur Denis Knoepfler*. Geneva. 533–66.

— 2015. *Le temps de Rhodes: Une chronologie des inscriptions de la cité fondée sur l'étude de ses institutions*. Munich.

Baslez, M. F. 1998. 'Les associations dans la cité grecques et l'apprentissage du collectif'. *Ktema* 23. 431–40.

— 2001. 'Entre traditions nationales et intégration: Les associations sémitiques du monde grec' in Ribichini, S., Rocchi, M. and Xella, P. (eds), *La questione delle influenze vicino-orientali sulla religione greca: Stato degli studi e prospettive della ricerca: Atti del Colloquio internazionale di studi (Roma, 20–22 maggio 1999)*. Rome. 235–47.

Bayliss, A. J. 2011. *After Demosthenes: The Politics of Early Athens*. London.

Bean, G. and Cook, J. M. 1957. 'The Carian Coast III'. *ABSA* 52. 58–146.

Benincampi, L. 2008. *I koina di Rodi*. (Unpublished dissertation, Università degli studi di Trieste).

Berthold, R. M. 1984. *Rhodes in the Hellenistic Age*. Ithaca, NY.

Blinkenberg, C. 1912. *La chronique du temple lindien. Exploration archéologique de Rhodes (Fondation Carlsberg) IV*. Copenhagen.

— 1941. *Lindos: Fouilles et Recherches 1902–1914: II: Inscriptions*. Copenhagen.

Bob, C. 2011. 'Civil and Uncivil Society' in Edwards, M. (ed.), *The Oxford Handbook of Civil Society*. Oxford. 209–19.

Boyxen, B. 2018. *Fremde in der hellenistischen Polis Rhodos zwischen Nähe und Distanz*. Berlin.

Bresson, A. 1980. 'Rhodes: Une famille camiréen de commerçants en blé'. *Index* 9. 144–9.

— 1988. 'Richesse et pouvoir à Lindos à l'époque hellénistique' in Dietz, S. and Papachristodoulou, I. C. (eds), *Archaeology in the Dodecanese*. Copenhagen. 154–74.

— 2016a. *The Making of the Ancient Greek Economy: Institutions, Markets, and the Growth of the City-States*. Princeton.

— 2016b. 'Women and Inheritance in Ancient Sparta: The Gortynian Connection'. *Studi Ellenistici* 30. 9–68.

Buskens, V. 2002. *Social Networks and Trust*. Dordrecht.

Calhoun, G. M. 1913. *Athenian Clubs in Politics and Litigation*. Austin.

Camia, F. 2011. 'Spending on the *agones*: The Financing of Festivals in the Cities of Roman Greece'. *Tyche* 26. 41–76.

Carlsson, S. 2010. *Hellenistic Democracies: Freedom, Independence and Political Procedure in Some East Greek City-States*. Stuttgart.

Chaniotis, A. 2005. *War in the Hellenistic World*. Oxford.

Coleman, J. S. 1990. *Foundations of Social Theory*. Cambridge, MA.

Coleman, W. D. and Skogstad, G. 1990. 'Policy Communities and Policy Networks: A Structural Approach' in Coleman, W. D. and Skogstad, G. (eds), *Policy Communities and Public Policy in Canada: A Structural Approach*. Mississauga, ON. 14–33.

Constantakopoulou, C. 2015. 'Beyond the *Polis*' in Taylor, C. and Vlassopoulos, K. (eds), *Communities and Networks in the Ancient Greek World*. Oxford. 213–36.

Cook, J. M. 1961. 'Cnidian Peraea and Spartan Coins'. *JHS* 81. 56–72.

Cotter, W. 1996. 'The Collegia and Roman Law: State Restrictions on Voluntary Associations 64 BCE–200 CE' in Kloppenborg, J. and B. Wilson (eds), *Voluntary Associations in the Greco-Roman World*. 74–89.

Cox, C. A. 1998. *Household Interests: Property, Marriage Strategies, and Family Dynamics in Ancient Athens*. Princeton.

Davies, J. K. 1971. *Athenian Propertied Families 600–300 B.C.* Oxford.

— 1981. *Wealth and the Power of Wealth in Classical Athens*. New York.

Dietz, S. and Papachristodoulou, I. C. 1988. *Archaeology in the Dodecanese*. Copenhagen.

Dignas, B. 2003. 'Rhodian Priests after the Synoecism'. *AncSoc* 33. 35–51.

Dmitriev, S. 1999. 'The *stratégos ek pantôn* in Rhodian Inscriptions'. *Historia* 48. 245–53.

— 2005. *City Government in Hellenistic and Roman Asia Minor*. Oxford.

Doyle, D. H. 1977. 'The Social Functions of Voluntary Associations in a Nineteenth-Century American Town'. *Social Science History* 1.3. 333–55.

Dyggve, E. 1960. *Lindos: Fouilles et recherches 1902–1914 et 1952 III: Le sanctuaire d'Athana Lindia et l'architecture lindienne*. Copenhagen.

Edwards, M. 2004. *Civil Society*. Malden, MA.

Erickson, B. 1997. 'Social Networks and History'. *Historical Methods* 30.3. 149–57.

Faraguna, M. 2012. 'Diritto, economia, società: Riflessioni su eranos tra età omerica e mondo ellenistico' in Legra, B. (ed.), *Transferts culturels et droit dans le monde grec et hellénistique: Actes du colloque internationale, Reims, 14–17 mai 2008*. Paris. 129–53.

Ferguson, W. 1944. 'The Attic Orgeones'. *HThR* 37.2. 61–140.

Finkielsztejn, G. 2001. *Chronologie détaillée et révisée des éponymes amphoriques rhodiens de 270 à 108 av. J.-C., environ*. Oxford.

Finkielsztejn, G. and Thomsen, C. A. forthcoming. Review of Badoud 2015. *Athenaeum*.

Foucart, P. 1873. *Des associations religieuses chez les grecs*. Paris.

Fraser, P. M. 1953. 'The Tribal-Cycles of Eponymous Priests at Lindos and Camiros'. *Eranos* 51. 23–47.

— 1972. 'Notes on Two Rhodian Institutions'. *BSA* 67. 113–24.

— 1977. *Rhodian Funerary Monuments*. Oxford.

Fraser, P. M. and Bean, G. E. 1954. *The Rhodian Peraea and Islands*. Oxford.

Fukuyama, F. 1995. *Trust: The Social Virtues and the Creation of Prosperity*. New York.

Gabrielsen, V. 1992. 'The Status of Rhodioi in Hellenistic Rhodes'. *C&M* 43. 43–69.

— 1994a. 'The Rhodian Associations Honouring Dionysodoros from Alexandria'. *C&M* 45. 137–60.

— 1994b. 'Subdivisions of the State and their Decrees in Hellenistic Rhodes'. *C&M* 45. 117–35.

— 1997. *The Naval Aristocracy of Hellenistic Rhodes*. Aarhus.

— 2000. 'The Synoikized *Polis* of Rhodes' in Nielsen, T. H., Rubinstein, L. and Flensted-Jensen, P. (eds), *Polis and Politics*. Copenhagen. 177–205.

— 2001. 'The Rhodian Associations and Economic Activities' in Archibald, Z., Davies, J. K., Gabrielsen, V. and Oliver, G. (eds), *Hellenistic Economies*. London. 163–84.

— 2007. 'Brotherhoods of Faith and Provident Planning'. *Mediterranean Historical Review* 22.2. 183–210.

Gabrielsen, V. and Thomsen, C. A. (eds), 2015. *Private Associations and the Public Sphere: Proceedings of a Symposium Held at the Royal Danish Academy of Sciences and Letters, 9–11 September 2010*. Copenhagen.

Gauthier, P. 1985. *Les cités grecques et leurs bienfaiteurs, IVe–Ier siecle avant J.-C.: Contribution à l'histoire des institutions*. Athens.

— 1993. 'Les cites hellénistiques' in Hansen, M. H. (ed.), *The Ancient Greek City-State*. Copenhagen. 211–31.

— 2000. 'Le décret de Thessalonique pour Parnasos: L'évergète et la dépense pour sa statue à la basse époque hellenéstique'. *Tekmeria* 5. 19–62.

Gottesman, A. 2014. *Politics and the Street in Democratic Athens*. Cambridge.

Grieb, V. 2008. *Hellenistische Demokratie: Politische Organisation und Struktur in freien griechischen Poleis nach Alexander dem Grossen*. Stuttgart.

Griesbach, J. 2016. 'Wechselnde Standpunkte: Griechische Porträtstatuen und die Neu-Konfiguration von Erinnerungsräumen' in Queyrel, F., von den Hoff, R. and Perrin-Samindayar, É. (eds), *Eikones: Portraits en contexte: Recherches nouvelles sur les portraits grecs: Koll. Freiburg, 13.-14. März 2015*. Venosa. 149–84.

Guarducci, M. 1942. 'Le iscrizioni di Venezia'. *Rivista dell' Istituto Nazionale di archaeologia e storia dell'Arte* 9. 7–53.

Habicht, C. 1995. *Athen: Die Geschichte der Stadt in Hellenistischer Zeit*. Munich.

Hamon, P. 2009. 'Démocraties grecques après Alexandre: À propos de trois ouvrages récents'. *Topoi* 16. 347–82.

Hann, C. 1996. 'Political society and civil anthropology' in Hann, C. and Dunn, E. (eds), *Civil Society: Challenging Western Models*. London. 1–26.

Hansen, M. H. 1989. 'On the Importance of Institutions in an Analysis of Athenian Democracy'. *C&M* 40. 107–13.

— 1991. *The Athenian Democracy in the Age of Demosthenes*. Oxford.

— 1997. 'The *Polis* as an Urban Centre' in Hansen, M. H. (ed.), *The Polis as an Urban Centre and as a Political Community: Acts of the Copenhagen Polis Centre 4*. Copenhagen. 9–86.

— 1998. *Polis and City-State: An Ancient Concept and its Modern Equivalent*. Copenhagen.

— 2006. *Polis: An Introduction to the Ancient Greek City-State*. Oxford.

Harland, P. 2002. 'Connections with the Elites in the World of the Early Christians' in Blasi, A. J., Duhaime, J. and Turcotte, P.-A. (eds), *Handbook of Early Christianity: Social Science Approaches*. Walnut Creek. 385–408.

— 2003. *Associations, Synagogues, and Congregations*. Minneapolis.

Harris, E. 2012–13. 'Review of Gottesman 2014'. *Classics Ireland* 19–20. 156–60.

— 2016a. 'The Flawed Origins of Democracy' in Havlíček, A., Horn, C. and Jinek, J. (eds), *Nous, Polis, Nomos: Festschrift Francisco L. Lisi*. St Augustin. 43–55.

— 2016b. 'From Democracy to the Rule of Law? Constitutional Change' in Tiersche, C. (ed.), *Die Athenische Demokratie im 4. Jahrhundert: Zwischen Modernisierung und Tradition*. Stuttgart. 73–87.

— 2017. 'Applying the Law about the Award of Crowns to Magistrates (Aeschin. 3.9–31): Epigraphic Evidence for the Legal Arguments at the Trial of Ctesiphon'. *Zeitschrift für Papyrologie und Epigraphik* 202. 105–17.

Harrison, A. 1968. *The Law of Athens: The Family and Property*. Oxford.

Higbie, C. 2003. *The Lindian Chronicle and the Greek Creation of Their Past*. Oxford.

Hiller von Gaertringen, F. 1895. 'Inschriften aus Rhodos'. *MDAI(A)* 20. 222–9.

Hiller von Gaertringen, F. and Saridakis, S. 1900. 'Inschriften aus Rhodos'. *MDAI(A)* 25. 107–110.

Hopkins, K. and Burton, G. 1983. 'Political Succession in the Late Republic (249–50 BC)' in Hopkins, K. (ed.), *Death and Renewal: Sociological Studies in Roman History*. Cambridge. 31–119.

Hudson McLean, B. 1996. 'The Place of Cult in Voluntary Associations and Christian Churches on Delos' in Kloppenborg, J. and B. Wilson (eds), *Voluntary Associations in the Greco-Roman World*. London and New York. 186–225.

Humphreys, S. C. 1983. *The Family, Women and Death: Comparative Studies*. London.

Ismard, P. 2010. *La cité des réseaux: Athènes et ses associations VIe–Ie siècle av. J.-C.* Paris.

Johnstone, S. 2011. *A History of Trust in Ancient Greece*. Chicago.

Jones, A. H. M. 1940. *The Greek City from Alexander to Justinian*. Oxford.

Jones, N. F. 1987. *Public Organisation in Ancient Greece: A Documentary Study*. Philadelphia.

— 1999. *The Associations of Classical Athens: A Response to Democracy?* Oxford.

Kaninia, E. 1998 'Χρυσά στεφάνια από τη νεκρόπολη της αρχαίας Ρόδου'. *AD* 48–9 (1994–5). 97–132.

Kloppenborg, J. and Ascough, R. 2011. *Greco-Roman Associations: Texts, Translations, and Commentary*. Berlin.

Kontorini, V. 1983. *Inscriptions inédites relatives à l'histoire et aux cultes de Rhodes au IIe et au Ier s. av. J.-C.: Rhodiaka*. Louvain.

— 1989. Ανέκδοτες επιγραφές Ρόδου II *(inscriptions inédites de Rhodes II)*. Athens.

— 1993. 'La famille de l'amiral Damagoras de Rhodes: Contribution à la prosopographie et à l'histoire rhodiennes au Ier siècle av. J. C.'. *Chiron* 23. 83–99.

— 2014. 'Inscriptions de Rhodes pour les citoyens morts au combat, ἄνδρες ἀγαθοὶ γενόμενοι'. *BCH* 136–7.1 (2012–13). 339–61.

Kruit, N. and Worp, K. 2000. 'Geographical Jar Names: Towards a Multidisciplinary Approach'. *Archiv für Papyrusforschung* 46.1. 65–146.

Lambert, S. D. 1993. *The Phratries of Attica*. Ann Arbor.

Launey, M. 1949–50. *Recherches sur les armées hellénistiques*. Paris.

Lawall, M. 2011. 'Socio-Economic Conditions and the Contents of Amphorae' in Tzochev, C., Stoyanov, T. and Boskova, A. (eds), *PATABS II: Production and Trade of Amphorae in the Black Sea: Acts of the International Round Table held at Kiten, Nessebar and Sredetz, September 26–30, 2007*. Sofia. 23–33.

Le Guen, B. 2001. *Les associations de technites dionysiaques à l'epoque hellénistique*. Paris.

Lewis, D. M. 1997. (ed. Rhodes, P. J.). *Selected Papers in Greek and Near Eastern History*. Cambridge.

Lund, J. 1999. 'Rhodian Amphorae in Rhodes and Alexandria as Evidence of Trade' in Gabrielsen, V., Bilde, P., Engberg-Pedersen, T., Hannestad, L. and Zahle, J. (eds), *Hellenistic Rhodes: Politics, Culture, and Society: Studies in Hellenistic Civilization (vol. 9)*. Aarhus. 187–204.

Lupu, E. 2005. *Greek Sacred Law*. Leiden.

Ma, J. 2013. *Statues and Cities: Honorific Portraits and Civic Identity in the Hellenistic World*. Oxford.

Maillot, S. 2005. *Les associations cultuelles d'etrangers dans la région de Rhodes à l'epoque hellénistique I–II*. (Unpublished dissertation, Université Blaise Pascal-Clermont II).

— 2009. 'Une association de sculpteurs à Rhodes au IIe siècle av. J.-C.: Un cercle d'intégration à la société rhodienne' in Bodiou, L., Mehl, V., Oulhen, J., Prost, F. and Wilgaux, J. (eds), *Chemin faisant: Mythes, cultes et société en Grèce ancienne*. Rennes. 39–58.

— 2015. 'Foreigners' Associations and the Rhodian State' in Gabrielsen, V. and Thomsen, C. A. (eds), *Private Associations and the Public Sphere: Proceedings of a Symposium Held at the Royal Danish Academy of Science and Letters, 9–11 September 2010*. Copenhagen. 136–82.

Maiuri, A. 1916. 'Nuove inscrizioni greche dalle Sporadi Meridionali'. *Annuario* 2. 133–79.

Mann, C. 2012. 'Gleichheiten und Ungleichheiten in der hellenistischen Polis: Überlegungen zum Stand der Forschung' in Mann, C. and P. Scholz (eds), *'Demokratie' in Hellenismus: Von der Herrschaft des Volkes zur Herrschaft der Honeratioren?* Mainz. 11–27.

Manville, P. B. 1994. 'Toward a new paradigm of Athenian citizenship' in Boegehold, A. L. and Scafuro, A. C. (eds), *Athenian Identity and Civic Ideology*. Baltimore. 21–33.

Migeotte, L. 1989. 'Democratie et entretien du peuple à Rhodes après Strabon, XIV.2.5'. *REG* 102. 515–28.

— 1992. *Les souscriptions publiques dans les cités grecques*. Geneva.

— 2013. 'Les souscriptions dans les associations privées' in Frölich, P. and Hamon, P. (eds), *Groupes et associations dans les cité grecques*. Geneva. 113–28.

Millett, P. 1991. *Lending and Borrowing in Ancient Athens*. Cambridge.

Mitchell, J. C. 1969. 'The Concept and Use of Social Networks' in Mitchell, J. C. (ed.), *Social Networks in Urban Situations*. Manchester. 1–50.

Momigliano, A. 1936. 'Note nella storia di Rodi'. *RFIC* n.s. 14. 49–63.

Morelli, D. 1959. 'I Culti in Rodi'. *SCO* 8. i–x, 1–184.

Morricone, L. 1949–51. 'I sacerdoti di Halios: Frammento di catalogo rinvenuto a Rodi'. *Annuario* n.s. 11–13. 351–80.

Most, G. W. 2018. *Hesiod: Theogony; Works and Days; Testimonia*. Cambridge, MA.

Ober, J. 1989. *Mass and Elite in Democratic Athens: Rhetoric, Ideology, and the Power of the People*. Princeton.

— 1993. 'The *Polis* as a Society: Aristotle, John Rawls and the Athenian Social Contract' in Hansen, M. H. (ed.), *The Ancient Greek City-State*. Copenhagen. 129–60.

Ogilvie, S. 2004. 'The Use and Abuse of Trust: Social Capital and its Deployment by Early Modern Guilds'. *CESifo Working Paper Series* 1302, <http://ssrn.com/abstract=614822> (last accessed February 2012).

O'Neil, J. L. 1981. 'How Democratic was Hellenistic Rhodes?' *Athenaeum* 59. 468–73.

— 1995. *The Origins and Development of Ancient Greek Democracy*. London.

Ostrow, S. E. 1990. 'The Augustales in the Augustan Scheme' in Raaflaub, K. A. and Toher, M. (eds), *Between Republic and Empire: Interpretations of Augustus and his Principate*. Berkeley. 364–79.

Ostwald, M. 1986. *From Popular Sovereignty to the Sovereignty of Law: Law, Society and Politics in Fifth-Century Athens*. Berkeley.

Pakkanen, P. 1996. *Interpreting Early Hellenistic Religion: A Study Based on the Cult of Isis and the Mystery of Demeter*. Helsinki.

Papachristodoulou, I. C. 1983. *Symboli stin archeologiki Erevna ton Dimon tis archaias Rodiakis politias: I: Ialysia*. Ioanina.

— 1986. 'Νέα στοιχεία για βιβλιοθήκες στην αρχαία Ρόδο: Επιγραφή σχετική με τη βιβλιοθήκη του αρχ. Γυμνασίου'. *Dodek. Chron*. 11. 265–71.

— 1989. Οἱ ἀρχαίοι Ροδιακοί δῆμοι: Ἱστορική ἐπισκόπηση: Ἡ Ἰαλυσία. Athens.

— 1990. 'Das hellenistische Gymnasium von Rhodos' in *Akten des XIII. Internationalen Kongresses für Klassische Archäologie, Berlin 1988*. Mainz. 500–1.

— 1999. 'The Rhodian Demes Within the Framework of the Function of the Rhodian State' in Gabrielsen, V., Bilde, B., Engberg-Pedersen, T., Hannestad, L. and Zahle, J. (eds), *Hellenistic Rhodes: Politics, Culture, and Society: Studies in Hellenistic Civilization (vol. 9)*. Aarhus. 27–44.

Papakonstantinou, Z. 2016. 'The Hellenistic *agonothesia*: Finances, Ideology, Identities' in Mann, C., Remijsen, S., and Scharff, S. (eds), *Athletics in the Hellenistic World*. Stuttgart. 95–112.

Parker, R. 1996. *Athenian Religion: A History*. Oxford.

— 2009. 'Subjugation, Synoecism and Religious Life' in Funke, P. and Luraghi, N. (eds), *The Politics of Ethnicity and the Crisis of the Peloponnesian League*. Cambridge, MA. 183–214.

Paton, W. R. 2012. *Polybius: The Histories, Volume V: Books 16–27* (revised by Walbank, F. and Habicht, C.). Cambridge, MA.

Patsiada, B. 2013. *Μνημειώδες ταφικό συγκρότημα στη νεκρόπολη της Ρόδου: Συμβολή στη μελέτη της ελληνιστικής ταφικής αρχιτεκτονικής (Ρόδος III)*. Rhodes.

Peters, B. G. 1998. 'Political Institutions, Old and New' in Goodin, R. E. and Klingemann, H.-D. (eds), *New Handbook of Political Science*. Oxford. 205–20.

Poland, F. 1909. *Geschichte des grechische vereinswesens*. Leipzig.

Poma, G. 1972. 'Ricerche sull'adozione nel mondo rodio (III sec. A.C./III sec. D.C)'. *Epigraphica* 34. 169–305.

Porro, G. G. 1916. 'Bolli d'anfore rodie del Museo Nationale Romano'. *Annuario* 2. 103–24.

Pugliese Carratelli, G. 1942. 'Per la storia delle associazioni in Rodi antica'. *Annuario* n.s. 1–2 (1939/40). 147–200.

— 1949. 'Alessandro e la constituzione rodia'. *PP* 12. 154–71.

— 1951. 'La formazione dello stato rodio'. *SCO* 1. 77–88.

— 1953. 'Sullo stato di cittadinanza in Rodi' in *Studi in onore di Vincenzo Arangio-Ruiz nel XLV anno del suo insegnamento* 4. 485–91.

— 1956. 'Ancora sui damoi di Rodi'. *SCO* 6. 62–75.

Putnam, R. 2000. *Bowling Alone: The Collapse and Revival of American Community*. New York.

Quass, F. 1993. *Die Honoratiorenschicht in den Städten des griechischen Ostens: Untersuchungen zur politischen und sozialen Entwicklung in hellenistischer und römischer Zeit*. Stuttgart.

Rackham, H. 1926. *Aristotle: Nikomachean Ethics*. Cambridge, MA.

Rahe, P. 1984. 'The Primacy of Politics in Classical Greece'. *American Historical Review* 89. 265–93.

Rauh, N. 1993. *The Sacred Bonds of Commerce: Religion, Economy, and Trade Society at Hellenistic Roman Delos*. Amsterdam.

— 1999. 'Rhodes, Rome, and the Eastern Mediterranean Wine Trade, 166–88 BC' in Gabrielsen, V., Bilde, B., Engberg-Pedersen, T., (eds), *Hellenistic Rhodes: Politics, Culture, and Society: Studies in Hellenistic Civilization (vol. 9)*. Aarhus. 162–86.

Reader, D. 1964. 'Models of Social Change with Special Reference to Southern Africa'. *African Studies* 23. 11–33.

Rhodes, P. J. 1972. *The Athenian Boule*. Oxford.

Rhodes, P. J. with Lewis, D. M. 1997. *The Decrees of the Greek States*. Oxford.

Rhodes, R. A. W. 2011. *Everyday Life in the British Government*. Oxford.

Rice, E. E. 1986. 'Prosopographika Rhodiaka'. *BSA* 81. 209–50.

— 1988. 'Adoption in Rhodian Society' in Dietz, S. and Papachristodoulou, I. C. (eds), *Archaeology in the Dodecanese*. Copenhagen. 138–44.

Robert, L. 1969. 'Théophane de Mytilène a Constantinople'. *CRAI* 1969. 42–64.

Robinson, E. W. 1997. *The First Democracies: Early Popular Government Outside Athens*. Stuttgart.

— 2011. *Democracy Beyond Athens: Popular Government in the Greek Classical Age*. Cambridge.

Rostovtzeff, M. 1941. *The Social and Economic History of the Hellenistic World*. Oxford.

Roy, J. 1999. '*Polis* and *Oikos* in Classical Athens'. *Greece and Rome* 46.1. 1–18.

Rubinstein, L. 1993. *Adoption in IV. Century Athens*. Copenhagen.

Ruffini, G. 2008. *Social Networks in Byzantine Egypt*. Cambridge.

Salviat, F. 1993. 'Le vin de Rhodes et les plantations du dème d'Amos' in Amouretti, M.-C. and Brun, J.-P. (eds), *La production du vin et de l'huile en Méditerranée*. Athens and Paris. 201–11.

Schaps, D. M. 1979. *Economic Rights of Women in Ancient Greece*. Edinburgh.

Schmitt, H. 1957. *Rom und Rhodos: Geschichte ihrer politischen Beziehungen seit der ersten Berührung bis zum Aufgehen des Inselstaates in römischen Weltreich*. Munich.

Sealey, R. 1976. *A History of the Greek City States 700–338 B.C.* Berkeley.

— 1987. *The Athenian Republic: Democracy or the Rule of Law?* Pennsylvania.

Sebillotte, V. 1997. 'Les Labyades: Une phratrie à Delphes?' *CCG* 8. 39–49.

Segre, M. 1936. 'Dedica votiva dell'equipaggio di una nave rodia'. *Cl. Rhodos* 8. 227–44.

Seligman, A. B. 1992. *The Idea of Civil Society*. Princeton.

Shear, T. L. 1908. 'A New Rhodian Inscription'. *The American Journal of Philology* 29.4. 461–6.

Sickinger, J. 2009. 'Nothing to Do with Democracy: Formulae of Disclosure and the Athenian Epigraphic Habit' in Mitchell, L. and Rubinstein, L. (eds), *Greek History and Epigraphy: Essays in Honour of P. J. Rhodes*. Swansea. 87–102.

Sinclair, R. K. 1988. *Democracy and Participation in Athens*. Cambridge.

Smith, D. R. 1972. '*Hieropoioi* and *hieropythai* on Rhodes'. *L'Antiquité Classique* 41.2. 532–9.

Smith, M. S. 1967. 'Greek Adoptive Formulae'. *CQ* 17. 302–10.

Smith, R. R. R. 1988. *Hellenistic Royal Portraits*. Oxford.

Solokowski, F. 1955. *Lois sacrées des cités grecques*. Paris.

Sosin, J. 2005. 'Unwelcome Dedications: Public Law and Private Religion in Hellenistic Laodicea by the Sea'. *CQ* 55. 130–9.

Steinhauer, J. 2014. *Religious Associations in the Post-Classical Polis: Potsdamer Altertumswissenschaftliche Beiträge 50*. Stuttgart.

Stolle, D. and Hooghe, M. 2003. 'Conclusion: The Sources of Social Capital Reconsidered' in Stolle, D. and M. Hooghe, *Generating Social Capital*. New York. 231–48.

Thompson, D. J. 2015. 'The Ptolemaic *ethnos*' in Gabrielsen, V. and Thomsen, C. A., *Private Associations and the Public Sphere: Proceedings of a Symposium Held at the Royal Danish Academy of Science and Letters, 9–11 September 2010*. Copenhagen. 301–13.

Thomsen, C. A. 2015. 'The *eranistai* of Classical Athens'. *GRBS* 55.1. 154–75.

— 2018. 'The "Thirteenth" Deme of Lindos' in Nowak, M. (ed.), *Tell Me Who You Are: Labeling Status in the Graeco-Roman World: Studia źródłoznawcze. U schyłku starożytności 16*. 283–306.

— forthcoming a. 'The Place of Honour: Association Sanctuaries and Inscribed Honours in Late Classical and Early Hellenistic Athens' in Cazemier, A. and Skaltsa, S. (eds), *Private Associations in Context: Rethinking Associations and Religion in Context*.

— forthcoming b. 'Family Reunions: The Dedication and Reuse of Statues on the Lindian Acropolis' in Fejfer, J. and Kristensen, T. M. (eds), *Sacred Treasures: Inscribing and Collecting Art in Greek and Roman Sanctuaries*.

— forthcoming c. 'The Religious Typology of Private Associations' in Jensen, J. and Schultz, P. (eds), *Aspects of Early Greek Cult II: Architecture – Context – Music*. Copenhagen.

Tilly, C. 2005. *Trust and Rule*. Cambridge.

Tod, M. N. 1932. *Sidelights on Greek History*. Oxford.

Trümper, M. 2002. 'Das Sanktuarium des "Établissement des Poseidoniastes de Bérytos" in Delos'. *BCH* 126. 265–330.

— 2006. 'Negotiating Religious and Ethnic Identity: The Case of Clubhouses in Late Hellenistic Delos' in Nielsen, I. (ed.), *Zwischen Kult und Gesellschaft: Kosmopolitische Zentren des antiken Mittelmeerraumes als Aktionsraum von Kultvereinen und Religionsgemeinschaften* (*Hephaistos* 24). Hamburg. 113–50.

van Bremen, R. 2013. '*Neoi* in Hellenistic Cities: Age Class, Institution, Association?' in Frölich, P. and Hamon, P. (eds), *Groupes et associations dans les cité grecques*. Geneva. 113–28.

van Gelder, H. 1900. *Geschichte der alten Rhodier*. The Hague.

Van Nijf, O. 1997. *The Civic World of Professional Associations in the Roman East*. Amsterdam.

Veligianni-Terzi, C. 1997. *Wertbegriffe in den attischen Ehrendekreten der Klassischen Zeit*. Stuttgart.

Venticinque, P. 2010. 'Family Affairs: Guild Regulations and Family Relationships in Roman Egypt'. *GRBS* 50. 273–94.

Verboven, K. 2007. 'The Associative Order'. *Atheneaum* 95. 1–31.

Vérilhac, A.-M. and Vial, C. 1998. *Le mariage grec du Vie siècle av. J.-C. à l'époque d'Auguste: Bulletein de Correspondence Hellenique Supplement 32*. Athens.

Vestergaard, T., Hansen, M. H., Rubinstein, L., Bjertrup, L. and Nielsen, T. H. 1992. 'The Age-Structure of Athenian Citizens Commemorated in Sepulchral Inscriptions'. *C&M* 43. 5–21.

Veyne, P. 1990 [1976]. *Bread and Circuses*. London.

Vikela, E. 1994. *Die Weihreliefs aus dem Athener Pankrates-Heiligtum am Ilissos: Religionsgeschichtliche Bedeutung und Typologie*. Berlin.

Vlassopoulos, K. 2007. 'Free Spaces: Identity, Experience and Democracy in Classical Athens'. *Classical Quarterly* 57.1 33–52.

Vondeling, J. 1961. *Eranos*. Groningen.

Walbank, F. W. 1979. *A Historical Commentary on Polybius: Volume 3: Commentary on Books XIX–XL*. Oxford.

Whitehead, D. 1986. *The Demes of Attica, 508/7-ca. 250 B.C.: A Political and Social Study*. Princeton.

Wiemer, H.-U. 2002. *Krieg, Handel und Piraterie. Untersuchungen zur Geschichte des hellenistischen Rhodos (KLIO Beihefte 6)*. Berlin.

Wilson, P. 2000. *The Athenian Institution of the khoregia*. Cambridge.

Yardley, J. C. 2018. *Livy: History of Rome, Volume XI: Books 38–40*. Cambridge, MA.

Young, J. H. 1956. 'Studies in South Attica: Country Estates at Sounion'. *Hesperia* 25.9. 122–46.

Ziebarth, E. 1896. *Das griechische Vereinswesen*. Leipzig.

Index Locorum

EPIGRAPHIC SOURCES

LITERARY SOURCES

39.14, 131
42.45, 24
44.23, 38
45.10, 20

Lys. *Frg.*
53, 159

Pl. *Leg.*
771a-d, 96
909d-e, 96

Pol.
15.23, 24

16.4, 112
16.5, 112
20.6, 129
21.7, 112, 156
22.5, 51
25.5, 19, 24
27.3, 24
27.4, 24
27.7, 23, 25, 51, 76
28.2, 51, 127
28.16, 127
28.17, 19
29.10, 19–20, 38
29.11, 20, 24

30.4, 76
30.9, 38
30.21, 19
30.31, 48
33.15, 76

Strabo
14.2, 26, 72, 113

Thuc.
8.54, 159

General Index

adoption, 59–64
  and demes, 60–3
  double sonship, 60–4
  within the family, 59–60, 63–4
  see also inheritance
agriculture, 45–6
Amioi (deme), 46n
Amnistioi (deme), 82n64, 85
anagraphe, 72–5
Aphrodisiastai Hermogeneioi, 97, 102, 134
Aphrodisiastai Soteriastai, 31, 141
Archokrates son of Archipolis (Lysistratos), 62–3,
  100, 120
Argeioi (deme), 83–4, 86
Aristotle, 9–14, 158, 160
Arkaseis (deme), 66–7
Arkesine (Amorgos), 47
Arioi (deme), 45, 84–6, 117n49, 123–4
Aristombrotidas son of Aristombrotidas, 55–6, 76,
  84–6, 120–5, 138, 153–5
Asklapiastai hoi en Kamiroi, 138, 153–5
Asklapiastai Nikasioneioi Olympiastai, 28n46,
  90–3, 97n, 102–3
assembly
  of demes, 66
  federal, 19–25, 37–9, 67, 78–80, 86–7, 147, 151
  Kamirean, 22, 76–9
  of *ktoinai*, 67, 139–40
  Lindian, 22, 119, 146–7
  of private associations, 95, 98–101, 159
associations *see* private associations
asty see Rhodes (city)
Astymedes son of Theaidetos, 37–8, 49n1, 51, 76,
  86n, 152–3, 156, 160
Athana Lindia *see* priesthood: of Athana Lindia
Athens, 1–7, 11–13, 21, 39–41, 56n, 59–61, 94–5,
  108, 110–11, 127, 150n, 159

benefactors
  of associations, 90–3, 100–4, 112, 118–28,
    132–6, 139–44, 150–6
  of demes, 84–8
  demes and associations as, 86–7, 137–9, 148
boula, 19–21, 24, 37–8, 72, 79–80, 120, 132–4,
  141, 157
Boulidai (deme), 83, 87
Brasioi (deme), 65–6, 83, 86
brothers, 32n, 39, 42, 44, 49–50, 52, 55, 63–4, 76,
  85, 102n, 110n, 115, 120, 122n, 124, 153–5
Brykountioi (deme), 79, 86
Bybassioi (deme), 39, 66, 86n70, 151n64

choragia, 40, 105–9
  foreigners, 146
  at Lindos, 146–8
  winning, 107
choragos see choragia
choruses, 40, 78–9, 105–6
  professionals, 107–9
civil society, 156–62
corporate *polis*, 11–14, 160–2
council *see boula; mastroi*
cousins, 55, 58, 64, 122, 155
crowns
  announcement, 77–9, 86, 120
  by associations, 136, 98–103, 138, 140, 142–5,
    148, 152–9
  list of, 143–4
  petition for, 79–80, 114–17
  by public associations, 67, 76–80

damiourgos, 23, 31–2, 34, 36, 40, 42–5, 50–2, 55–6,
  60, 76, 82n65, 85, 121–3, 138, 140, 153
damos see assembly; demes
daughters, 53–61, 64, 87, 90, 95, 99

CPSIA information can be obtained
at www.ICGtesting.com
Printed in the USA
LVHW022058110820
662939LV00004B/15